Trade Unions and the Age of Information and Communication Technologies in Kenya

African Governance and Development

African Governance and Development identifies and elaborates on the strategic place of governance and development within the African studies. Reflecting the fact that life in Africa continues to change; particularly in political, development, and socioeconomic arenas; this series explores issues focusing on the ongoing mobilization for good governance and the search for sustainable and economic development. The *African Governance and Development* series address gaps and larger needs in the developing scholarship on African and the African Diaspora. This series provides scholarly monographs and edited collections in the humanities, social science, and social scientific traditions. Contributors are encouraged to submit book-length manuscripts that encompass, besides the above-named topics, those focusing on: Africa's political economy and economic development, Africa's place in world trade development, democratization of African countries, the inclusion and representation of ethnic minorities, and the role of gender in Africa's development. Works can be focused on a single African country, a region of African countries, or the African continent's place as a global player.

Recent Titles

Pan-African in Modern Times: Challenges, Concerns, and Constraints, edited by Olayiwola Abegunrin and Sabelle Ogbobode Abidde
Nigeria, Africa, and the United States: Challenges of Governance, by Olayiwola Abegunrin
Human Rights in Nigeria's External Relations: Building the Record of a Moral Superpower, by Philip C. Aka
Nigeria's Niger Delta: Militancy, Amnest, and the Post-Amnest Environment, by Sabella Ogbobode Abidde
Trade Unions and the Age of Information and Communication Technologies in Kenya, by Eric E. Otenyo

Trade Unions and the Age of Information and Communication Technologies in Kenya

Eric E. Otenyo

LEXINGTON BOOKS
Lanham • Boulder • New York • London

Published by Lexington Books
An imprint of The Rowman & Littlefield Publishing Group, Inc.
4501 Forbes Boulevard, Suite 200, Lanham, Maryland 20706
www.rowman.com

Unit A, Whitacre Mews, 26-34 Stannary Street, London SE11 4AB

British Library Cataloguing in Publication Information Available

Library of Congress Cataloging-in-Publication Data

Names: Otenyo, Eric Edwin, author.
Title: Trade unions and the age of information and communication technologies in Kenya / Eric E. Otenyo.
Other titles: African governance and development.
Description: Lanham, Maryland : Lexington Books, 2017. | Series: African governance and development | Includes bibliographical references and index.
Identifiers: LCCN 2016056373 (print) | LCCN 2016057248 (ebook) | ISBN 9781498548793 (cloth : alk. paper) | ISBN 9781498548809 (Electronic)
Subjects: LCSH: Labor unions--Kenya. | Labor unions--Political activity--Kenya. | Labor unions and education. | Information technology--Economic aspects--Kenya.
Classification: LCC HD6866.5.Z65 084 2017 (print) | LCC HD6866.5.Z65 (ebook) | DDC 331.88096762--dc23
LC record available at https://lccn.loc.gov/2016056373.

™ The paper used in this publication meets the minimum requirements of American National Standard for Information Sciences Permanence of Paper for Printed Library Materials, ANSI/NISO Z39.48-1992.

Printed in the United States of America

I dedicate this book to the memory of my brother James Arthur Otenyo (JAO) who put me in contact with several union members in the Rift Valley, Nyanza, and Western Kenya regions.

Contents

Preface

Any discussion about the new economy has to start with an understanding of the roles of information and communication technologies (ICTs) in the emerging changes. Unions and other stakeholders engage policy-making processes to find the right balance between the effects of ICTs on the economy and the benefits to accrue for members. This means we have to describe and outline actual ways in which unions participate in collaborative governance frameworks. Whether the issue is saving jobs or improving productivity, ICTs are now a core part of human social and economic experiences. Still, unions are core actors in collaborative governance strategies and must be aware of full capabilities of new information technologies in developmental discourses. There are many dimensions of focused attention to ICTs in development and governance. For instance, the role of unions in leveraging policy toward ICTs is inevitably political, which really is about the allocation of values in society. To understand ICTs, unions and other members of civil society must raise critical questions about efficacy—do ICTs produce values that move the interests of workers forward? Unions have to interrogate the context of ICTs in Kenya's Vision 2030 and find ways to navigate the globalized new economy.

It so often is easy to dismiss the role of labor unions in this age of globalization, in which the dominance of ICTs is self-evident. Critics view globalization as making it easy for businesses to move to any part of the world where labor is cheap. Moreover, technological advances make it relatively easy to substitute much of what labor does with automation. ICTs can facilitate the substitution by shortening or eliminating distance through which products and services are moved. This action can also weaken job security of those in the sector involved. Without appropriate understanding of how best to leverage ICTs to the way we live and work, policy makers may operate from a weaker standpoint.

Unions and their members can have completely divergent views on ICTs. In some cases, union members are ambivalent about ICTs. Yet, they majority of union members use these ICTs in daily operations. At any given moment, a union member is on her mobile phone, texting, emailing, surfing the web, telecommuting, or doing a host of other chores that were unheard of in the 1950s, and 1960s, when most of the trade unions in East Africa were established.

Good discussions about ICTs and the unions are important not only in developed countries, but especially so in the developing world. For it is the developed world which has greater need to develop systems that safeguard against any threats that technologies may pose to their economies. Developing countries, with lower GDPs, need to be fully aware of the roles ICTs play in advancing their economic wealth. The unique disadvantages of the digital divide provide even stronger reasons for engaging ICTs to help workers do their jobs better.

The emerging new economy has the potential to further marginalize developing countries, if they do not leverage ICTs to their advantage. In a sense, this book tells the story of how ICTs are being embraced in the nation's productive capacity. The book shares approaches with human resource management and education, history, economics, communication, and politics. Indeed, the politics of ICTs in Kenya's economy are central to the country's future, and unions have a part to play. That is the area this book explores in some detail.

The book's plan and chapter layout is as follows: chapter 1 sets the stage of the context of the growth of Internet cultures and the genesis of union activism in matters of national politics and governance. Chapter 2 suggests the role of trade (labor) unions in public policy and governance is traced back to the formative years of the nation. Kenya's politics is characterized by patronage and attendant expansion of public sector jobs, which in turn, affects the national wage bill. This chapter sheds light on emerging discourses in light of expanded political spaces. In addition, new opportunities have emerged in the age of ICTs, which influence everyday living.

Chapter 3 considers the power of technological diffusion and explores the contention that diffusion of ICTs from private sector (MNCs and local industry-technology transfer) is weak or underexploited. The technology diffusion thesis suggests that countries and organizations learn from each other. The author argues that e-government platforms learned from corporate applications are gaining currency in Kenya. But the question remains, do unions learn from internationalism? The chapter refers to weak capabilities in Kenya's lower rate of industrialization and full absorption of ICTs, highlighting historical trends of industrialization based on MNCs and international capitalism.

Chapter 4 focuses on the question of digital platforms and education and barriers to ICT applications, especially questions of the digital divide. The chapter considers the Laptop Project in Kenya and the ability of trade unions to support projects that will narrow the digital divide.

Chapter 5 discusses the attitudes of public trade unions to ICTs, drawing from qualitative and quantitative research tools. Use of various apps like M-PESA, cashless transportation systems, email, and other applications is explored. The chapter underscores the need for union leaders to find strategies of engaging the emerging benefits of ICTs at the workplace and in society at large.

Chapter 6 explores the question of productivity in African management systems and the role of ICTs. The chapter considers the question: have unions addressed the question of technology and its role in enhancing productivity? In addition, the chapter offers insights on the roles of training in worker empowerment strategies.

Chapter 7 is the conclusion and a statement about the future of trade unions and internationalism in a global and digitized world. The chapter argues that while Kenyan trade unions are relatively weak organizations, there is room for ICTs to be leveraged for greater benefit of the workers. The arguments for technology substitution are presented as a way of explaining that labor-rich economies can still survive changing environments. The chapter discusses the implication of ICTs for management of unions and their effectiveness in collective bargaining. Failure to play roles in the era of globalization in policy management has some costs that are explored.

In sum, throughout this book, the aim is to tell a narrative about trade unions and the age of ICTs in Kenya's development process. I try to fill in gaps in the literature on collaborative governance in Africa by highlighting the special place of trade unions, within political and economic contexts, but recognize the task is incomplete. There is room for scholars to explore roles of trade unions in other African countries, particularly how unions embrace the new world in which new technologies threaten job security in some sectors while they offer new opportunities in other economic endeavors. Hopefully, *Trade Unions and the Age of Information and Communication Technologies in Kenya* is an invitation to scholars and practitioners alike to have conversations on what has been said and done about the sweeping role of ICTs in everyday lives of union members.

Acknowledgments

I am grateful to Lexington Books, the publishers of this book. I want to especially thank Professor Olayiwola Abegunrin, editor of the African Governance and Development series, the editorial staff, Ms. Kathryn Tafelski and Madhumitha Koduvalli, for their kind support. I have also spent decades following the activities of unions in Kenya and elsewhere and thank union members that I was privileged to meet and share idea about their different causes. For all who participated in the production of this volume, you deserve credit for the positive features of the end product, but I alone am responsible for any shortcomings.

ONE

Trade Unions and the Age of ICTs in Kenya

An Overview

INTRODUCTION

As will soon be apparent, this book underscores the role of trade or labor unions in public affairs and the emergence and growth of information and communication technologies (ICTs) in Kenya. The relationship between unions and government policy on ICTs suggests that a form of partnership exists in the nation's governance networks. Although there exists academic literature on public governance in Africa, not much attention has been focused on specific components of existing policy networks. This means there is room for understanding key concepts of the strategic place of unions as partners in governance and development within African nations. Unions, in turn, need to understand the unfolding ICT-driven governance regimes, which profoundly impact all modern economies.

Since we have to seek out influences on Africa's development, it is imperative to explore the place of ICTs within the new economy. Scholars and development assistance partners concerned about Africa's development constantly refer to the need for governments to embrace administrative reforms and democratic rule as a means to achieve development. The World Bank (1989, p. 60), for example, links good governance, defined as the exercise of political power to manage a nation's affairs, as a key ingredient for achieving development. And stakeholders in the development process all recognize the need for inclusion of citizens, political leaders, community organizations, nonprofits, media, corporations, government ministries, and trade unions in efforts to ensure good governance occurs (Bovaird & Loffler, 2009, p. 219; Lee, 2007). This realization is not new and has been well developed in both developed and developing nations. In fact, because unions predate the independence of all African nations and were a part of the coalitions that took responsibility for expansion of human rights and development, there is an implicit obligation to periodically appraise unionism in relation to society growth and development. Perhaps, the importance of revisiting union attitudes and actions in the furtherance of activities that promote development should receive greater academic scrutiny and evaluation. Moreover, unions have to find ways to engage ICTs for their own survival as organizations with an enduring mission to promote workers' rights.

It is well understood, from Victor Feather's (1971) account, that the origins of trade unions can be traced to the changed conditions of workers stemming from the Industrial Revolution in the eighteenth century. Now that a new information and communication technology revolution has occurred, new ways of engaging the world of work have to evolve. ICTs challenge ideas about time and space in more than one profound way. Workers now have to function as parts of a wired and cloud-based and virtual reality. In fact, the changing ICT policy environment mirrors the modernization and integration of the country into the globalized and networked new economy. In an attempt to show the political context of the unfolding ICT-driven society, we draw attention to the country's administrations and challenges to absorptions of new technologies.

Trade or labor unions are active players in public affairs. In East Africa, trade unions are associations purposefully organized for improving the terms and conditions of work for members. As a subset of human resource management systems, unions are tasked within the law to conduct negotiations to eliminate arbitrariness in managerial actions (Otenyo, 2016). Unions also maintain terms of service for workers when employers seek to impose conditions perceived to be detrimental to worker interests and welfare. It is not uncommon for unions to act as pressure groups and collectively mobilize for a political cause. This often translates into adversarial relationships with the state, especially when unions use strikes and other forms of work stoppages as a bargaining tool.

Historically, unions engage public affairs and policy in many arenas, in the service of members. Union participation is mostly determined by leaders' interpretation of the urgency of the situation. Among the goals is to represent members in grievance processes, defend them, represent them in media relations, and occasionally involve them in political action (Shostak, 1991, p. 19). Unions are also key players in policy advocacy in areas such as human rights, slave trade prohibition, discrimination, and protection of children from exploitation (Compa & Diamond, 1996). Unions may in many instances be invited, as stakeholders, to be a part of the public policy making process. As such, unions are members of the collaborative governance processes that implement neoliberal economic policies. Although the manner in which neoliberal policies are articulated remains stable among different elite factions, some form of pragmatism has emerged in the more digitally savvy administrations governing Kenya.

From the outset, we can argue that the Silicon Age (new millennium) overlaps with the age of neoliberalism and concepts such as privatization and globalization. The age of rapid ascendancy of the market brought along increased consumerism and increased struggles between state powers, often in alliance with corporations and unions. All over the world, there was recognition that workers bear the brunt of neoliberal policies, privatization, and globalization (Ratnam, 2007, p. 622). The global neoliberal ideology has visible consequences, foremost of which is the tendency of employers to favor individualized employment contracts. In the old order, bargained plans were at the heart of union negotiations and activities.

Globalization, which includes China's emergence as a key player in African economies, has contributed to the rapid transfer of technologies throughout the developing world. Transfers in terms of hardware are both material, in the forms of equipment, and cultural, expressed in art forms such as music and movies. Technology transfers include reorganizations of the workplace as well as use of data storage and retrieval software packages. Much like had been posited in Kraemer and Perry (1999), information systems and other applications in areas of policy evaluation and monitoring supported efforts to enhance service delivery. Computers and other ICTs not only led to workplace reorganizations but also added new functions and jobs in government and other sectors.

Kenya and other African countries received technological transfers through trade, multinational investments, and technical assistance, especially from international organizations including the World Bank, European Union, (EU), United Nations (UN), United States Agency for International Development (USAID), and bilateral donor agencies. From a global standpoint, aid programs after World War II, through the Marshall Plan, ushered in a new wave of development logic in which technology transfer was considered a path through which the least developed countries would "take off" and attain development, much as had been witnessed in Europe (Fredland, 2000; Rostow, 1971).

Development assistance programs come with Western tools of work including computers, fax machines, and the Internet, as well as work organization frameworks. These technologies have no doubt enhanced efficiency and productive capacity in the world's business and government operations. For instance, a click of the mouse can generate list of persons on no-fly lists at most airports. New technologies have also made it easier to track packages shipped across the globe. And in industrial sectors, it is much easier to govern the global markets for all goods and services.

But these spectacular innovations have come at a price not excluding weaker environmental protections and fragmentation of labor markets (Frundt, 2002). Sheth (1996) argued, "the global wind of liberalization and flexibility with its accompaniment of consumerism, greed and selfishness" was likely to generate divisions in society (p. 14). Liberalization also promoted individualism and advanced the interests of technological and ideological products of the global market (Sheth, 1996, p. 14). Of course, the new information and communication technologies (ICTs) are obvious examples of these new products. These products could be used for both good and bad causes. In sociological terms, these products, which include computers, may also influence power dynamics in society and workplaces (Hakken, 1993).

While the proliferation of ICTs has changed the way we live, the rapid pace of social change is manifest in several ways. Take for instance the manner in which Sunday worship is conducted. Traditionalists still carry old bible books to church. The same is not true of tech-savvy churches. Here is how a newspaper commented on worshiping at Nairobi's Jubilee Christina Church, whose leaders, Bishop Allan Kiuna and wife Pastor Kathy Kiuna, preferred to use Apple iPads and smartphones at church. At their church, "There will be a few Bibles in sight. Here, faithful come with iPads and smartphones. In these gadgets the worshiper can access all that will be needed during the service—Bibles in various versions and commentaries—at the tap of a finger." There are reading plans, commentaries, daily encouragements, songs of worship, and much, much more from the ever-expanding world of Internet applications." (Wesangula, 2012). The writer adds: "There is even the e-confession, an application by Apple that was approved by the Vatican early last year to guide the users through the process of confession and allow them to keep track of their sins." (Wesangula, 2012). The fact that churches now fully engage the world of ICTs means that most core aspects human society are integrated into the maturing globalized ICT-driven world.

Marshall McLuhan's concept of the Global Village has come to pass and is exceeded by new technologies to the extent that "one might live anywhere on earth and still communicate interactively with anyone else on earth" (Garson 2006, p. 8). Futurists, who include Manuel Castells, (2000), Raymond Kurzwell, (2005), and Alvin Toffler (1981) were spot on as we continue to be amazed by the power of search engines that can put together a person's full-life profile in a matter of seconds. Furthermore, mobile phones have easily superseded land telephones and created possibilities beyond simple calling and texting, to providing avenues for exchanges of photographs and other digital images that can be shared with others anywhere in the world via the Internet. Thanks to the Internet we can watch whole series of drama through Netflix and Amazon, and video chat with friends throughout the world through Skype, Zoom, FaceTime, Firefox Hello, and other platforms available on mobile devices. These devices mean new ways of doing work and spending leisure time. Authors Snellen and Thaens (2008) add that thanks to the mobile devices—phones, laptops, tablets, and personal digital assistants, we live in the "always on" society. Such a society is characterized by mental multitasking blurring the division between work, family, and leisure times. Others focus on the "hyperlinked" nature of society where individuals are connected to a number of Internet and digitized applications on a 24/7 basis.

EMERGING INTERNET CULTURES: THE INTERNET OF THINGS (IoT) AND THE INTERNET OF EVERYTHING (IoE)

So dominant is the Internet culture that, through smart and mobile phones apps, we speak of the paradigm of the Internet of Things (IoT). IoT is based on machine-to-machine (M2M) technological logistics and relies on sensors, connectivity, and data processing and has wide ramifications on quality of life and business cost management. IoT impacts on how business is conducted, and unions and other participants in the economy ought to know what it is all about. For companies and employers, IoT means that data on fuel consumption can be captured and transmitted in real time to fleet operation managers.

At the regional government level, data tracking and transmission devices are proliferating. Numerous other tracking applications (apps) have emerged in Kenya that illustrates the complex nature of the emerging ICT regime. For instance, a mobile tool dubbed M-ship was introduced to detect problems in the shipping industry. Members of the public can report any shipping issues through the app, connected to the Safaricom network. The International Standing Committee on Shipping (Iscos) developed the app as a means to facilitate trade and identify hitches that occur in clearing cargo and transportation along key routes including the Northern Corridor (Mwangi, 2015).

At the local level, data on dysfunctional street and traffic lights is automatically reported to public works engineers. Within this Internet culture, citizens are constantly watched through cameras, Global Positioning System (GPS), facial recognition devices, and Radio Frequency Identification (RFID) chips installed in documents such as passports. Unlike a barcode, RFID devices do not have to be scanned and instead are automatically readable within a range of installed readers and may also be connected to mobile networks. RFID tags can also transmit data to wireless local area networks. Mobile devices and laptops are connected to video surveillance feeds and can report breaches to security direct to law enforcement officials. GPS-based tracking systems can provide real-time information about government- or company-owned vehicle locations.

Today, GPS applications exist in Kenya, much as they do in the advanced economies. For instance, in 2012, then Administration Police commandant Kinuthia Mbugua announced the introduction of GPS tracking devices to aid in the fight against cattle rustlers. GPS devices were to be fixed on animals so that owners would be able to monitor flock movements (*Daily Nation* Correspondent, 2012). GPS devices have also been used in wildlife tracking programs. These differ from geographic information systems (GIS), which are technologies that "allow governments to capture, manage, analyze, and use land-related data to solve complex planning and management problems" (Huxhold, 1991). GIS systems are increasingly being recommended and used in Kenya in the areas of mineral exploration, public transportation operations, and urban planning.

In March 2015, Kenya was placed on the "App Map" after Jason Eisen, an American consultant, developed an app that rivals the Uber cab app. Although Uber was launched in Nairobi in January 2015, and is relatively safe, it did not fully persuade skeptics concerned about the trustworthiness of taxi drivers. Eisen's app, named Maramoja, was built based on a social trust model and applies to customers seeking taxi or cab rides in Nairobi. Maramoja has built-in tracking systems that show customers which taxis are close by and "assigns the drive a trust score, by scouring riders' contacts and social media" (Warner, 2015). Eisen was able to make use of social media like Facebook to help riders basically determine which taxi drivers are trustworthy. The entry of apps in the realm of taxis is just one of the many signature ICTs that has changed the interactions between people and machines. These applications can go further than just calling for taxis and can do more.

Applications of face-recognition software now transcend humans and have been extended to animals. Miami Dade Animal Services, in Florida, reported that its dogs could be integrated in the free Finding Rover App in which missing dogs are traceable through smartphones. Dog owners have to first register their dogs by loading the picture into a database from which face recognition software can match missing canines and notify owners (Teproff, 2015). Everything is connected anytime and anywhere through intelligent technologies, hence the terminology and references to Internet of Everything (IoE) when people, processes, data, and things are all connected. Mitchell, Villa, Stewart-Weeks, and Lange opine in their white paper "as more people and new types of information are connected, IoT becomes an IoE—a network of networks where billions or even trillions of connections create unprecedented opportunities as well as new risks" (2015, p. 2). It is an era of tech democracy, in which, winners and losers are announced on the Internet. But as Kranenburg (2008) warns, the IoT also signifies loss of autonomy and submission to control by those who *own* the technologies or powers that be. In essence, citizens have to basically choose between trusting and being controlled.

Most observers believe the grand idea and paradigm of IoT is unstoppable because the Internet is now an infrastructure, connecting humans to their home grids, gates, maps, merchants, vehicles, iPhones, Ipads, health apps, telemedicine, and much more. Things are so connected that the Internet is mainstream and affects our quality of life. According to data from Verizon (2015), the factors driving adoption of IoT include the need for faster and better delivery of goods and services. Customers are also looking for more personal services on devices that are accessible to all and available everywhere. Perhaps the motivation stems from increased use of social media and mobile technology, which has changed public expectations of realizing what is possible in an age of rapid transformation (Brown, 2015).

On the other hand, industry leaders predict, "that by 2025, organizations that adopt IoT extensively will be at least 10 percent more profitable than companies that don't. By 2025 smart cities capabilities will become a critical consideration for companies deciding where to invest and open facilities" (Brown, 2015). Most observers regard smart cities as a future reality for municipal centers around the world (Clarke, 2013). Cities are considered fertile ground for realizing IoE. Cities are increasingly using ICTs and the Internet to address urban problems. As the world's rural landscapes decline and cities grow, ICTs are the go-to tools for addressing social and economic problems. ICTs are critical resources for city planning and for bringing people together for collective action through such platforms as social networks and smartphones. The proliferation of social media and creation of a culture of the Internet is boosted by government action, which in the case of Kenya includes facilitation of hubs and attendant infrastructures.

For countries like Kenya, the idea of Konza Techno City in Machakos County is a realization of the global trends toward smart cities. But it is also a manifestation of changing expectations from generations that have grown within a connected world. As seen from its architectural design, upon completion, Konza City will have elements of network integration. The architecture brings together interactions between sensors and hosts of devices embedded in multiservice infrastructure that will host numerous city services. Probably linked to idea of control as described in Kranenburg (2008), is the thought that ICTs enable governments to have knowledge about every individual's digital activities and transactions.

Announcements that the government of Kenya is indeed planning on developing a master data bank of all citizens' transactions is a realization of the IoT's control function. In November 2014, the government announced it would set up an electronic registry for all Kenyan nationals. The government contracted an Israeli firm to develop the integrated system. Nationals would be issued with an e-card, which would capture complete biometric data and contain unique digital identifiers referenced from birth to death (Ligami, 2014). In addition, the e-card would hold information about each individual's bank account, relatives, property, driving license, passport numbers, and personal identification numbers used for tax purposes. It is not hard to figure out that e-cards can be detectable and hence feed into other IoT systems. In 2015, the government launched the Integrated Population Registration System (IPRS), which was construed as a "super database" or more appropriately, the National Master Database that would provide state agencies personal data of all individuals in the country. IPRS was set up to capture critical data that include birth certificates, national identity cards, passports, Kenya Revenue Authority tax status, National Hospital Insurance Fund (NHIF), and Social Security Fund (NSSF), information accessible through the click of a button (Jamah, 2015). Therefore, moving toward IoT is a function of politics, economics, technological, and social realities.

Indeed, as Christine Bellamy and John Taylor (1994) observe, ICT's impact is ubiquitous in enabling the rise of an information polity. This polity, sometimes manifest as an information society, information age, and information economy, has created a dynamic that elicits reactions from human societies. The reactions affect relationships among different groups that include citizens, workers, employers, customers, and suppliers. ICTs, from the perspective of pessimists, may challenge job security. Profoundly, the fear of robots has increased rather than diminished.

Machines, especially, those that are self-driven and can think, are increasingly changing the workplace. Artificial intelligence has brought forth a new world in which words are increasingly being replaced. Gone are the days when humans programmed computers to perform certain duties. Today, S-Voice, Siri, and Watson-like devices are capable of autonomous actions, much like we have witnessed the first generation of autonomous driving cars. And not surprising, Japan has begun to experiment with replacing doormen and hotel janitors with robots. In Nagasaki, a hotel purchased androids (called Actroids) to greet guests, carry luggage, and clean rooms. The actroids were designed with capabilities to mimic human breathing, blinking, and speaking in languages like English, Korean, Chinese and, of course, Japanese. The hotel president, Hideo Sawada, was quoted in the *Japan Times* expressing hope that 90 percent of labor in the hotel would be replaced with robots (Government Technology, 2015).

In other words, the substitution of labor with machines is real and, as we shall note, will have effects on developed and developing countries like Kenya. The worst nightmares of some of the world's pioneers of computer devices at IBM have been realized. Back in the 1950s, some of the inventors of the thinking machines feared that computers would replace humans and, hence, Stanford University's IT expert Jerry Kaplan remarked during an interview over the National Public Radio (NPR) station (2014) that artificial intelligence systems (AI) have made it possible for roughly 47 percent of all jobs to be replaceable with machines. ICTs are at the core of AI systems and the displacement of labor with robots, hence the fear of the robot armageddon. Andrew McAfee of MIT also expressed a similar view on American science radio correspondent David S. Kestenbaum's National Public Radio show (2015). According to McAfee,

> Twenty or forty years from now, I believe we will not need the labor of a lot of the people alive in order to have a very, very productive economy. In terms of the amount of human labor that you need to get the stuff out of the ground and off the farms and through the factories and into our homes and tables—next to home. (Kestenbaum, 2015).

Top scientists in advanced economies have expressed the fear of the robot armageddon. For instance, Swiss scientists warned in 1998 that artificially intelligent robots threatened the very existence of human beings. The scientists predicted that by 2008, microprocessor-based autonomous robots would be as clever as humans and even capable of "taking over from humans, their creators" and "end the human race as we know it" (Kelly, 1998). As inventor of an artificially intelligent machine, Hugo de Garis went as far as claiming that global politics, in future would "be dominated by the question of should humanity build ultra-intelligent machines or not." (Kelly, 1998).

ICTs, Governance, and Unions

With such fears, debates over rules of human engagement with intelligent machines will force political debates over a whole range of issues that include meaning of work, freedom, liberty, and governance. As artificial intelligence forms the basis for a good deal of ICT development, human relations, including collective bargaining, will change. From the current advancements, there are practical concerns. Today, ICTs invoke thoughts of unwarranted intrusion on privacy, political control, dehumanization, and de-skilling employees. ICTs, especially those of the robotic kind, can displace labor and render millions unemployed. Perhaps it is the latter that draws most attention from members of labor unions.

In the new economy, workers' unions found that whichever party controlled governments pursued policies that somewhat challenged labor power. In many instances, the state ceased to be an ally to trade unions. Thanks to neoliberalism and globalization, the state-union relationship seems to have changed significantly (Frundt, 2002). However, for the most part, exploitation of labor in the informal sector and agriculture continued unabated (Sheth, 1996). The prevailing global changes notwithstanding, labor unions must engage the competitive and globalized world (Reid, 1990). Most certainly, the new economy seems to have strengthened the role of unions in engaging the policy making process (Flood, 1995). Unions are lead players in promotion of policies that grow the economy and provide jobs without squeezing the public worker (Flood, Scheuerman & Plotkin, 1995, p. 151). Crucial to this debate is the displacement of labor by machines. In some ways, the displacement of labor forms a core part of trade unions' discursive legitimacy in matters concerning ICTs in the economy.

Scholars debate union influence over diffusion of technology. Tauman and Weiss (1987) found that unionization was not necessarily at odds with the adoption of labor-saving technologies and instead served to encourage use of technology, provided that the improvements were mild and demand for the products was high. Unions were likely to discourage technological diffusion only if new technologies suppressed wages.

Stephen Peitchinis (1983, p. 104), explored the possibility that unions abhorred technological change and ruled that not to be the case. Instead, unions embraced new technologies and equipment, especially if the changes resulted in increases in wages and other benefits. He summarized the debate over technological changes and unions:

> In reality evidence suggests union are not opposed to technological change. They are aware of the close relationship between technological change and productivity, and since rising productivity enables them to deliver to their members increases in wages and improvements in benefits, they cooperate with management in the implementation of technological changes. There are exceptions, of course, but exceptions should be treated as exceptions, not as the basis for general conclusions. (Peitchins, 1983, p. 104)

Jeffrey Keefe (1991) further investigated this matter and concluded that unions that are larger in membership have greater abilities to use technology. However, his study did not sample larger Kenyan unions and, therefore, his conclusions must be seen in context of Western society. Using statistical methods, Keefe wondered whether unionized plants were more likely than nonunion plants to use advanced technologies. Again, he found no direct effect of union membership on abilities to use advanced technology. Unions, he argued, utilized technology to improve productivity but at the same time preferred higher wages and efficient bargaining. A most significant finding of Keefe's work was recognition that different unions operated in different political settings and environments. The political and leadership environments accounted for the distinction in dissimilar policies toward technology, "ranging from encouraging to opposition" (Keefe, 1991, p. 261).

In the new economy, unions' role is heightened in areas such as deindustrialization, taxation, and combating recession and persistent poverty. In recent history, generally, the new economy marginalized manufacturing enclaves with detrimental effects to unionized workers

(Nissen, 1995). The best example of the deindustrialization in Kenya was in the case of closure of some of the premier manufacturing zones—RIVATEX Eldoret, KICOMI Kisumu, and Pan Paper Webuye, among several state-owned enterprises.

Plant closings in many of Kenya's state-owned enterprise systems were occasioned through undercapitalization and managerial failures (Grosh, 1991). Loss of jobs is never good news for unions. It leads to loss of union members and their dues (Flood, 1995, p. 3). Without resources, unions cannot do well in their battles for benefits such as medical care, pensions, social services, and suitable working conditions. Resources are the oil that lubricates the labor movement and the ensuing militancy manifest in strikes. And it is here that we have to interrogate the means of organization, information, and communications. New technologies have provided avenues for experimenting with now tactics and programs. ICTs applications are now key to outreach efforts. Unions use new technologies to match management and be empowered. Without laptops for data management, computers for dissemination of union programs, and email applications, networking and exchange of ideas would be impaired.

Email and other computer-mediated communication systems are widely used in business operations and activities. Albert Huang (2002) observes that emails are invaluable for activities like "marketing, intelligence gathering, negotiating, relationship building, and payment processing." More importantly, emails serve as a tool for "internal management, horizontally connecting peers and vertically linking supervisors and their subordinates" (Huang, 2002). Huang adds that email communications are vital for knowledge workers who telecommute (p. 193). But, as we shall note in our discussion on productivity, emails must be used correctly for organizations to make the most cost benefit from the media (Carson, 2015).

Perhaps the simplest way to appreciate the new tools for labor advocacy is to note the advantages of a simple application like email. Email, as we know, is faster than snail mail. Email is also cheap and more reliable than fax machines, which were fairly expensive in Kenya. As Eric Lee observes, email is neutral in terms of being accessible to both the rich and poor, powerful and powerless (Lee, 1997, p. 21). Perhaps it is this ability that makes it a widely used by-product of the new ICTs.

In general terms, ICTs contribute to economic growth in various ways. As in the case of email, ICTs lower costs of doing business and facilitate access to various services in all sectors. Electronic learning, health, and banking applications are now a prominent feature in modern lifestyles. Just to reflect on ICTs in education, most observers note that ICTs redefined learning processes and created new opportunities for networking within the sector. Africa was included this process and like elsewhere, ICTs in education were linked to modernized learning (Alic, 1997; Denning, 1996). Overall, ICTs are now major contributors to economic growth, especially in the context of increasing efficiencies and effectiveness of work. Developing countries now have indispensable tools to "participate effectively and efficiently in the information economy and compete in global e-market places," in the process making strides toward reducing poverty (Indjikian & Siegel, 2005, p. 696).

Another aspect of ICTs is to facilitate transparency and accountability in government. Ward and Lusoli (2002) examined some of the ways in which British trade unions use the Internet generally and whether unions applied ICTs for political participation and mobilization. They observed that although union membership had declined, ICTs provided an avenue for unions to directly engage the political process. Union members have not hesitated to use e-voting, e-referenda, and e-discussion for increased union outreach possibilities. There is also the possibility that ICTs have reshaped traditional hierarchical structures to affect decision-making. Unions as service providers are also inclined to use ICTs as tools in administrative modernization. Union memberships are available online. Websites are designed as interactive platforms for information storehouses and sharing organizational, personnel, and policy news releases. Unions have also utilized ICTs for recruitment of members, and for building their own image, especially among the youth. As we shall show, union members as individuals and organizations, including the Kenya National Union of Teachers (KNUT) and the Central Organization of Trade Unions (COTU), use social media platforms like Facebook and LinkedIn for both semi-official and social purposes. Both unions publicize their activities and positions on various economic policies on social media.

From the societal democratization perspective, new applications in e-participation and e-democracy enable society to engage its leadership. Besides the well-publicized social networking platforms, ICTs serve an important human need for interaction. ICTs probably lower the cost of participation in civic matters. Electronic meetings are convenient and allow greater participation than brick-and-mortar town halls do.

All over the world, small businesses drive economic activities. For example, in the United States, the Small Business Administration (SBA) reported that small and midsize businesses (SMBs)—businesses with fewer than five hundred employees—were engines that drove the economy and accounted for about half of the jobs in the private sector. To get most out of these investments, SMBs have changed their culture to enhance productivity through embracing new information and communication technologies. The Internet, in particular, has become an essential tool for twenty-first century living. Elsewhere, the World Bank's 2004 report detailed some of the paths taken by Small Business Enterprises (SBE) in developing countries to utilize the new forms of telecommunications.

Similarly, the United Nations Conference on Trade and Development (UNCTAD) recognized that the large small or medium enterprises, or Jua Kali Sector, in Kenya need Internet resources for marketing and research. This important component of the world's workforce is increasingly connected to the Internet and making use of mobile phones and email communications.

The growing importance of the Internet is highlighted through global initiatives that address the United Nation's Millennium Development Goals (MDG). Today, following the leadership of a 2011 UN Special Rapporteur, the UN considers Internet access a human right. Member nations that do not adequately invest in Internet resources deny their citizens a key resource for their livelihood and thereby stifle productivity. The vast array of resources available on the Internet also provides labor unions the additional ability to network globally.

Political Roots of the Internet in Kenya and Offline Union Activism and Political Engagements

The origins of the Internet in Kenya are well documented. One can argue that several factors working together gave Kenya an advantage in its quest to be linked to the global superhighway. A simplistic view would suggest that location matters. Yet, as host to the United Nations Environmental Program (UNEP) and Habitat, there was certainly substantive push from the country's international partners to move quickly and build an ICT infrastructure. But there was also a small but sizeable ICT savvy workforce, thanks to previous investments in the telecommunication sector. Kenya has been home to the African Advanced Level Telecommunication Institute (AFRALTI) and government-run Kenya Communications Institute (KCI). These centers maintained contacts with the International Telecommunication Union (ITU) and other worldwide ICT institutions that shared knowledge and current developments in the sector.

Although enough linkages existed, Kenya's ICT policy framework remained disjointed and lacking in identifiable focus. In Etta and Elder's (2005) edited work *At the Crossroads: ICT Policy Making in East Africa*, several authors, including Tim Waema (2005), note that the journey to providing a policy framework to absorb new technologies had many false starts. One of the challenges was the availability of seed money and committed technical knowhow, infrastructure, regulation, and cultural issues to lay the groundwork upon which the country would join the information superhighway.

The origins of the Internet in Kenya are well documented. Kenya's integration into the global village and information superhighway was, initially, the effort of a small group of individuals led by engineer Randy Bush supported by the U.S. National Science Foundation. Steve Goldstein of the U.S. National Science Foundation spearheaded the provision of equipment, as did Peter Sutherland of the UK Overseas Development Agency (ODA), which paid for the leased telephone lines. Among the key players in the movement was Shem Ochuodho, who served as the nation's first domain administrator. Ochuodho hosted Kenya's first DOS-based Internet Service Provider (ISP). In 2000, the Computer Society of Kenya named Ochuodho the "Father of Internet in Kenya." And in December 2010, on the occasion honoring him for linking Kenya to the world, Ochuodho acknowledged the inputs of several techies like Martin Koyabe, Paul Olendo, Alfred Orimbo, and their colleagues at the African Regional Center for Computing (ARCC). He also acknowledged Michael Joseph for his instrumental role in the process (Ochuodho, 2012, p.xv).

At the time Kenya received its first Internet signal, in 1994, union leadership was remarkably mute in articulation of its policy toward ICTs. Unions seemed to feature in the maintenance of the Kenyan state-run capitalist system, seeking to conform to the Kenya African National Union's (KANU) ideology of state domination of the nation's productive capacity. Unions limited their interventions by way of agitation for price stability, checking inflation, and supporting economic growth with the ultimate aim to secure job creation.

Although in 1994, the country was still participating in World Bank and International Monetary Fund (IMF)–led structural adjustment programs, it became one of the early African leaders in connectivity. In the face of intense global competition for markets and foreign exchange earnings, African governments were conditioned to regulate markets in all sectors. Driven by the desire to reduce debt repayment, the IMF promoted policies that undermined unionization, like price controls and higher wages. That the debt crisis and globalization of markets are associated with anti-unionization is well documented in Martin and Brady's work (2007).

All productive sectors were included in the structural adjustments and, in particular, the strategic communications sector was a prime candidate for divestiture. As a result, the Kenya elite promoted a neoliberal agenda and begun to open up telecommunication markets across the board. Although organized labor unions resisted the neoliberal agenda, the balance of power tilted toward business and the International Finance Institutions (IFI). Furthermore, the pressure by business to weaken labor unions was manifest in government's interference in trade union movements.

Thus, efforts to achieve control of the movement involved the politicization of the trade union leadership. It was a strategy to facilitate labor dependency on state largesse. The dependency thesis was well articulated in work done in Australia. According to W. A. Howard, the relationship forged between the state and unions was designed to shelter unions from fluctuations of the market and the prevalence of conflicts with employers. Since the state recognized unions, it was safeguarding union membership and ensuring that arbitration mechanisms curtailed the challenges of organizing. Dependency in Kenya's case guaranteed that union amalgamations and restructuring did not threaten state power. For proponents of the dependency school, reorganizations and rebirths were about reliance upon state assistance (Cooper, 2002, p. 44).

President Moi's administration had ensured that there was little room for workers' political mobilization. He failed to ratify international conventions that guaranteed freedoms of association mandated in the International Labor Organization (ILO) treaties. President Moi's preoccupation with regime survival obscures his preindependence role in helping champion the rights of workers, especially teachers. During colonial days, communication technologies were rather weak and it was difficult for the various teachers' unions, mostly organized in different regions, to come together. For example, in Nyanza, teachers were represented through the Nyanza African Teachers Unions (NATU), in the Rift Valley there was the Rift Valley African Teachers Association (RATA), at the Coast, the Coast African Teachers Unions, and for Central Province, the Central Province African Teachers Union, frequently organized as the Kikuyu Teachers Union (KTU). It took efforts from teachers like Daniel Moi, in the late 1950s, to bring together the different associations and have the Legislative Council (Legco), the forerunner to the National Assembly, to pass a bill that helped create a single national body for teachers. Kenya National Union of Teachers (KNUT) emerged in 1957 with Ignatius Mkok as its first interim president and Stephen J. Kioni as interim secretary general. After the official registration of KNUT in May 1959, Samwel Ayany was elected its first president, with Kioni leaving his full-time position at Kilimambogo Teachers Training College to join KNUT's administration. These early trade union leaders enjoyed close association with Daniel Moi throughout his service in the formative years of the nation's administrative apparatus. When he was president of Kenya, from 1978 to 2002, Moi's administration did not tolerate criticism, especially from a trade union with membership spread throughout the country.

Like President Jomo Kenyatta, his predecessor, Moi sought to neutralize all workers because he detested Marxism and associated the left with workers' movements. During the cold war era, Kenya was among the few countries in the region to denounce communism as inappropriate to its development goals. Since teachers were associated with the intelligentsia, they aligned with political aspirations that demanded greater political freedoms in the country. Workers' association with intellectuals was particularly frightening hence Moi's discomforts with unions like the Universities Academic Staff Union (UASU), whose leaders were closely monitored by the Special Branch, a notorious unit in the country's law enforcement machinery known for its brutality and disregard for human rights. In most of the 1980s, Kenya's economy weakened as single-party authoritarianism took its toll. Arguably, then, union activism in 1994 was a reaction to the decline in academic freedom and deterioration of worker terms of service and wages.

Kenya's collective bargaining structure was enshrined in the statutes. The Central Organization of Trade Unions (COTU) represented private sector workers while the Federation of Kenya Employers (FKE) negotiated and stood for employer interests. Unions' main concern was in employment stability and matters of retrenchments orchestrated through the structural adjustments. Under Moi, there was an attempt to merge the then ruling party Kenya African National Union (KANU) with the Central Organization of Trade Unions (COTU). One of the trade union leaders incorporated into this scheme was Ali I. Mohamed, the General Secretary of the Union of Posts and Telecommunication (UPT). His proposal to affiliate unions with the ruling party included a change in the curriculum at Tom Mboya Labor College (TMLC) to offer politics courses that would promote the interests of the ruling elite. The affiliation plan also promoted the idea of COTU members providing support for KANU party policies. As the KANU-COTU National Liaison Officer, Ali Mohamed appeared to support regulation of the airwaves and other communication avenues. Therefore, through policy, ruling elites monopolized the national radio and other broadcasting instruments. By this time, KANU had established a national newspaper network (with the assistance of the Robert Maxwell Communication Corporation of London) through which it would offer official versions of its management of public affairs and policy. In other words, KANU would participate in liberalized communications markets in a confined structure.

Although the "merger" or "affiliation" with KANU was brought to a halt in 1993, a year before Kenya's first Internet service providers (ISPs) linked the country to the world, the cooption of trade unions into the policy making apparatus remained unchanged. After 1991, international pressure caused President Daniel arap Moi to end the one-party rule. With the rise of multiparty politics came a renewed sense of openness. There was consensus within the donor community that without political conditionality, foreign investments were insecure. Neoliberal regimes were seen as the chosen strategy to ensure maximum profits for Western corporations doing business in Kenya.

Single-Party Dictatorship, ICTs, and Coalition Politics

In terms of the impact of ICTs on governance, perhaps, we should reflect on the academy's initial depiction of ICTs as enablers of two scenarios, the Orwellian model, which means governments would curtail political freedoms, and the Athenian perspective, which implies greater freedoms would stem from investments in emerging technologies (de

Donk & Tops, 2006). To some extent, both models were applicable to Kenya. ICTs have proved to be helpful tools in promoting democratic values and through various social media and online platforms, have made governments more responsive to citizen needs. In Athenian terms, ICTs enabled NARC to defeat KANU and opened greater democratic space in Kenya. At the opposite end, new technologies threaten power elites, who seek to restrain the power of institutions like unions, which are often aligned to progressive agendas and demand more freedoms and transparency in government operations. Arguably, the Orwellian surveillance system whereby governments monitor citizens' online activities is manifest in the continuation of symbiotic relationships between ruling elites and corporate leaders in the ICT sector.

The Internet arrived in Kenya in the mid-1990s amid the rise of single-party dictatorships in several African states. In fact, for Kenya, considerable resistance toward expansion of airwaves and other new communication technologies existed throughout the duration of President Daniel Moi's administration. Thus, according to Ochuodho, the KANU regime, fearing the decentralized and interactive nature of ICTs, attempted to block the development of the Internet in Kenya. The elite aversion to free media was not, however, unique to developing countries. Interest in controlling sensitive information has some implications for political stability. Not surprising, governments all over the world develop substantial interests in new methods of communication (Klotz, 2004, p. 5). It is perfectly understandable that President Moi's administration's survival was dependent upon its control of the communication infrastructure. Without having its finger on the information market, the regime feared its competitors would weaken its hold on other levers of power and the commanding heights of the state-centered economy. Predictably, a memo from the Head of Public Service to all Permanent Secretaries, Heads of the Military, Special Branch, and other government agencies warned against government departments connecting to ARCC/Internet/UNEP without the approval of the Office of the President. Ochuodho and his colleagues' breakthrough came only as a result of direct intervention and support from three members of President Moi's administration, Benjamin Kipkorir, then ambassador to the United States, Micah Cheserem, then governor of the Central Bank of Kenya, and Brigadier Wilson Boinnett, then head of National Security Intelligence Service (NSIS), the notorious police Special Branch (Ochuodho, 2010; 2012, p. xv).

Before the entry of ICTs, Kenya's government promoted the World Bank and IMF agenda, which supported industrialization based on foreign investments. The idea of creating a suitable investment climate guided the entire framework for encouraging investments in ICT sector. Thus actors in the ICT sector, as we shall note, applied time-tested concepts and approaches and was on the path to integration into the national economic fabric. In fact, ICT platforms were increasingly applied in the cause of politics. Ochuodho (2012) reported members of the opposition used Internet platforms to craft their progressive agenda and remove Moi's party from power.

In 2002, the Mwai Kibaki–led National Rainbow Coalition (NARC) pushed KANU out of power. President Mwai Kibaki developed a more pro-business approach than his predecessors. He previously served as Minister for Finance and Planning and gave the green light to rehabilitation of the debilitated infrastructures and further opening up of the telecommunications markets. To further promote the country's ICT agenda, Kibaki signed into law the Science, Technology, and Innovation Act of 2002. His administration also initiated the National Commission for Science Technology and Innovation (NACOSTI) and the Kenya National Innovation Agency (KENIA) to help formulate innovations based on ICT development. As a result of these and other efforts, the profile of Kenya as an emerging African ICT leader was enhanced. Subsequently, under the coalition government, Kenya became the most wired economy in the East African region. Massive informatization processes were launched. Both workers and employers were able to access a host of communication platforms that had been previously unavailable.

However, the relative successes in building ICT infrastructure were not matched by increased union attention to policy implications for members and broader questions about apparent weakening of union power. From the perspective of government, public union demands were embedded in budgetary perspectives. Officials continuously voiced concerns about rising wage bills. Thus, in terms of engaging unions for policy management, the NARC government appeared to favor a policy of fragmentation of trade unions to offer a counternarrative on the necessity for wage bargaining. As a strategy, fragmentation achieved some goals. Not unexpectedly, by the end of 2002, government registered the Kenya Civil Servants Union (KCSU), rationalizing its decision in terms of the constitutional rights of workers.

Although Kibaki favored freedom of assembly for unionized workers, his government relegated the role of the Ministry of Labor to one of the nonstrategic departments. He preferred to let the FKE, the National Tripartite Consultative Committee, the Joint Industrial and Commercial Consultative Committee, the Labor Advisory Board, and the National Advisory Committee on Occupational Health and Safety and Ministry of Labor became the lead actors in articulation of labor matters.

Although labor unrest was common after 2004, Kibaki preferred labor disputes to be addressed at the Industrial Court and not through strikes. Still, teachers took to the streets in 2009 and 2011 demanding higher wages. Most of the unrest was occasioned by the weakening purchasing power of teachers and other workers and not by substantive policy disagreements. It is only the Kenya Socialist Democratic Alliance (KSDA) party that publicly articulated an alternative approach to labor issues in the country. KSDA saw itself as a "workers' party" that challenged the IMF and World Bank for promoting policies that undermined creation of jobs and workers' dignity.

The Emergence of Safaricom and National Politics

Through structural adjustments, the government promoted market liberalization in all sectors, including the information and communication technology industries. Arguably, the biggest winner in the liberalized ICT market was Safaricom, a company partly owned by Britain's Vodafone, which hired chief executive Michael Joseph in 2000 to increase mobile phone subscribers from 500,000. By 2005, Joseph's Safaricom became one of the largest companies in Kenya, netting more than 5 million subscribers. And by the time he retired in 2010 Joseph's leadership had turned the telecom firm into East Africa's largest company by market capitalization (Reuters, 2010). Joseph enjoyed excellent relationships with the Kenyan administration and was influential in promoting the board vision for Safaricom products including M-PESA and other electronic money transaction platforms.

Through government's symbiotic relationships with Safaricom, the national bureaucracy gave full support to the company's growth. High-level Ministry of Information and Communication Technology (ICT) officials within Kibaki's administration led by then Permanent Secretary Bitange Ndemo and Mutahi Kagwe, then minister, persuaded President Kibaki to further relax business opportunities within the ICT sector, favoring the relative dominance of Safaricom. Ndemo, hailed by many observers as one of the key players in the development of ICT platforms in the country, was receptive to the symbiotic relationships between government and the few private sector actors in the ICT sector. Clearly inspired by the need to transform the country, he advocated for greater preparations toward a mature ICT regime and hastened the nation's e-readiness (Ndemo, 2013).

For his part, President Kibaki saw these initiatives as a symbol of modernization (Bowman, 2010; Nduati & Bowman 2005). Following a stakeholders' conference in 2006, which President Kibaki attended, the initial development of the ICT Master Plan was established. The conference laid out what was to become the framework of the country's ICT development. Underlying the framework was the strategy to build an ICT infrastructure based on the public/private partnership (PPP) model. President Kibaki gave full support to the development of ICT platforms to include development of MB broadband, which materialized in 2009 when the first-ever undersea fiber optic cable was installed in Mombasa. After the initial layout of the infrastructure, the Ministry of Communications worked with other stakeholders, culminating in Kibaki's support and implementation of Kenya Open Data platforms.

At the core of open data initiatives is the concern for transparency and reduction of workers' time when processing information requests from the public. Open data goes beyond just providing data and extends into the realm of entrepreneurship. Creative minds use the data to develop new apps for public consumption. Apps can range from citizens having at their finger tips bus routes, availability of parking spaces, housing affordability, land value, schedules of municipal street cleanings, and much more. In developed countries, open data portals serve to provide information on a whole range of services. Open data is about engaging members of society through a whole range of apps enabled through new information technology devices. The government of Kenya saw an opportunity in ICTs and framed initiatives as means to create jobs and increase national productivity.

Although Kenya's ICT infrastructure vastly improved after 2010, the key concern for trade unions was to safeguard national stability, ensure security, and maintain living wages for the lowest paid workers. Fragmentation and the cooption of the labor movement continued after the 2007 elections. Still, the coalition government resulted in the growth of patronage positions in the public sector. As a result, the wage bill grew out of proportion, prompting the government to consider a return to downsizing. As we shall observe, the high wage bill led government to adopt better personnel tracking software and improve on personnel data services.

From the perspective of union leaders, new technologies not only encouraged awareness of transparency concepts but offered members platforms for civic engagement, self-reflection, and education. With increased use of mobile communication devices, workers were empowered to mobilize and respond to calls for action. New social media like YouTube also served as an important repository for information useful to union members and leaders. In an interview with Jeff Koinange, on the former CNN International journalist's show *The Bench,* Francis Atwoli of COTU expressed his displeasure with bureaucratic corruption in the country. But at the same time, he appeared to share more than was necessary by bragging on his great personal wealth, which would give the impression that being a union leader was akin to being a corporate CEO (see, Atwoli, 2014). Later, speaking another function in Khwisero, Atwoli quipped about his wealth and social status, "Western Community has faith in me. I have money, two wives and 15 children, traditional cows and homestead" (Chepkoech, 2015).

New technologies, therefore, serve to increase awareness of national problems and illustrate in clear terms, the everyday toils of workers in the country. In particular, the Internet published government statistics on economic growth and gave workers insights into comparative wage levels. Information widely available through Google searches seemed to serve as a catalyst for worker agitation, especially as members could now track down the expenditure patterns of their leaders.

Arguably, at the end of President Mwai Kibaki and Prime Minister Raila Odinga's coalition government, the incoming Jubilee Alliance, which had dubbed itself as the digital leadership, found itself unable to maintain a momentum of economic growth. As a result, the material conditions of workers deteriorated, as evidenced by increased labor unrest and public frustration over the quality of government services. Kenya ushered in 2013 with some of the worst labor-government relations in the country's history.

Initially, the President Uhuru Muigai Kenyatta–William S. Ruto administration was confronted with labor unrest and a host of security and public safety challenges. Among the most obvious disasters included when fire gutted a section of Jomo Kenyatta International Airport in August 2013. Although the incident occurred on the fifteenth anniversary of the terrorist bombing of the U.S. Embassy in Kenya, no association with global terrorism was established. The second and major breach of security was more profound. In September 2013, a group of Somali Al-Shabaab Jihadists attacked Westgate Mall in Westlands, living more than sixty-seven dead. Among the dead was Mbugua Mwangi, a nephew of President Uhuru Kenyatta.

Uhuru Kenyatta's administration started on a weak footing after his main rival unsuccessfully sought court action to nullify his election. And, as persons named by the International Criminal Court (ICC) as war criminal suspects, their administration initially faced legitimacy issues, especially among Western countries. As alluded to, the country experienced among the worst security challenges in its modern history. Al-Shabaab terrorist and other criminal gangs seemed to rule the major towns and attacked residents of Mpeketoni Lamu, among other areas. Agitation for better security policies and effective policing became an important area of union concern after the 2013 election. For example, KNUT officials urged teachers not to go to work in areas such as Mandera and areas bordering Somalia unless the government guaranteed students' and teachers' safety (Ongeri, 2013).

In a similar move, leaders of Kenya Union of Domestic, Hotel, Education, Institutions, Hospitals and Allied Workers (KUDHEIHA) toured hotels in Kenya's coastal region to see for themselves the effects of massive job losses that resulted from travel advisory warnings issued by Western governments. The United States and its Western allies advised their citizens against traveling to Kenya in 2014, noting that security conditions were unacceptable after Al-Shabaab intensified attacks in the country. KUDHEIHA raised its concern over loss of jobs in the tourist sector and joined civil society in calling for the government to improve its policy on security. Such direct action meant that unions were not averse to public policy as important as security and safety.

But the focus on public safety did not alter traditional union causes. Instead, a good number of COTU affiliates like the KUDHEIHA, Kenya Plantation and Agricultural Workers Union, Dock Workers Union, Kenya Local Government Workers' Union, and Kenya Union of Food and Allied Workers Union with strong collective bargaining and training portfolios, continued to pressure employers for other benefits. For example, unions like the Kenya Building, Construction, Timber, Furniture and Allied Employees Union, Communication Workers Union, Kenya Local Government Workers Union, and the Kenya Union of Commercial Food and Allied Workers Union were successful in achievement of benefits such as pension schemes, paternity house allowances, medical, legal protection, and terminal benefits. On the other hand, problems in the vital and predominantly public sector areas of education and healthcare continued throughout the administrations of Kibaki and Uhuru Kenyatta. Teachers, nurses, and other workers demanded pay rises and went on strike in 2013. Also, the Kenya National Union of Nurses and other health workers called a strike in late 2013. The Kenya Health Professionals Union (KHPU), the Kenya Medical Practitioners, and Pharmacists and Dentist Union (KMPDU) joined them.

In 2014, students across the nation took to the streets to demand the government rescind its decision to increase university fees. The representatives of university faculty (Universities Academic Staff Union [UASU] and Kenya Universities Staff Union, [KUSU]), issued further threats to strike, claiming that government had failed to implement collective bargain agreements agreed upon between unions and the Inter-Public Universities Council Consultative Forum (IPCCF). Additionally, the Union of Kenya Civil Servants (UKCS) threatened industrial action over poor terms and conditions of service.

Labor militancy continued well into 2014 and 2015 as operators of public transport vehicles and commercial trucks demanded government withdraw rules they deemed as raising operational costs. Among the regulations were use of paperless cards for payment, removal of tinted windows, and ban of night travel by certain classes of transportation vehicles.

Although wage policy remained the most visible concern for trade unions, a token increase was announced during Labor Day 2013. No pay raise was announced for the May 1, 2014, Labor Day. Instead, the Jubilee Alliance began to prepare workers for possible retrenchments and reduction in force in the public sector. Of course, labor unions reacted by threatening to mobilize for action and also, through the COTU secretariat, called for policies that would reduce waste through government corruption and a revisit of the Value Added Taxes (VAT) revenue policy.

In July 2013, the Deputy President William Ruto initiated talks with COTU and sought workers' support in efforts to cut down the huge national wage bill. Upon realization that worker support would not be forthcoming, the Jubilee resorted to supporting further union fragmentation. The government encouraged the Kenya Police Union to be registered. It also, through the Teachers Service Commission, supported the rivalry between KNUT and KUPPET.

There were allegations that the government encouraged the formation of the National Union of Kenya Parastatal Employees (NUKPE) as a strategy to tame COTU. Officials from several affiliates of COTU, including the Kenya Ferry Services, Kenya Ports Authority, Kenya Union of Commercial Food and Allied Workers (KUCFAW), Banking Insurance and Finance Union (BIFU), Dock Workers Union, and Communication Workers' Union (CWU) issued statements denouncing NUKPE as a "government project."

For the most part, union members in Kenya recognized the need for utilizing citizen apps for various causes that included solving problems society. In most cases, union members as citizens did not wait for the government's to draw policies on capture of data for public service. Applications of ICTs within Kenya's civil society gained international attention in a backhanded way. After the disputed presidential election of 2007 and the ensuing violence, a group of Kenyan bloggers developed an app that helped people to report hot spots where grisly killings were taking place. The app, dubbed Ushahidi (Kiswahili for witness), helped members of nonprofit and voluntary organizations respond to distress calls. The tool was originally built from a website and morphed into a real-time app that gave the media and relief organizations pictures of what was happening on the ground. This was accomplished through aggregation of texts, tweets, photo images, and messages available on desktops and smartphones. Ushahidi's crowd-sourced data documented maps of places where the election violence and fraud occurred. Ushahidi was one of the positive impacts of new technologies that gave the country a better appreciation of ICTs. As far as delivery of public services was concerned, government corporations were now experimenting with payments of utility bills and employing websites for announcing information helpful for members of the public and businesses.

A key change in modern society is the increased use of ICTs in provision of public services. Through ICTs, employers and employees are becoming more technologically proficient and learning how to integrate older technologies such as fax and copy machines into a vast network linking business operations. Today, even older technologies like surveillance systems, tracking systems, road traffic police enforcement systems, various radar devices, weather monitoring, and hundreds of other appliances are integrated within a mosaic of the "Internet of things."

New ICTs have the capacity to efficiently reach larger populations and are characterized by greater sensory integration involving audio and images. Perhaps political communication scholar Robert Klotz's account explains this characteristic most eloquently.

> The Internet is at once like no other communication device and like every other communication device. It is a personal and mass medium of communication. It is capable of transmitting communication in any format—print, audio, or video. Of course, these dimensions of communications have been available previously—just not through the same medium. By harnessing the power of the computer to previous communication advancements, the Internet has become the most versatile of media. (Klotz, 2004, p. 1)

At the same time, e-governance builds on the logic of availing ICTs for use in state affairs more generally. In that regard, governance institutions work within well-defined networks that include private and nonprofit organizations. In e-governance, ICTs and other digital platforms enable and/or enhance political and social developments. In many ways, the virtual state is a manifestation of the e-governance framework. Kenya has made enormous progress in integrating ICTs into the country's governance systems.

Powered by easy access to mobile phones, the communication space between the government and its people had shrunk to unprecedented levels. Mobile phones have rapidly taken over from the problematic and unreliable landlines. In a past study, Kenya had one phone line for every one hundred people (Wresch, 1996, p. 39). The availability of software and devices that transmit data signals from cellular phones to computers resulted in building an ICT community that has wide ramifications for politics. The point is, that with these devices, the potential for political interaction between the governed and ruling elites was at least in a theoretical sense far more possible than hitherto.

Under the Mwai Kibaki administration, the applications of ICTs for political management increased tremendously to the extent that Kenyans were among the first in Africa to create a website to monitor MPs, in 2006, to track bills and parliamentary debates.

The number of MPs who had developed their own websites also increased, but the interactive capacity of the websites was weak. Many of Kenya's MPs rarely interacted with their constituents outside of the social media frameworks like Twitter and Facebook. As for the mobile phones, Harvard University's Kennedy School of Government Professor of Practice Calestous Juma (2010) documented the use of these devices for purposes of political mobilization. Thus, the ICTs were now major facilitators of public discourses and avenues for governance.

The entries of overseas and diaspora Kenyans into the vast array of political blogospheres were one way of holding MPs accountable and enhancing the quality of governance generally. Several blogs were created to share information on political issues of the land (for example, www.kenyapundit.com and mzalendo.com, among many others). The administration enhanced its online presence through several government-administered institutional websites. Nearly all ministries, public universities (including online [web] teaching through African Virtual University [AVU] platforms, in collaboration with donors), and other public organizations offered opportunities for online public presence. An early impressive initiative was the www.kenya.ke website, which was a one-stop portal with informational and interactive features. More important, the Office of the President (OOP) established the Directorate of e-Government as the road map and gateway to a future robust e-government structure (www.e-government.go.ke). Briefly, there are at least eight main reasons for making the leap toward e-government in Kenya. First, Internet portals have the ability to streamline data management processes, which leads to more customer-centered service delivery. Second is the nonspecific need for modernization, which speaks of the embracing twenty-first century technologies. Third, is to satisfy powerful donors and ICT corporations who are major players in matters of economic development. Fourth, government officials are attracted by efficiencies accrued from electronic transfer of petty cash (G2B) in local municipalities. Fifth, is to use the Internet as a tool for political mobilization to reach the youth. Sixth, is to satisfy powerful local political elites and franchises allied to the political elites. Seventh, is the need for e-participation and for civic education purposes.

The ramifications of engaging ICTs in governance are well understood. Just for the record, in January, February, and March 2008 Kenyans saw the application of ICTs for negative political action. Then, mobile phones and Internet services were the carriers of hate messages, which added fuel to ethnic rivalries in the aftermath of the December 2007 hotly contested general and presidential election.

Aside from the negative uses of ICTs for ethnic mobilization, applications in formal politics are well known. For instance, members of parliament (MPs) have often lobbied each other using email and mass list serves (computer-mediated communication), electronic data interchange Systems (EDI), and text messaging (phone devices). The political establishment's embrace of ICT platforms signaled the entry of a new form of digitalized consciousness and creation of space to reshape national social capital. One would argue that the ICTs also helped provide bridges to help different community leaders engage each other in a non-physical manner. After all, the Internet provided social networks through which groups on opposite sides of policy issues could, at least, deliberate anonymously. Digital politics offered a platform clearly absent from face-to-face meetings.

Now, with e-governance and e-government integrated into the national socio-technical systems, the platform for union engagements was well established. Unions, as members of society, embrace ICTs within the larger context of values and national psyche. The question was just how complex and to what ends would the engagement with technologies be effected?

The growing use of ICTs in organizations is seen as a form of modernization. Kenya's heavy investment in ICTs raises obvious questions concerning the role of new technologies in labor affairs. This is particularly true, as more use of ICTs requires adjustments in labor markets. As part of Africa's pressure group systems, trade unions often realize that they have to understand the changes brought about by the proliferation of ICTs in society. But union leaders must provide clear incentives to members to be able to fully leverage new ICTs for their own advantage. The slowness to embrace ICTs in union functions limits the leadership's ability to effectively steer unions toward effective participation in national ICT policy.

Traditionally, trade unions are aware of the use of ICTs as resources that promote workplace modernization. Throughout the world, trade unions have grappled with the growth of different technologies, especially the benefits of technology for the union membership.

Union members seek to understand the role of technology in terms of organizational rationality as promoted by management. The proliferation of ICTs when promoted by management can be included in labor-management negotiations.

CONCLUSIONS

In summary, the chapters that follow are about the promise and perils of ICTs and the role of trade (labor) unions in Kenya's search for policies for development. This role assumes Kenya's governing elite has embraced, to some extent, consultative and participative governance models. The volume speaks to issues that concern the new economy and how best unions, as key players in governance, can engage with the penetration of ICTs in daily lives of workers and employers. The unfolding proliferation of ICTs requires that practitioners, union leaders, and union members fully educate themselves about the possibilities of leveraging technology for raising the standards of living of workers. Gaining clear insights into the fast-changing world of ICTs is not easy. Since these changes are occurring at a fast pace, my purpose is to enhance the understanding of the politics, policy, and economic discourses around ICTs for unions. The main themes captured in this book include the role of ICTs, union engagements with policy and politics, and the factors and attitudes that affect the interactions between new technologies and Kenyan workers. The book outlines the critical need for unions to recognize the changes brought about as a result of emerging new information technologies. The framework offered here considers the critical role of unions in collaborative governing structures and describes and reveals the political and policy context through which ICT policies are situated.

TWO

Trade Unions, ICTs, and Public Policy in the New Economy

INTRODUCTION

As was previously stated, trade or labor unions are active players in public affairs and influencing policy. Historically unions engage public affairs and policy in many arenas in the service of members. Among the goals is to represent members in grievance processes, defend them, represent them in media relations, and occasionally involve them in political action (Shostak, 1991, p. 19). Unions, as stakeholders in national governance, voice concerns about corruption and maladministration. Furthermore, unions speak for vulnerable members of society and are responsive to economic forces that determine quality of life for members and other citizens alike. And the new economy seems to have strengthened the role of unions in engaging the policy making process (Flood, 1995). Unions are lead players in promotion of policies that grow the economy and provide jobs without squeezing the public worker (Flood, Scheuerman & Plotkin, 1995, p. 151).

One of the defining features of unions in Kenya is the tradition to align its core interests with those of the "government of the day." This rather conservative position means the unions do not challenge assumptions about public authority and instead regard the state as the agent of public interest. Increasingly, in ethnic-driven politics, state interests are not at odds with those of big business. A symbiotic relationship between private and state interests complicates the nature of the labor-management-state relationships in Kenya. From the time of independence, pioneer trade unionists navigated the thin line between unionism and national politics. Makhan Singh, who in 1949 founded the East Africa Trade Union Congress (EATUC), was the father of the labor movement in the region. He was also a freedom fighter, whose clarion call Uhuru Sasa (Freedom Now), served both union members and parties agitating against colonial rule. Moreover, trade union leaders like Dennis Akumu, Bildad Kagia, and Fred Kubai befriended other nationalist and freedom fighters including left-leaning Pio Pinto Gama. Together they opposed the leadership of American-leaning union members, especially Thomas J. Mboya, a nationalist and avid supporter of the capitalist economic system.

As a visionary trade unionist, Mboya supported and promoted free enterprise alongside state-led capitalism. He asserted that trade unions were obligated to "freely contribute to the social and economic development" of Kenya (Mboya, 1963). Mboya's view was that the working class was to be involved in policy and management decisions for the good of the country. To some extent, the history of the country's labor movement reflects the desire of union leaders to align their policies with those of the national government. And the foremost unions—the Central Organizations of Trade Unions (COTU), and Kenya National Union of Teachers (KNUT)—organized their movements along economic issues.

Also, since most of the early unions were concerned with wage labor in occupational industries like railways, plantations, hotels, and teaching, the movement's struggles revolved around a limited and narrow struggle. Union leaders viewed themselves as champions of workers' rights and also sought to promote safety in the workplace. Occasionally, union leaders would pay "impromptu visits" to factories in the name of occupational health and safety in the private sector.

But, remarkably, the tendency of union leaders to transition from union activism to direct engagements with the ruling political party, as alluded to in the efforts by KANU to merge with COTU, complicated the ability of unions to be impartial representatives of their members' interests. Moreover, union leaders throughout the Jomo Kenyatta and Daniel arap Moi administrations joined the ruling elite, serving as cabinet ministers, as in Tom Mboya's case, or as elected members of parliament and assistant ministers. For example, Dennis Akumu, Bildad Kaggia, and Fred Kubai all joined the establishment, thereby receiving platforms to articulate labor goals. In Kaggia's case, he also served as Assistant Minister for Labor and Social Services in 1969–1974 (Nguli, 2013). Then and now, COTU's top leadership seemed more persuaded to use union experience in parliamentary politics. For instance COTU General Secretary Juma Boy and his successor Joseph Mugalla both served as members of parliament. Likewise, Kimani wa Nyoike, who was head of the Union of Kenya Civil Servants (UKCS) also joined national politics after clashing with the Moi administration, in 1982 which banned the UKCS. The organization had become the most powerful single union in the country, posing a direct threat to Moi's single-party rule (Berg-Schlosser, 1992, p. 261; Chege, 1987).

Also, after independence, there was a proliferation in the number of public service jobs, thereby giving financial might to public unions. As a result of the entry of civil servant unions, a shift in the emphasis in the government's labor relations occurred. The law governing labor relations gave public sector workers the rights to collectively bargain. And with unions seeking to bargain over pay and benefits for lower-level civil servants, a new personnel system had to be nurtured. Later, constitutional changes in 2010 made collective bargaining an element of the Bill of Rights. Still, prior to 2010 and beyond, labor markets in Kenya experienced major realignments and changes in organization occasioned by global shifts in employment practices. Perhaps not surprisingly and in addition to the big two umbrella unions, the pool of workers increased to include professionals that had been reluctant to form unions.

Historically, union collective bargaining agreements appeared to yield more benefits for public servants, as opposed to private sector workers, who were at the mercy of a much more challenging policy framework. Changes in global financial investments weakened workers' capacity to challenge the strengths of corporations wishing to locate in countries that lacked capital. In this chapter, we explore the nexus between trade unions and the policy making environment. The discussion considers the changes brought about by the new economy, whose main driver is the information and communication technology (ICT) sector. The emerging ICT-driven economy has provided opportunities for unions in both public and private sectors to participate in national development policy processes. As key stakeholders in governance, unions have achieved some measures of success in shaping policy discourse in areas such as in public health and security management.

Unions and Participation in Governance: Challenges in Policy Advocacy

In policy advocacy, trade unions, as key actors in governance, frequently agree with the private sector in fighting for common interests, which may include combating endemic corruption and the protection of property and contract rights. The one huge difference in Kenya is that, over the years, unions have not had the same autonomy enjoyed by corporations. Major unions such as the Kenya National Union of Teachers (KNUT) have strongly rejected the ideological bent toward "market solutions" in national education policy. KNUT, in particular, has publicly opposed the privatization of education, arguing that it leads to commercialization and is antithetical to the idea of public education. KNUT regards public education as a key human rights issue and has routinely framed the urge for privatization of schools as externally driven. KNUT's contention was that the World Bank, Commonwealth Development Corporation, and investors such as Facebook, Microsoft, and Omidyar Network promoted the ideology of privatization for their own reasons.

While KNUT was not against participation of low-cost private schools in the country's education sector, it was opposed to curriculum development not approved by the Kenya Institute of Curriculum Development (Sossion, 2016).

The challenge for KNUT is to be able to act as a catalyst against large-scale privatization of education in Kenya. In many instances, unions are under attack and must ward off pressures from more powerful local and international ruling elites. Some of the largest trade unions in Kenya are in the public sector—teachers and civil servants. The lack of autonomy from the state weakens the ability of union work. Corporate power does not surrender its economic and political position in society. Because government has to provide a climate for business to invest in the country, urban and rural workers are traditionally kept under control and the state utilizes the judiciary to encourage business and economic accumulation. Finding the right wage policy is a challenge that Kenya has continued to face (Vandemoortele, 1984).

However, in a broader sense, labor is not sympathetic to business' tendency to call for a shrinking of state apparatus. Instead, labor unions place much faith in the competency of the government. Traditionally, the government in Kenya has a larger role to play in the economy than in the advanced countries, where labor is relatively expensive. As a result of the dominant nature of the urban formal and government sectors, economic policy has to contend with massive unemployment and underemployment, which are forces of disequilibria (Killick & Sharpley, 1985). By conservative estimates, the unemployment situation in Kenya is bleak and continues to be a policy challenge. Especially problematic is that sociologists see a direct link between persistent unemployment and deviant youth behaviors including lawlessness. Of the 841,600 jobs created in 2015, only 128,000 were in the formal wage sector, which lags behind the 450,000 youths graduating from colleges (Achuka & Okoth, 2016; Federation of Kenya Employers' [FKE], 2016). Overall, over 80 percent of workers were in the vulnerable informal sector, which also produced the so-called "casual" laborers. The casuals are mostly outside the purview of unionization and long coveted by COTU, which seeks to grow its numbers and political muscle (Mwembe, 1989).

At the same time, unions have joined with civil society to call for reforms to expand human rights and the dignity and human rights of the workers (ICFTU, 1998). Labor is quick to support bureaucratic growth if the state's regulatory framework ensures that business acts in the public interest. Profound mistrust between unions and the state has ensued where the state bureaucracy is corrupt, without integrity, and inefficient.

Ironically, the challenge today is that global capitalism reaps more profits where the regulatory framework is weak and corrupt. Thus, in a sense, labor unions must navigate a thin line in seeking to embrace "job creators" on one hand and the "regulators" on the other. Because capital is internationally mobile, unions cannot be seen to articulate democratic socialism and other left-leaning ideologies without risking being labeled "anti-development" or "job-killers."

In terms of trade union mobilization, while sympathetic to workers causes, the government has persistently rejected the expansion of union power. Unions have often sought to expand power against government and business infringements on workers' rights. Through various means like cooptation and fragmentation, the state has not allowed unions to create a powerful political force. Through legal mechanisms, unions do not have discretion to challenge corporations in Kenya. As a result, the allocation of corporate capital and price-control regimes are largely out of reach of labor unions. Without this power, Kenya's labor union was relatively constrained as it watched the country's industrial sector shrink in the new economy of the 1980s and 1990s.

The New Economy

Arguably, Kenya entered into the global markets in pre-independence times through trade and cultural exchanges. That said, the new information technologies take globalization to a whole new level. As the literature suggests, "the electronic integration and digitization of the world economy is but one aspect of globalization" (Kobrin, 2000, p. 134). As the University of Namibia's Maggy Beukes-Amiss remarks, "ICTs have brought Africa into the heart of the global economy, giving our businesses a unique opportunity to expand" (2014, p. 16–17). Indeed, observers associate the new economy with the rise of ICTs around 1990.

At the end of 1990, the world witnessed a rapid proliferation of computer software and hardware products that drove literally all facets of human civilization. Then, high-tech tools and computer-enabled devices became common features of the marketplace. There was also a huge proliferation of financial institutions investing in technology companies. The new economy thrived, with globalized marketing strategies built around the Internet. Especially important was what Richard Sennett (2006) referred to as "gold plating" or the idea of branding items that are inherently similar. For example, the difference in appearances of the different brands of mobile phones was based on emotion and aesthetics rather than functionality. ICTs were highly personal and facilitated the notion that information was a key value in the post-manufacturing era. As such, the transition from manufacturing-based services accelerated the drive toward more developments in areas such as telematics and bionics. The ripple effect of the new ICTs spread to other industries and became a key feature of decision making in nanotechnologies as well. ICT changed the structures of most organizations and made it relatively easy for service industries to substitute capital for labor. Although the causal relationships are not easily discernable, service industries prospered in the new economy.

And even if the "old" industries, including those in the service sector, survive, they must adopt to new ways of doing business. New ways involve embracing technologies of the day. For one, modern technologies render existing organizational structures and behaviors obsolete. The rapid growth in ICTs changes how both manufacturing and service industries deliver products and meet customer and client needs. New technologies enable managers to reach global markets in unprecedented ways. As such, in this increasingly flattened word, "old school" postal services and other traditional ways of conducting economic ventures must be revised. And because, as Milakovich (2012) observes, American and other global corporations "outsource certain segments of their operations to lower cost labor market," the vehicles of communications must adapt. Of course, forces of flattening result in loss of jobs, even in advanced countries like the United States (Milakovich, 2012, p. 225). The fear of adaptability to new global trends is not lost to Kenya's policy makers, who, in various policy pronouncements, remind state-owned corporations of the need to learn about ICTs and also embrace the new ICTs at work.

A good example of organizational adaptation to new technologies in a flattened world is the postal service. Otenyo and Lind (2011) pointed out that Postal Services are forced to redefine their core functions to survive the new world. In their book, *E-Government: The Use of ICTs in Administration*, public administration scholars Eric Otenyo and Nancy Lind observe:

> During the paper age, postal services were government monopolies and, in many parts of the world, emerged as the quintessential public service. Market forces have changed this old reality, and in the new ICT-driven age, postal services are on the decline. (Otenyo & Lind, 2011, pp. 275–76)

That reality is well understood in Kenya's postal service sector. Reports showed that Postal Corporation of Kenya actually lost revenues due to increased use of mobile phones. Data from the Communications Commission of Kenya (CCK) points to troubling times, if the management and other stakeholders did nothing. For example, in the first quarter of 2012, ending March, "16.7 million letters were sent compared to 19.5 in the three months to December" (Mugwe, 2012). Outgoing international letters dropped from 2.2 million to 1.7 million in 2012. However, the number of incoming international letters increased by 135,212, a rate of 68.6 percent (Mugwe, 2012). The decline in package and letter delivery was attributed to competition from a host of courier services including security firm G4S, Nation Media Group, Roy Parcels, and even county bus companies. The CCK also observed that increased "preference in the use of the Internet compared to letters" was a key factor affecting the decline in postal services (Mugwe, 2012). For instance, the mobile telephone services accounted for over a billion short text messages in just one quarter, reflecting a 53 percent growth above the 2011 figures.

Not unexpectedly, in 2015, cabinet secretary for the Ministry of Information Communications and Technology (MICT), Fred Matiangi, reminded officials of the General Postal Office of the need to embrace technology if their operations were to remain sustainable. Speaking at a Nairobi conference on leveraging ICTs in transformation of postal and courier sector attended by officials from the Pan African Postal Union and the Universal Postal Union, Matiangi observed:

> The ICT sector today is undergoing tremendous changes, thanks to increased liberalization, competition and emergence of new technologies. The changing environment calls for adjustments in operations to survive the intense competitive pressure from other ICT-enabled services such as instant messaging technologies. Posta still has an opportunity despite the coming of new communication technologies. (Ngila, 2015)

His statement reinforced the government's position concerning the importance of trade unions in the development of new ways of doing business. In his remarks, Matiangi reminded postal service enterprises that they risked going out of business, if they did not devise ways to engage ICTs (Ngila, 2015). Such an eventuality would lead to job losses and incomes, as business would turn to private providers. Already, the Internet and mobile phones had cut into revenues of the previously unified Kenya's Postal and Telecom Service.

In the new economy, unions' role is heightened in areas such as deindustrialization, taxation, and combating recession and persistent poverty. Unions, as part of society, were involved in the social-media campaigns for greater corporate social responsibility, green industries (green capitalism), animal rights, and the climate change and sustainable growth movements. In other words, the new economy coincided with these progressive movements for improved social developments.

On the global stage, the International Labor Organization (ILO) took part in helping direct union engagement in the economy through promotion of a Job Creation and Enterprise Development Project that encouraged sustainable development (McFellin, 2013). ILO's union members, including those in Africa, were encouraged to consider utilizing pension funds for investment activities that would empower members. The ILO strategy promoted investment vehicles and innovative financial services that would include worker-owned small and medium entities including those supporting the proliferating ICT industries.

In its report, the ILO emphasized the link between ICTs and global economic growth and wealth creation.

> Recognized as among the major drivers of economic growth and wealth creation, ICT are raising productivity, reducing costs and increasing the speed of communications to help shape the new global economy. The effects of ICT on the emergence of new enterprises and the demand for new skills and knowledge are profound, and this study illustrates how they have changed labor market conditions and industrial relations as well. (ILO, 2001)

The ILO argued that ICTs would transform the "old economy" and influence employment relations (ILO, 2001, p. 2). The transformative nature of the new economy is seen in ways beyond the impact of new technologies like iPhones, Ipads, smartphones and so on. The impact is visible in the very characteristics of the ICT industry. For one, those involved in the ICTs sector are, for the most part, youthful members of society. This realization implies the ICT sector will expand and continue to drive the global economy.

Already, an ICT-based corporation like Apple Computers made history in 2015 by becoming the first major business firm to build a market value worth $710 billion on Wall Street (CBS Dallas, 2015). The accomplishment was based on the value of its stocks at the close of trading Tuesday February 10, 2015. Apple's market capitalization surpassed that of oil corporate giants like ExxonMobil mainly as a result of iPhone sales in China (Wakabayashi, 2015).

The growth in the global ICT sector has come at a cost for social and economic order. A few sentences are not enough to capture the changes and impact of the growth in the sector. As futurist Manuel Castells (1996) observed in his work on the network society, the new information technologies have led to an emergent "networking logic," in sharp contrast with past linear relationships. Thanks to ICTs, the workplace is different because employees can telecommute and interact with others across the globe at the touch of a button or click on their devices. The ensuing networks allow for networks to grow beyond the workplace and to delve into the social realm as well. The complex organizational architecture around the networked society means that employees have to work differently.

Likewise, corporations now require new skills to engage their employees for optimal productivity. ICTs gave the world a new economy in which ICTs are a primary resource and countries lacking such skills would be disadvantaged. While one may not attribute plant closings and industry relocations to a single variable alone, chances are that the new information technologies must be present in a country that seeks to maintain its industrial base. The network logic implies putting in place ICT infrastructures to facilitate market planning and development in all other sectors. It is entirely possible that industry relocation can occur if all or a single piece of the infrastructural bases including ICTs, electricity, utilities, governance, and skilled labor are dysfunctional or ill-prepared. It is not a coincidence that in the post-1990 world, industry realignment and transformations have occurred globally and not skipped developing countries like Kenya as well.

In recent history, generally, the new economy marginalized manufacturing enclaves with detrimental effects to unionized workers (Nissen, 1995). As alluded to, among the examples of deindustrialization in Kenya was the case of closure of plants in the Western region, including garment industries RIVATEX Eldoret, and KICOMI Kisumu, and paper making industry—Pan Paper in Webuye. In 2014, two important companies closed their doors. Eveready East Africa, a dry cell battery manufacturer, transferred its business to Egypt, citing competition from cheaper imports. Cadbury Kenya, a chocolate, Oreo, and Trident chewing gum maker with over sixty years' presence in Kenya relocated plants from Kenya. Cadbury's parent company, Mondelcz International, cited changes in its transformation strategy. It also relocated its plant to Egypt. Reckitt Benckiser, Procter & Gamble, Bridgestone, Colgate-Palmolive, Johnson & Johnson, and Unilever are among the numerous companies that closed production factories in the country (Njiru, 2014).

Plant closings in many of Kenya's state-owned enterprise system were occasioned through undercapitalization and managerial failures (Grosh, 1991). While unions desire full employment, they are not naive about changes in the national and global economies. Unions recognize that changes brought about by technologies can lead to job losses and hence pay attention to policies that promote economic growth. Therefore, trade unions engage government and cooperate whenever policies enhance job growth, especially in regions where unions draw most membership.

Unions in Kenya took action to voice displeasure over introduction of technologies that led to job losses. When a MNC, Mitchell Cotts, introduced machines that could pick tea leaves in the Kericho and Nandi districts, union leaders vehemently protested (*Sunday Times*, March 4, 1984, p. 1; *Kenya Times* March 22, 1984 p. 8, and March 26, 1984, p. 14). In an address to the 100th Session of the International Labor Organization (ILO) conference June 2011, COTU leader Francis Atwoli remarked:

> COTU has been on record as opposing mechanization of enterprises, so long as the goal is not value addition but reduction of Labor force with a view to maximizing profits for capital. This is what has been happening in Tea plantations in some parts of Kenya and we ask that the same be curtailed in order to help in growing sustainable enterprises and an all-inclusive growth. (Atwoli, 2011)

Sub-Saharan Africa faces high unemployment, especially among the youth. Various ILO reports suggest a possible existence of a "lost generation" of workers, referencing young people who detach themselves from the labor markets. This fallout not only causes social strife but also creates other problems in the workplace, especially if in the event of downsizing and recession the younger employees are first out and last in, as has been the case in the Kenyan reduction-in-force and job-cut initiatives.

Loss of jobs is never good news for unions. It leads to loss of union members and their dues (Flood, 1995, p. 3). Without resources, unions cannot do well in their battles for benefits such as medical care, pensions, social services, and suitable working conditions. Resources are the oil that lubricates the labor movement and the ensuing militancy manifest in strikes. And, it is here that we have to interrogate the means of organization, information, and communications.

New technologies have provided avenues for experimenting with now tactics and programs. Information and Communication Technologies (ICTs) are now key to outreach efforts. Unions use new technologies to match management and be empowered. Without laptops for data management, computers for dissemination of union programs, and email applications, networking and exchange of ideas would be impaired.

Perhaps the simplest way to appreciate the new tools for labor advocacy is to note the advantages of a simple application like the email. Email as we know is faster than snail mail. Email is also cheap and more reliable than fax machines—which were fairly expensive in Kenya. As Eric Lee observes, email is neutral in terms of being accessible to both the rich and poor, powerful and powerless (Lee, 1997, p. 21). Perhaps it is this ability that makes it a most applied by product of the now not so new ICTs. The vast array of resources available on the Internet also provides labor unions leadership the additional ability to network globally.

Kenya's collective bargaining structure was enshrined in the statutes. The Central Organization of Trade Unions (COTU) represented private sector workers while the Federation of Kenya Employers (FKE) stood for employer interests. Founded in 1959, within the framework of the Trade Unions Act Cap 233, the FKE sought to organize employers to counter demands from unionists. By 1989, FKE represented more than three thousand employers (Mwembe, 1989). Unions' main concerns were in employment stability and retrenchments orchestrated through the structural adjustments.

Trade unions participated in policy issues including economic security through participation in the National Social Security Fund (NSSF) and health policy through involvement in the National Hospital Insurance Fund (NHIF). Unions were coopted in the food policy arena through board presence in the country's food marketing institution—the National Cereals and Produce Board (NCPB). It was always a KANU strategy to control urban food prices as a means to forestall labor unrest. The country's leadership assumed that rural hunger would be contained through tribal and community support systems and never really developed policies that targeted the alleviation of rural hunger and poverty. In most instances, the government's core policies were based on World Bank prescriptions, which privileged market-based solutions and disadvantaged poorly paid workers. Although it voiced those concerns, its mechanisms for negotiating better deals for workers were hampered by the need to protect existing jobs, now under threat of being relocated to other labor-rich countries.

By 2000, the country's economy was deeply entrenched in the globalization market space. The government sought to calm the labor waters through controlling the labor movement. The structure of trade union management was unchanged. The ruling party ensured that labor peace was structured by an Industrial Relations Charter, agreed upon between on the one hand, COTU, as workers' representatives, and the Federation of Kenya Employers (FKE) on behalf of employers. Both COTU and FKE supported the government's neoliberal policy actualized through growth of Export Processing Zones (EPZs). The government established the EPZ Authority to manage the zones. By 2002, at least 26,447 were employed in the enclaves. In 2004, at least forty-one factories were associated with EPZs. In most of these Export Processing Zones, factory workers were subjected to poor work conditions, including low pay (Mushita & Thompson, 2007, p. 117).

For its part, Kenya's government turned a blind eye to the worsening terms of employment in the EPZs. As a result, in 2003 more than 9,200 textile workers organized in strikes and demanded better pay instead of what the Kenya Human Rights Commission (KHRC) termed as "poverty wages" (KHRC, 2004). Later, the KHRC prepared a report that claimed some EPZ workers were denied the right to unionize and such basic rights as sick leave. Neither the FKE nor COTU supported the KHRC's report. However, COTU continued to offer statements in support of workers in the EPZ. COTU, FKE, and the government seemed to be in agreement concerning reduction of unemployment. Policy makers were concerned that the donor community had cut aid funding due to massive corruption. In 1997 the IMF, noting rampant corruption, had suspended Kenya from receiving the Enhanced Structural Adjustment facility. Without sufficient external funding, elites lacked largesse to maintain stability. Realizing that his power base was weakening, Moi sought to build alliances with workers' leaders.

COTU was a prime target because its members associated with the now powerful civil society. The administration invited the Secretary General of COTU to be part of the team coordinating the IMF and World Bank's National Poverty Reduction Plan (NPEP). The World Bank and IMF typically extended invitations to trade union officials to coopt them in drafting policies aimed at promoting growth and reducing poverty.

Upon the urging of donor agencies, COTU participated in the permanent commission that produced the National Poverty Eradication Plan (NPEP) and launched in 1999. COTU, then, as the sole federation of trade unions represented over 300,000 workers. Although COTU has a full-fledged research unit, its role as stakeholder was more symbolic than concrete. According to COTU's Director of Research, COTU representatives were provided very little information before crucial meetings (COTU, 2003). In most cases, deliberations between the Ministry of Finance and Economic Planning and the trade unions were rushed. In the end, the majority of trade union members knew very little about national poverty reduction goals (Chune, 2003).

Evidence suggests that local trade unions were weak participants in the supposedly collaborative policy making initiatives. Union representatives were not privy to all information concerning the plight of workers. Although Kenya's Ministry of Finance and Economic Planning took the lead role in articulation of national policy toward role of technology and labor in achieving growth, union leaders were concerned with larger strategic goals. Unions sought to engage in the policy process by serving a key role in the review of labor laws, promoting social dialogue and involvement in HIV prevention and AIDS management. COTU's Plan of Action did not privilege issues of implementation of technology policy. If it existed, it was tangential and in relation to promotion of social dialogue.

One may make the argument that weak representation of workers is not confined to Kenya. The problem was that COTU and other unions lacked the technical capacity to produce their own economic growth blueprints. By 2000, COTU had at least thirty-one affiliated unions. Non-COTU unions included the giant Kenya National Union of Teachers (KNUT), whose members include most teachers in the country. According to the Teachers Service Commission (TSC), the number of unionized teachers was well over 288,060. Of this number, approximately 206,000 were primary school teachers and the rest, about 34,000, were secondary school teachers. According to the TSC, among the nonunion members of the teaching profession are about 48,060, mostly school head teachers spread across the country (Wanzala, 2015). KNUT self-identified as a representative of the intelligentsia and not a blue-collar outfit. KNUT leadership felt it had greater capability to engage the policy process through implementation of national education policies. Arguably, KNUT was best suited to promote the development of the Science, Technology, Mathematics, and Engineering (STEM) curriculum that is essential for the growth and applications of ICTs in national development. Although much is expected from KNUT, the question becomes, did KNUT seize the moment to promote use of emerging new technologies? This question will be central to our discussion of the role of union members in influencing the direction of government policy toward digitization of schools and the supply of laptops and tablets to primary schools.

Perhaps a more nuanced answer may be extrapolated from KNUT's own actions with regard to the country's overall governance outlook. While KNUT voiced concerns over lack of transparency in management of national affairs, its priority was to help teachers earn better salaries and only in rare occasions produced policy publications to help government find solutions to the country's relatively weak digital footprint. One would expect KNUT to promote the use of ICTs for advancing transparency in government institutions. It is also reasonable to argue KNUT's ability to engage the policy process was considerably weakened by internal wrangles that culminated in the formation of a splinter union—Kenya Union of Post Primary Teachers (KUPPET). The splinter caused the TSC to require both KNUT and KUPPET to use an online system (http://payslip.tsc.go.ke) for validation of members. The TSC had concerns that some of the union members did not observe the procedures laid out in the Labor Relations Act of 2007 to switch membership from one union to another.

From a comparative perspective, the splinter seemed contrary to the theoretical position that in the changing economic circumstances, mergers would transform unions into more prominent organizations. Specifically, during recessions and unemployment, and declining manufacturing, unions would need to consolidate and take advantage of economies of scale offered through mergers. Mergers would provide fragmented unions with resources to deal with membership losses and hostile government (Chaison, 1996. p. 1). A close observation of Kenya's labor history reveals that the conditions for fragmentation have more to do with national politics than union-management relations and the economy.

Ruling elites in Kenya saw labor as an inconvenient disruption to the bid to control and consolidate power in all spheres of the economy. Fragmentation of unions in Kenya is, therefore, not an economic or organizational decision to enhance efficiency and effectiveness. If that were the case, the narrative on fragmentation would be expressed in rational argumentation of economies of scale and claim that a unified organization was a weaker labor negotiator on behalf of members. On the contrary, national politicians saw decentralization of collective bargaining as offering huge benefits in terms of dividing the body of workers. Further, having different unions fight it out for membership dues was a strategy for draining union resources and time. To illustrate, available reports indicate that each month the TSC remitted, per month, between KSh 120–130 million to KNUT and approximately KSh 20–35 million to KUPPET respectively (Oduor, 2015; Wanzala, 2015). Annually, KNUT collected from teachers' unions over KSh.1.6 billion per year (Wanzala, 2015). Although not announced in official government policy documents, some members of the ruling elite regarded reduced resource base a method for controlling labor power.

In theoretical terms, things may look different when fragmentation occurs. Following Chaison (1996, p. 3), it is acknowledged that smaller unions are not necessarily ineffective. However, the point is, the smaller unions are likely to bargain for only a few agreements. Thus, in the case of KNUT and KUPPET, the division implies that the KUPPET would represent the narrow interests of secondary school teachers. Evidence of weakening union power is easy to decipher. For example, during the January 2015 teachers' strike over pay and benefits, it was clear that the two unions were agreed on the need for raising base pay for teachers but had differences in ideas about harmonization of various benefits like commuter allowance, responsibility allowance, medical, house, and leave allowances. The two unions also had varied responses toward TSC's offers of car, mortgage, and responsibility allowances.

Another point of reference is, unlike in the United States, Australia, Britain, Canada, and New Zealand, unions are fairly independent of political control by power elites such as cabinet ministers. Autonomy confers to workers a better deal in negotiating collective bargains. Chaison (1996) contends that when workers have greater autonomy, they have a free hand in deciding whether to join or fragment their unions. In other words, government or parties cannot compel unions to merge or fragment (Chaison, 1996, p. 2).

As if the divorce between KUPPET and KNUT was not enough of a distraction in the national labor movement, another splinter occurred in 2011. This time around, the Kenya Union of Special Needs Teachers (KUSNET) was registered, thereby fragmenting teachers' collective bargaining power. KUSNET contended itself a leader in advocacy for matters concerning teachers of children with special needs. It has yet to develop a comprehensive blueprint of how teachers will engage new technologies for the benefit of their constituency.

Although the two unions separated, efforts to merge were considered with the intention to increase the union's bargaining capacity. Among the proponents of a merger is the Education International (EI) group with headquarters in Brussels, which conducted a study, that favored co-operation among members. Education International's African headquarters is in Accra, Ghana. The organization works to promote the principles of trade unionism and works with the Global Union Federations and the Trade Union Advisory Committee (TUAC). Although talks on merger were stalled, KNUT and other unions come together over issues of mutual interest.

Unions were coopted in food policy discussion through board presence in the country's food marketing institution—the National Cereals and Produce Board (NCPB). In a twisted way, it was always a well-known KANU strategy to control urban food prices as a means to forestall labor unrest. Unions also collaborated on matters of economic security and participation in deliberations over the National Social Security Fund (NSSF), and health policy through involvement in the National Hospital Insurance Fund (NHIF).

THE NATIONAL HOSPITAL INSURANCE FUND (NHIF)

For example, KUPPET came together on common interests like demanding pay hikes and negotiating on teachers' medical insurance and opposition to certain elements of the NHIF deductions (Oduor, 2015). Opposition to rate increases also came from Kenya University Staff Union (KUSU), which demanded the rates be suspended. KUSU argued that in the past NHIF had misappropriated contributions and there was no assurance that would stop. In addition, the Federation of Public Service Trade Unions of Kenya (FPSTUK) and affiliated Trade Union Congress of Kenya regarded the new NHIF rates as an unmerited taxation. Although unions came together over the NHIF rate increases, as a general statement, fragmentation within the trade union movement was the norm rather than the exception. Thus, in 2011, the Kenya Union of Special Needs Teachers (KUSNET) was registered, thereby fragmenting teachers' collective bargaining power. KUSNET contended itself a leader in advocacy for matters concerning teachers of children with special needs. It has yet to develop a comprehensive blueprint of how teachers will engage new technologies for the benefit of their constituency.

Vision 2030: The Current Policy Blueprint

In consultation with various development partners and the support of the World Bank, Kibaki's administration promulgated Kenya Vision 2030 as the umbrella blueprint for 2008–2030. The blueprint acknowledged the previous development plans, which sought to recognize the role of information technologies in development. For example, the 5th Development Plan, 1984–1988, sought to modernize the postal and telecommunications services. At that time, Kenya had only 746 post offices and had access to an Indian Ocean submarine cable (Kenya, 1984, p. 129). The 6th Development Plan, 1989–1993, committed to update and adopt information technology systems to the changing needs of Kenya (Kenya, 1989, p. 95). The Development Plan stated:

> Kenya is fully committed to exploiting existing possibilities in these fields for the advancement of her people. Consequently, a range of institutional arrangements in the fields of statistical data bases and retrieval services, telephone telegraphic, telex, and facsimile services, satellite communication, radio, and TV broadcasting networks, mail courier services, books, newspapers, journal, and a system of shows, exhibitions and extension services has been put in place to take advantage of existing technological possibilities. Government will continue to provide the necessary back-up for the development of relevant information and data generation, collection, processing, storage, retrieval and dissemination facilities. (Kenya, 1989, p. 95)

Although in the 1980s the use of computers was restricted mainly to uses in statistical and data management areas, the government had already indicated its readiness to exploit benefits of these types of technologies. Jules-Rosette (1990) discusses the role of the state in the spread of new technologies emphasizing the salience of computers in Kenya and other African nations. Vision 2030 reinforced the state's eminence as a mover of social changes structured through increased use of workplace technologies.

In addition, although Vision 2030 was based on the previous development plans and economic policy documents, it was more specific in acknowledging the role of ICT in driving the development agenda. For example, Vision 2030 promotes the strategy of Business Process Off Shoring (BPO) (or outsourcing), which revolves around providing business services via the Internet to international and local companies. The goal is to make Kenya one of the top three BPO destinations in Africa (Republic of Kenya 2007, p. 9). Observers of Kenya's ICT sector attribute the setting up of institutions like the Information Communication and Technology Board (ICT Board) to the government's commitment to achieve top marks as a BPO destination (Manono, 2012). Best practices manuals would indicate the key ingredients to making Kenya a top BPO destination to include variables such as: "labor cost, technological advancement, infrastructure, language, education system, competent manpower, host government support, data security, political and economic environment, cultural compatibility and legal maturity" (Manono, 2012). The country's pitch for its establishment as a BPO destination can be summarized in Table 2.1 below.

Since 2004, in some measures, the overall architecture of the road to robust BPO has been to frame policy along meeting specific goals in the key variables identified above. With at least eighteen licensed call centers and a liberalized telecommunication sector, the country signaled its readiness to attract investments and enhance its competitiveness. However, the country has a long way to go in terms of offering incentives that attract Foreign Direct Investments (FDIs).

In addition, Vision 2030 observed that Kenya's education institutions were to aim for globally competitive quality education. This would be achieved through modernization and training in ICT skills at primary, secondary, and university levels. Vision 2030 gave special emphasis to expanding knowledge in sciences, technology, and innovation (STI) (Republic of Kenya, 2007. p. 12). Kenya's planners identified STI as emphasis areas that would guide the country's drive to a Middle Income Country status. Subsequent actions and planning reflect Vision 2030's goals. Since 2008, the expansion of the education sector has been remarkable.

KNUT recognized that under Vision 2030's Education Pillar objectives, teachers were key players in pushing forward the integration of ICTs in the profession. KNUT was concerned about providing quality

Table 2.1. Kenya's Attractiveness as Business Process Outsourcing, BPO Destination

Attractiveness Variables	***Existing achievements and ongoing plans***
Labor cost	Abundant cheap and youthful human resources. Kenya has domesticated ILO conventions regarding labor and wages.
Technological advancement	Ongoing plans to establish BPO Park in Nairobi, entry of tech giants like Accenture, Cisco, IBM, and Microsoft added to human capital and transfer of skills. Vodafone subsidiary Safaricom also contributed to technical knowledge transfers.
Infrastructure	Fiber optic cables and broadband capacity exists; undersea fiber optic cable SEACOM connecting through South Africa; East African Marine Systems (TEAMS), the East African Sub-marine Cable System (EASSY), and the Lower Indian Ocean Network (LION2) cable all reduced bandwidth costs and made the Internet cheaper.
Language	Majority speaks English and it is the primary official language in all government activities. School systems actively promote English, the global business language.
Education System	Over twenty universities and growing influx of Diaspora-assisted initiatives strengthened education. E-learning platforms have proliferated. Government provides loans to increase access to university and higher education. But government acknowledged Kenya lacks technical competence in ICT assignments. Ongoing reforms in education actively being sought. Government complements ICT infrastructure with investments in railways and roads transportation networks. Research and development infrastructure and policy framework still weak, in relative terms.
Competent manpower	Growing expansion of IT skills but still work-in-progress.

Attractiveness Variables	***Existing achievements and ongoing plans***
Host government support	Vision 2030 Pillar includes ICTs with flagship projects that include the Konza Technology City. Government promotes ICTs as driver of new economy. Government laws and regulations favor free markets. President Kenyatta launched the Presidential Digital Talent Program. Promotion of idea of innovation hub but more stakeholder collaboration including union participation required.
Data security	Ongoing government interest in IT security sector but pipeline of highly skilled IT security professionals nonexistent.
Political and economic environment	Predictable elections and participation in political processes; economic incentives required for incentivizing viable business plans for early start-ups and development of venture capital funds in the ICT sector. Environment has led to opportunities for growth in the mobile money sector.
Cultural compatibility	Western values dominate urban landscape. Cultural sensitization initiatives still at infancy but political establishment promoted transformation by employing narratives of changes from analogue politicians to digital politics. Kenya's media coined the term the Silicon Savannah to create a brand for Kenya's ICT sector.
Legal maturity	2010 constitution strengthened the judiciary. Government recognizes international conventions that govern intellectual property rights.

Source: Compiled and created by the author.

education and supported government's efforts to equip schools with advanced technologies. According to Wilson Sossion, then KNUT's national chairman, teachers were ready to use smart boards instead of using blackboards for "health reasons" (Koross, 2013).

Several universities offer ICT training and are well connected to the Internet. However, unions at all levels have been slow at presenting a plan for members' engagement with new technologies. Union members in the education sector were among those who opposed the introduction of laptops in primary schools, arguing that the policy was flawed or not a priority. Education sector trade unions instead preferred to call for increased pay and hiring of more teachers.

Although Kenya's ICT infrastructure vastly improved after 2010, the key concern for trade unions was to safeguard national stability and ensure security and maintenance of living wages for the lowest-paid workers. Fragmentation and the cooption of the labor movement continued after the 2007 elections. As expected in underdeveloped political systems, the coalition government resulted in the growth of patronage positions in the public sector. As a result, the wage bill grew out of proportion.

With increased use of mobile communication devices, workers were empowered to mobilize and respond to calls for action. Widespread use of social media has enlarged democratic space for union members to engage the political establishment. At the same time, new technologies increase union-related debates and news outlets and political blogs shape overall perceptions about the role of unions in society.

New technologies also served to increase awareness of national problems. In particular, the Internet published government statistics on economic growth and gave workers insights into comparative wage levels. Information widely available through Google searches seemed to serve as a catalyst for worker agitation, especially as members could now track down the expenditure patterns of their leaders. Beyond economic growth, information systems are now becoming necessary for ensuring public safety and security.

Security: What Has It Got To Do with IT?

Arguably, at the end of the Mwai Kibaki and Raila Odinga coalition government, the incoming Jubilee Alliance found itself challenged with the need to maintain the momentum of economic growth. Security topped the agenda of the government. Likewise, the tourism sector deteriorated. In addition, the government faced teething problems with devolution and a declining manufacturing base. As a result, the material conditions of workers deteriorated. Kenya ushered in 2013 with some of the worst labor-government relations in the country's history. Crisis after crisis characterized the President Uhuru M. Kenyatta and William S. Ruto administration.

As persons named by the International Criminal Court (ICC) as war criminal suspects, the government faced integrity questions. Although charges against Uhuru Kenyatta were dropped, the case was a great distraction from efforts to build cohesion in the country as well as a blot on national psyche and pride. Regardless, the country experienced some of the worst security challenges in its modern history. Security had always been a problem for Kenya. And even in the months before the 2007 election, COTU, through its secretary General Francis Atwoli, had released statements to the effect that trade unions would support President Kibaki's reelection bid on condition that his administration tackled insecurity in Kenya (Ali, 2007). COTU specifically raised specific concerns about the rise of the Mungiki sect and the Sabaot Land Defense Force that had caused much panic in the country (Ali, 2007). Yet, going by government investments in the security sector, the rise of Al-Shabaab and other international terrorist organizations were a much more troublesome threat than the domestic gangs.

Al-Shabaab terrorist and other criminal gangs seemed to rule the major towns. Agitation for better security policies and effective policing became an important area of union concern after the 2013 election. For example, KNUT officials urged teachers not to go to work in areas such as Mandera and areas bordering Somalia unless the government could guarantee students' and teachers' safety (Ongeri, 2013). In November 2014, terrorists and bandits attacked passengers aboard Mekka Bush en route from Mandera to Nairobi. This attack triggered further exodus of non-indigenous teachers from the area.

As a result of security concerns, Kenya invested in Closed-Circuit Television (CCTV) cameras in key business centers. In advanced countries, surveillance technology covers most small and large businesses, malls, casinos, banks, and a good number of central business centers. Additional systems recognize vehicle number (license) plates, monitor traffic movements, and report violators of traffic laws. CCTV operate on the premise that images are transmitted to a central monitor or recorded by video cameras connected in closed-circuit. Kenyan policy opted for installation of surveillance cameras to provide real-time footage of events to the existing National Police Operations Command Center. According to information released to the public, the bulk of the contract to provide CCTV was awarded to Safaricom.

Safaricom's chief executive officer, Robert Collymore, argued that the system would be an "intelligent solution that harnesses the power of technology to enable law enforcement officers to effectively coordinate and deploy their resources in response to threats to national security and, indeed, emergency situations requiring the interplay of competencies from the National Police Service and various disaster response teams" (Waitathu, 2014). The new system would be based upon the LTE security communications network and not be run on Safaricom's commercial network. The deal to set up a National Surveillance, Communication and Control System for Nairobi and Mombasa was worth over KSh 15 billion. At least two thousand CCTV cameras would be installed in locations around the two selected cities.

Safaricom did not disclose whether or not the closed-circuit television cameras were casted in bullet-proof materials and or had night-vision capability. Sophisticated systems not only include such features but also have advanced zoom and tracking capabilities. Variations of the CCTV configurations include those that have the ability to transmit images over the Internet and those operated by motion-activated sensors, with limited facial recognition capacities.

As from December 2014, the closed-circuit television cameras in Nairobi were housed at Jogoo House. The cost of the equipment and installation was at least KSh 437 million. By early 2015, almost eighty screens and fifty-one cameras were operational. Additional backup CCTV systems, operated by the Nairobi City County (NCC), were in the works. And by early 2015, a control room at City Hall Annex was functional. Officers assigned to the room were expected to report to police incidents that threatened public safety.

Yet, skeptics, including members of parliament, doubted the efficacy of the gadgets. After Kabete MP George Muchai, a former deputy general secretary of COTU, was murdered in downtown Nairobi, several MPs felt the CCTV system was not worth the money or that police were underprepared to use new technologies (*Daily Nation*, 2015). Reports also emerged that officials assigned to man the CCTV control room at City Hall Annex "may have been asleep when armed men attacked and killed Kabete MP George Muchai on February 17" (Mwangi, 2015). Nairobi Traffic Police spokesman confirmed that the CCTVs had not been of much help in the management of operations but city officials argued to the contrary and claimed traffic police and marshals ignored City Hall reports (Mwangi, 2015).

In communications prior to launching, Safaricom revealed it involved Huawei, a China-based ICT international corporation. At the same time, the government deported from Kenya two persons associated with ZTE, another Chinese company that had legal battles with Huawei. The contracting of the Integrated Public Safety Communication and Surveillance System also suffered from administrative problems.

As a part of the plan to enhance security, the government also demanded mobile phone operators to register SIM cards of all subscribers in Kenya. The Ministry of Interior and Coordination of National Government oversaw the primary agreement. These measures did not drastically reduce national crime rates. Workers took security concerns to opposition political party platforms and union leaders. However, in spite of government assurance that security was "under control," more regions faced public safety challenges. In May 2013, Kenya National Union of Teachers (KNUT) asked teachers in Garissa, Mandera, and other areas on the Kenya-Somali border to stay away from their posts until security was restored. Al-Shabaab mujahedeen killed villagers including a schoolteacher in Damajaley and Abdisugow villages within Garissa County.

In November 2014, Al-Shabaab attacked and killed more than twenty-four teachers in Mandera County. Teachers' unions, Kenya National Union of Teachers (KNUT) and Kenya Union of Post Primary Education Teachers (KUPPET), directed their nonresident members stationed in the northeastern region to withdraw services from such areas. Union leaders also demanded compensation for bereaved families.

Still, in early 2015, KUPPET demanded that government compensate teachers killed. KUPPET argued that it was unfair for police killed in the line of duty to receive compensation while teachers killed in Mandera and other regions were uncompensated (Kipsang 2015). And again, in April 2015, after Al-Shabaab militants killed 147 students and security personnel and wounded seventy individuals at Garissa University College, a constituent college of Moi University, KNUT repeated the call for its members to leave the area if they felt insecure. KNUT also asked the government to close down the college and called for the resignation of Education Cabinet Secretary Jacob Kaimenyi (Kamau, 2015). KNUT also raised funds to assist in the burial arrangements for the students killed in Garissa. In the end, more than one thousand teachers in Garissa, Mandera, and Wajir counties refused to return to work for fear of threats from Al-Shabaab militants. According to KNUT sources, ninety-five public schools in the northeastern region were closed for fear of terrorists (Jubat, 2015).

On the other hand, the Kenya Union of Post Primary Education (KUPPET) also issued a notice to its members to withdraw services from northeastern and other regions where the government had failed to provide security (Dareel, 2015). KUPPET's leadership gave the government an ultimatum to convene a stakeholders' peace meeting for purposes of providing sufficient security to teachers and students in all schools. In protest to the government, Julius Korir, KUPPET's national vice chairman, remarked:

> As a union, we are calling on the Government to take matters concerning security involving teachers and students very seriously. What we have learnt in the last few weeks is that some of our learning institutions have been turned into IDP camps and barracks for bandits, which should not be the case. (Ochieng & Kipruto, 2015)

In Baringo County, the local KNUT chapter documented over 38,000 school-age children were kept out of school due to security concerns. Thousands of families in Baringo South and Baringo North fled May and early June 2015. A school watchman at Baragoi Boys Secondary School was reportedly shot and killed by bandits.

Concerns over deteriorating security in public education were reported in numerous locations in Baringo. In South Baringo County alone, at least twenty-eight schools were closed down due to insecurity. These challenges highlighted the importance of security and public safety as a major preoccupation in public policy. In Kenya, it is arguably the pillar upon which other public policies are anchored. In other words, security undergirds policy development in all other areas such as food security, health care, and infrastructure. Any intensification in insecurity, therefore, undermines potential achievement of all goals set for national governance.

Further evidence of troubling safety concerns was also raised in the case of demonstrations at the University of Eldoret, Uasin Gishu County. In February 2015, Musalia Edebe, organizing secretary of the Universities Academic Staff Union (UASU) reported that faculty were "in danger" after students and villagers threatened the security of employees following claims of ethnic bias in recruitment and selection of personnel at the university (Wanyoro, 2015). Similar ethnic-driven confrontations had occurred at Karatina and Kabianga as well. Unions responded by calling for security and strengthening the rule of law in the country.Unions recognized the role of direct action as an obligation to the nation's goal for achievement of human development and dignity.

Pocketbook Policies are Main Agenda

Pocketbook policy issues are concerned with bread-and-butter financial resources. If you as members of unions what their top priority agenda for collective bargaining is, the answer is most likely wage increases. Many union members have agitated for the government to bring relief to workers who still struggle with stagnant salaries, a dysfunctional health delivery system, uncertain economic security during retirement, youth unemployment and perennial bureaucratic corruption. Many of these issues are not mutually exclusive from the security challenges. And many of the challenges experienced in the national labor movement have indicated a great deal of moral dilemma on the part of union leaders' decisions to call for work stoppages, especially in public union like government doctors and police. Strikes by doctors, especially in 2016, have caused immense suffereing and triggered debates over the trade off between pocketbook issues and commitment to public safety and health, especially prevention of death.

Labor militancy has increased, as evident in 2015 when KNUT called for a strike citing pay disparity among public officials. The union demanded a 150 percent pay raise, but the Industrial Court ordered a pay increase of 50 to 60 percent. Although professional unions, including the Inter-Public Universities Council Consultative Forum (IPUCCF) representing various universities also desire academic freedom, salaries remain a top priority. IPUCCF and other professional unions like the Kenya Health Professionals Union (KHPU) and Kenya Medical Practitioners and Pharmacists and Dentist Union (KMPDU) traditionally peg salary negotiations to international compensation levels. These groups expect remuneration to be reflective of global trends where their professional skills are transferable.

Until recently, ruling elites did not problematize economic stagnation in terms of unionization. Instead, the government regarded expansion of employment in the public sector as an obligation and in most cases an unintended consequence of the patron-client relationships that foster political stability. After 2008, and with the rise of the Jubilee Alliance Party, the government framed the huge wage bill as a problem, which required attention from unions. More specifically, the government proposed to bring back retrenchments thereby invoking counter reactions from labor unions. COTU, in particular, demanded a revision of the Value Added Tax (VAT), and elimination of corruption to restore economic equilibrium.

At the same time, union leaders presented counter arguments that increased wages and elimination of waste in government spending was key to achievement of economic growth. As key stakeholders in economic development, unions made the case for reforms in governance and especially, in the systems incentive structures for both workers. Unions also focused on issues of political legitimacy, especially the perception that actions of the government were appropriate and within constitutional parameters. Most importantly, the ability of the government to refrain from unfair labor practices and interference in administration of trade unions was strongly denounced.

On its part, government promoted emergence of new splinter unions such as the National Union of Kenya Parastatal Employees (NUKPE) to weaken labor power. With this in mind, government could suppress growth in wages and impose its will on unions. Also by encouraging power struggles within union leadership, the public would be less enthusiastic to support any form of union militancy. The urgency within which splinter unions were registered suggests discomfort with unions generally, and there is reason for that.

Public policy making is frequently understood in game theoretical terms. This means the government attempt to undermine union strength also weakens union ability to influence policy making. And it is here that we see the power of communication, especially in terms of framing of policy issues and problems. One would argue, the need to use modern communication technologies by both sides has been heightened. More than ever before, ICT devices can speed up processes of union mobilization and help in providing platforms for decision making for entire groups, rather than a few individuals. Through ICTs, unions found platforms for strategy development and in some instances outmaneuvering government operatives.

From a policy standpoint, government encouraged civil society to subscribe to new ICT platforms. At no time did it curtail e-participation within the movement. An ICT-driven governance system expanded was within the imagination of the ruling elites. And no matter the political rhetoric concerning failed collective bargaining efforts and increased labor unrest, there was sufficient issue salience for government policy to encourage emerging applications of ICTs. At no time did government discourage unionist, including teachers from e-activism.

Regardless of the economic challenges, President Uhuru Kenyatta's administration showed much courage by supporting investments in the ICT arena. Uhuru himself became an avid user of social media, frequently sending out tweets on various subject matters. He also led through creation of cabinet-level positions to the Ministry of Information Technology and personally oversaw several ICT initiatives, including the move toward digital biometric platforms for civil service identification and also participation in workshops to encourage senior officials in government to continue to embrace ICT platforms.

Significantly, in early February 2015, President Uhuru Kenyatta attended a high-level seminar on National Security Strategy at the Kenya School of Government, which involved the expertise of Microsoft and the University of Albany's Center of Technology in Government (CTG) (Ministry of Defense, 2014). The 4Afrika SOG seminar targeted policy-level officials and provided knowledge on best practices in ICT policy and practice. Such training sessions sought to strengthen e-government platforms and also assist in refining policy making and implementation in ICTs. His administration also produced the first comprehensive National Information and Communication Technology (ICT) policy with the intention of tying together the various pieces to the country's overall development blueprint. The draft policy document was released to the public in June 2016 (Republic of Kenya, 2016).

With government's full embrace of ICTs in development and delivery of services, perhaps the larger strategy ought to include units involved in governance, such as trade unions and civil society groups. Clearly, as all groups were consumers of government services, publicizing e-government platforms was a priority of the nation's leaders.

E-government, and its variations, was increasingly integrated into the national socio-technical systems. Mobile government through applications available on mobile phone devices that are now part of the Kenyan psyche, have reached a level at which there was no turning back, in terms of leveraging the technologies for societal development. Unions, as members of society and part of the governance networks, could not afford to be outside of the proliferation of ICTs in the larger context of diffused values and national psyche.

It follows that the growing use of ICTs in organizations is seen as a form of modernization and a key component of the drive to a knowledge economy. Labor must respond to the shift from mass commodity production to production of knowledge.

Kenya's heavy investment in ICTs raises obvious questions concerning the role of new technologies in labor affairs. This is particularly true since increased use of ICTs requires adjustments in labor markets. As part of the Africa's pressure group systems, trade unions often realize that they have to understand the changes brought about by the proliferation of ICTs in society.

Governance Networks and Policy Activism

Traditionally, trade unions, as organs in complex governance networks, are aware of ICTs as resources that promote workplace modernization. Throughout the world, trade unions have grappled with the growth of different technologies, especially the benefits of technology for union membership. Union members seek to understand the role of technology in terms of organizational rationality as promoted by management. Proliferation of ICTs when promoted by management can be included in labor-management negotiations.

Scholarly literature on networks reveals that organizations can collaborate to successfully implement policies for societal growth and development. Unions are a part of the information diffusion network, which aims at sharing information with government and employers to mitigate numerous employment problems. In addition, unions are also apart of problem-solving networks whose purpose is to solve problems in sectors like security and public safety, governance, education, and health and income security. Unions have contributed to policy issues and form part of the cooperative relationships and networks in managing different problems. COTU and KNUT leaders have traditionally raised objections when government excludes unions from policy making in matters of vital importance to workers.

An excellent example was in January 2015, when COTU leader Francis Atwoli publicly disclosed his displeasure at being left out of a four-day conference on social protection held in Nairobi. Also excluded was the Federation of Kenya Employers (FKE). COTU claimed that as custodian of workers' interests and contributors to the National Social Security Fund (NSSF) and other pension schemes, they should have had a seat at the table to help draw out the National Action Plan for income security for the poorest members of Kenyan society. The meeting had brought together stakeholders including members of international financial institutions and local financial interests like Kenya Commercial Bank (KCB). President Uhuru Kenyatta announced that the cash transfer program Inua Jamii would utilize KCB-issued smart biometric cards and other technologies to minimize fraud and promote accountability and transparency. COTU also rejected the implementation of the new Kenyan National Social Security Fund Act (2013), which became effective July 1, 2014. The law required employers to deduct and contribute 6 percent of the employee's monthly pensionable earnings to the fund. Thousands of workers, including members of the uniformed services regarded this deduction as unacceptable. Previously, (under Cap 258), uniformed employees, including military personnel, were exempted from making contributions.

Although the case of union engagements with government over the National Hospital Insurance Fund (NHIF) was previously mentioned, it represents an area of intense policy debates over use of workers' salaries. Kenyan workers rejected the Jubilee administration's policy change that raised NHIF rates. Through the Trade Union Congress of Kenya (TUC-K), workers demanded that government refund monies it had deducted from workers from April payday after new rates were gazetted in February 2015. According to TUC Secretary General Wilson Sossion, the increases in NHIF deductions were unconstitutional and workers were not consulted in the decision to increase the rates. TUC proposed an increase in the number of workers' representatives on the NHIF's management board. TUC's approach was more radical than hitherto and included joining the opposition party's Okoa Kenya Movement (OKM) that unsuccessfully sought to change the country's constitution. Besides, TUC threatened a nation-wide strike affecting both the private and public sectors. Sossion's remarks capture the union's mood: "We are opposed to the labor policy and habit of government secretly generating policy and launching them colorfully. We will bring them down in a day" (Guguyu, 2015).

Another example of COTU's policy activism concerned the Jubilee administration's decision to switch off TV stations that had not migrated from analog to digital signals. Kenya's decision was in line with recommendations from the International Telecommunications Union (ITU) to end analog systems by end of June 2015. TV stations demanded more time to install relevant equipment. The matter went to court thanks to an injunction from various TV providers, namely Standard Group, Nation Media, and Royal Media Services, seeking a stay of action and orders to continue broadcasting in analog formats. In September 2014, the Supreme Court of Kenya ruled the Communications Authority of Kenya (CAK) comply with certain procedures and set the analog switch off time lines ahead of the June 17, 2015, ITU recommendation. Basically, the Supreme Court did not stop the CAK from switching off the analog signals on its schedule. CAK set a phased process in which it would first turn off analog devices in the Nairobi area, by end of December 2014. The second phase would cover TV transmitters in other urban centers including Mombasa, Kisumu, Nakuru, Eldoret, Londiani, Meru, Malindi, Nyahururu, Kisii, Machakos, Narok, Kakamega, Webuye, and Nyeri, among others. The final phase would cover the remaining parts of Kenya and would be effected by the end of March 2015.

In February 2015, the Communication Authority of Kenya (CAK) turned off countrywide signals for four of the major TV stations, namely Citizen TV, NTV, QTV, and KTN. TV station owners had requested the date for migration to digital signals be extended to May 30 but the CAK rejected the request. Instead, the Jubilee administration was accused of favoring Chinese-owned Pan Africa Network Group (PANG), which was licensed to own national infrastructure for digital transmission. The TV stations favored migration to digital platforms but were opposed to handing over content to PANG. The decision to switch off the signals resulted in a news blackout throughout the country and massive loss of revenue for leading media houses. COTU's Secretary-General Francis Atwoli, issued a statement in which he described the decision as undemocratic, a "big shame," and not in the interest of the nation's workers (Odunga, 2015).

According to Atwoli, to switch off communication systems undermined the country's image as an attractive destination for both local and foreign investors. Atwoli remarked the decision would result in unemployment: "The government is playing very retrogressive, dangerous and selfish politics with our leading TV stations. It should protect and provide employment to most of our citizens who remain largely unemployed" (Odunga, 2015). Several commentators regarded the government's action as "careless" and regarded the CAK as a biased agency whose decision did not make it any easier for businesses to move to Kenya (*Standard*, 2015).

As far as being involved in governance networks, unions do participate in political debates—speaking on such issues as security, devolution, corruption, and accountability. As will be discussed, corruption is a critical issue that has a direct bearing on productivity. And when it comes to governance, unions recognize that new technologies are a key tool in facilitating citizen participation in political debates and issues of regime legitimacy.

Some trade unions do not play a big role in management of national affairs. Others like COTU and KNUT are actively involved in income distributive debates. As part of the organizational networks involved in finding policy solutions, unions have proven to be a very valuable resource with critical mobilization skills. In the era of globalization, government wants to be seen as solving societal problems and creating conditions for economic growth. Governments want unions on their side and prefer that unions do not compete against the political elite in terms of political mobilization. Instead, the preferred strategy is for union leaders to collaborate with government in ensuring peace in labor relations. What holds the network together are loose goals—employee welfare and peaceful coexistence between labor and management. However, the networks also include informal structures, frequently associated with ethnic affiliations. It is the informal structures, composed of ethnic elites, that work independently to exchange information and ideas about the roles of unions enhancing ICT programs.

In the arena of ICTs, government and unions have not understood the nature of the new economy. Government and union managers should ordinarily find ways to collaborate on productivity issues and especially the flow of information of the use of ICTs and the impact of the new technologies on work processes. However, without the two parties building trust in each other, the networks cannot objectively fulfill the dream of leveraging ICTs for development. Another element of cooperation is reciprocity in the network; in this case, there is need for labor leaders to build capacity in collaborative skills that alleviate the enormous development challenges facing the country.

To succeed, unions and government as members of development-oriented networks should ordinarily narrow their value difference. Therefore, as relates to the fight against corruption, the unions and government cannot afford to be on different planes. To illustrate, when the government launched the Laptop Project for elementary schools, there was much public outrage with the implementation process. Critics claimed the project was mired in less-than-transparent dealings. Unions were disjointed in their public discussion of the criteria used to award contracts worth billions of taxpayers' monies to well-connected firms. The Jubilee Government's interest in providing computers to students was in direct opposition to raising salaries for elementary school teachers. These competing values can lead to differing views about the network's effectiveness as an advocate of leveraging ICTs for development.

CONCLUSIONS

In conclusion, the interest here is to encourage us to conceptualize unions and government ministries as belonging to, first and foremost, problem-solving networks. Under this framework, union members and government managers should set the agenda for ICT policy development. The network of actors should also solve existing complex problems of poor productivity and low quality of education and other public services. In doing so, the goal is for members of the networks to share information and develop relationships that address issues emerging from a globalized and Internet connected world. Networks are more flexible and adapting than narrowly defined government ministries that are controlled through rigid red tape.

In terms of information sharing, unions, NGOs, government, and private-sector actors (like Safaricom) are in the network to solve important problems, like insecurity in Kenya. When teachers' unions called upon members to leave their workstations in Mandera and other northern counties for lack of security, there was evidence that the governance networks were not in sync with one another. In terms of knowledge about the potential uses of ICTs in law enforcement and public safety, there appears to be a mismatch in how the government and members of the security network can shape policies to respond to the problem of insecurity. Without communication and collaboration, the implementation network cannot lead to improved services produced by each member of the network. Shared information between the Office of the President, community groups, nonprofits like charity organizations, and unions all benefit from sharing information on Al-Shabaab and other groups that disrupt peaceful coexistence of communities in the northern part of the country.

Given the predictability of gangs attacking innocent civil servants, it makes sense to plan for those challenges to public safety in the regions where the incidents are frequent. Lack of collaboration and weak incident command systems frustrate the achievement of peace in regions like Mandera, Tana River, and Wajir in the face of continued Al-Shabaab attacks. Unions have to be proactive members of the information diffusion networks and be positioned with knowledge about ICTs that help reduce the prevalence of terrorist criminal attacks.

When debating about who should lead both the information-sharing and problem-solving networks, the government itself, as was evident in the September 2013 terrorist attack at the Nairobi Westgate Mall, appeared confused. But it still has the constitutional responsibility to protect its citizens. Unions have to play the support role, but developing critical expertise in providing strategies for employee wellness, helping out in building trust between union members and government lead agencies and supporting other members with informational logistics, frequently enabled by ICT platforms. Unions have to be proactive through helping other actors such as universities in capacity building and contributing to social capital development. The opportunities for building social capital are enabled through social networks that, thus far, are inadequate.

Proactive union efforts mean greater public awareness of issues. Unions like KNUT have greater outreach and presence than most other organizations. Problem solving networks may voluntarily monitor and evaluate government progress in creating structures for peaceful coexistence of communities. ICT tools are ideal for sharing these efforts and for getting people to talk about how best they can be served. Software that maps out areas of high crime can be applied to solving some of the challenges discussed above. Areas that are isolated from government services can be monitored and information shared among all the stakeholders with the goal of developing strategic plans to reduce incident occurrences.

THREE

Industrialization and Technology Diffusion

State Capacity in the Age of ICTs

INTRODUCTION

The first Industrial Revolution enabled humankind to shift from reliance on animals and human effort as sources of energy. At the end of the nineteenth century, a new revolution occurred. In this second Industrial Revolution, electricity became a key form of energy and was responsible for massive changes in human capacity and civilization. After the 1950s, another industrial revolution designed around rapid computing and developments in digital systems formed the third Industrial Revolution. The fourth Industrial Revolution based on proliferation of cyber-physical systems presented entirely new ways in which technologies were embedded in society.

By 2013, more people in the world had access to mobile phones than toilets for sanitation. Industrialization conjures the image of mass production of goods, including those that enable information and communications. Armed with new technologies, societies have developed new forms of tools to facilitate daily interactions.

Technologies are therefore associated with industrialization and the existence of governance, and especially ways of leveraging public policy to support production of goods and services. In particular, today information and communication technologies (ICTs) are available to facilitate commerce and socioeconomic and political development. Indeed, while Africa indeed plays a huge part in the development of ICTs, the maufacture or assembly of ICT products is associated with international capital and multinational corporations (MNCs). Yet, commitment to promote technology transfers to African countries remains a mirage, despite efforts by various stakeholders. The challenges of doing so are still intractable in all sectors.

In the area of ICTs, technology transfers are contested and controversial. Discussions in various international forums tend to highlight the historical nature of the north-south divide, which assigns production and distribution according to dictates of the developed countries. And in many instances, policy frameworks that shape discourses on technology transfers revolve around issues of governance and the weak capacity existing in developing countries like Kenya. Often, developing countries are reminded that they have to provide economic and political environments that attract industrial and technological investments.

Notwithstanding the challenge of governance and state capacity, the discussion on ICTs and other forms of technology transfers is often naïve and excludes comparative elements across the global South. In addition, the understanding of neoliberal, pro-market doctrines and practices pushed into African political policy documents must be addressed, especially for ICTs, which are a key element in the knowledge-based new economy.

This chapter places the discussion about ICTs within the broader context of debates over Kenya's ability and capacity to industrialize. As is well known, ICTs represent technological advancements, which started with use of primitive tools (Stone Age), through the Bronze Age and the Iron Age's massive industrialization and now the Silicon Age. Framing the emergence of ICTs outside the context of industrialization minimizes the linkages of policy debates about the roles of capitalist structures. An important element in the emerging discourse is the continuation of the forces that drive the ICTs, especially the banks and other interlocking service industries. This chapter explores the capacity of African countries, such as Kenya to explore the diffusion of ICTs through the Multinational Corporations sector (MNCs) and its allies within the ruling national elite. Generally speaking, African countries are mostly associated with providing minerals, targeted markets, and labor to the technologically advanced countries of the North. That does not mean Kenya and African countries did not try to industrialize and be a full participant in the technology-driven world.

At independence, Kenya, Nigeria, and Egypt, among other African states had been considered prime candidates for rapid industrialization. Indeed, most donors and pundits were optimistic that African countries would, at least, modernize in the same fashion that had been experienced in Asia several decades earlier. The example of the so-called "Asian Tigers" had arguably provided a blueprint for developing countries to join the industrialized world. Commentators referenced South Korea as a country that in 1963 was at par with Kenya in terms of economic development. By 2015, South Korea's per capita income was $33,629 compared to Kenya's paltry $1,300 (Shimoli, 2016). The lessons of South Korea and other Asian Tigers' path to development can serve to put into perspective the current state of Africa's poverty. From the perspective of governance, reputable economists remind us that the Asian Tigers emerged from poverty to global powers because their ruling oligarchies enriched their societies as opposed to African leaders' whose industrialization strategies were organized around personal enrichment (Ndii, 2016). Moreover, the Asian Tigers inculcated Confucian ethics within their working classes. As a value system, Confucianism placed country above self and government supported the Chaebols (huge business conglomerates) as a matter of national interest. In addition, the phenomenal growth of these industries was sustained through discipline, which the Kenyan state lacks.

Thus, while South East Asian "Tigers'" recorded remarkable achievements in industrialization, African nations have sunk deep into a pre-industrial pit and continued to be suppliers and consumers of most products of technology, which include information and communication technologies (ICTs) like radios, TVs, fax machines, telephones, mobile phones, and a host of computer-mediated devices.

For illustrative purposes, the theoretical question is, why did Africa fail in joining the industrialized world? Perhaps one may be forthright and conclude that the question cannot be answered in a single book. Each discipline surely has an answer to this question, which means no single variable captures the complexity of the problem. One simple way out is to fully understand the structural issues shaping the framework for technological absorption and diffusion into the mix. And here is where we might see the role of trade unions in the whole food chain of industrialization and the absorption of various ICTs.

Unions are a part of the institutional framework that can provide support for industrialization. But unions must start from a position of strength, through organizational stability and capacity. To carry out transformations, unions need to support training members on organizational, technical, and managerial capacity. Technology and communication impacts innovation and provides opportunities for societies to find better ways of doing business. For example, in Africa, land telephone lines were highly dysfunctional and, with the advent of mobile telephones, greater efficiencies have accrued. In most cases, the ensuing diffusion of new technologies is a game changer.

By substituting old technologies for mobile smartphones, workers are able to be more productive. ICTs have transformed society by cutting down time for travel and created new virtual communities. Many of the new social networks are also avenues for business entrepreneurships and organizational reforms. Thanks to the Internet, the modern worker is now guaranteed the full benefits of a global knowledge base. Unions recognize the ever-increasing role of ICTs in national economic developments across the nations. ICTs are now a key driver of growth and development in all countries, and employers should leverage these emerging tools for work. Based on government support of ICT infrastructure, a country can attract businesses and thereby increase its Gross National Product (GNP).

Governments have a unique role to play in ensuring that the proper regulatory policies and business environments are in place for ICT penetration. Diffusion of technologies is mainly a function of government policies, private sector actors, and market dynamics. As Moses Kiggundu (1989, p. 191) underscored, the world's stock of technological innovations is concentrated in the advanced countries, which have oligopolistic control of new technologies as well. This means Kenya and other developing countries have to go to global markets to acquire these new information and communication technologies. And, the globalized world business environment makes diffusion of technologies an integral part of industrial policy making in African countries, which compete for investments from a restricted pool of corporate ventures. Authorities in Kenya who have debated ways of improving the country's preparedness as an investment destination know this. For instance, the coalition government, in reaction to a World Bank (2012) and International Finance Corporation (IFC) report that ranked Kenya as number 109 destinations, tabled a bill to simplify payment of taxes and regulatory climate through introduction of e-government tools. In 2012, then Finance Minister Njeru Githae introduced a bill to establish an online registration platform. Electronic registration of businesses was meant to bring order in the business regulation environment and end the rigidities associated with paper-based application and registration bureaucratic practices. At the front end, the Kenya Revenue Authority (KRA) also initiated automation of services in an effort to streamline ways of doing business in the country (Shiundu, 2012).

For their part, unions must continue to support the transfer of new technologies in the workplace. Without supportive input from unions, national competitiveness may not be achievable. ICTs, through Internet devices, are the contemporary glue that holds together corporate engagements and innovations across the nations. The new business and corporate environment empowers employees through web-based collaborate exchanges and networks. The ensuing networks are key to solidifying existing industrialization and other business processes. New medias are where corporations govern themselves and conduct business. It is also here that technology transfers are enabled. Technology transfers can be costly in terms of utilization and acquisition, but unions acting as stakeholders should demonstrate that new technologies are necessary for the industrialization to be achieved.

In this chapter, for better or worse, industrialization refers to the process whereby commodities are skillfully manufactured through power-driven machinery located in plants and factories. Regardless of scale in manufacturing, a key characteristic of industrialization is the marked acceleration in the output of goods. The intent by African countries to industrialize is well articulated in various policy documents and speeches of the political and power elite.

Kenya's defining policy documents convey the message that industrialization was to be determined by government planning. Government, and not the private sector, saw itself as the main agent for modernization, employment creation, and earning or saving of foreign exchange (Republic of Kenya 1965, p. 43; Republic of Kenya, *Development Plans*, 1966–1970, 1970–1974, 1979–1983). From the onset, planners in Kenya recognized there was a high positive correlation between income per head and the share of manufacturing in the Gross National Product (GNP). Perhaps, manufacturing capacity differentiated rich from poor countries. Although reforms have lessened the role of government in the manufacturing sectors, the mentality that development through industrialization can only be achieved through public sector growth is an enduring misguided elite philosophy. The huge administrative class associates every aspect of "development" with political context. This, in turn, has created a huge misallocation of resources in Kenya and partly explains the skewed path toward growth and evolution of ICT industries. Evidence of this overbearing state capacity is found in the numerous five-year economic development plans and parliamentary Sessional Papers.

Up until the 1990s, the state, in Kenya, through various initiatives and interventions, sought to promote industrialization as opposed to achieving growth through service and raw material (agriculture and minerals) driven economy. Initially the preferred strategy was import substitution—whereby the state emphasized location of plants in the country. However, import substitution was dependent on imported inputs and centered on the last link in the manufacturing chain, mixing or assembly of components. State intervention was managed through various ministries initially through the auspices of the Ministry of Commerce and Industry. Today, following the election of Uhuru Kenyatta in 2013, several ministries share oversight of various activities that are associated with manufacturing and industrialization. There are large departments concerned with mining, separated from Ministry of Natural Resources; there is also the ministry of Industrialization and Enterprise Development, and that of Commerce, Tourism and East African region. The Ministry of Information, Communications and Technology is now the organization responsible for policy management in the area of ICTs.

Several state-owned enterprises and commissions operate under the aegis of various ministries named above. In tandem with these are other agencies, especially the Financial Parastatals supervised by the Ministry of Finance and the Office of the President. Key among the state-owned institutions are the Development Finance Corporation of Kenya, the Industrial and Commercial Development Corporation, the Kenya Industrial Estates for small-scale industries, and various state banks. Barbara Grosh (1991) provides an excellent exposé of the performance of Kenya's parastatal sector.

Also the state instituted mechanisms that allowed for the private sector to play a key role in the drive toward industrialization. The government's big idea was to establish mechanisms for "providing a conducive climate" to foreign investors. Especially favored at independence way into the 1980s and early 1990s were British companies and later on Western and Japanese firms in general. Upon ascending to power in 2003, President Mwai Kibaki aggressively sought out non-European, especially Chinese and Indian, investors.

Likewise, Uhuru Kenyatta gave Chinese investors increased access to resources and opportunities for locating firms in Kenya. There were plans by China to host a clearinghouse for Chinese renminbi currency in line with Kenya's goal of creating a financial hub in Nairobi. The largest component of Chinese investments is in the areas of energy, infrastructures including stadiums (Moi International Stadium, Kasarani), roads, and railways that include a standard-gauge railway line from Mombasa to Malaba. The Chinese government based their industrialization strategy on the notion that centers for industry and commerce were essential for attracting investments. According to Chinese strategists, China industrialized by first building "a nest to attract the phoenix" (Liqiang, 2015, p. 1). Following adaptations from Ireland's opening-up models of the 1970s, China's embraced zoning practices. By some estimates, zoning now accounts for 22 percent of China's national GDP, 46 percent of its foreign investments, and 60 percent of the country's exports (Liqiang, 2015, p. 6).

Therefore, Chinese participation in Kenya's industrialization process is based on China's own experience. Support in the area of ICT industrialization has been limited through participation of corporations like Huawei Telecommunications. ZTE, another telecommunications giant, has already made inroads into neighboring Ethiopia and also seeks Kenya's markets. Critics argue that Chinese aid and investments do not translate into major job creation and resemble past colonialism. Still, China became the largest bilateral lender to Kenya's treasury. Other major lenders are Japan, France, and Germany. Kenya's major multilateral donors are the World Bank's International Development Association (IDA), Africa Development Bank (Af DB), and the International Monetary Fund (IMF).

Former Central Bank of Nigeria governor Lamido Sanusi, cited in a *New York Times* op-ed, argued that China used equipment and imported labor from their country (French, 2014). China's aid and investments were therefore not a major contributor to job creation. Although they use raw materials from Africa, there are few instances where the Chinese transfer skills and instead export manufactured goods. China has reacted to criticisms of doing little to transfer technology by encouraging partnerships with developing countries in the manufacture of ICT products. The

Chinese international ICT firm Inspur has supported Jomo Kenyatta University of Agriculture and Technology (JKUAT) to launch "Taifa," a laptop assembled in Kenya. It is envisioned that Taifa would be sold in East African markets at a cost of KSh. 40,000 apiece. Likewise, Huawei supported a program for training African students to gain knowledge and skills in ICTs. Kenyans have benefited from the Seeds of the Future initiative but because it is in its pilot stages, the gains are yet to be evaluated.

Context of Multinational Corporations (MNCs)

Notwithstanding Chinese aid and investments, multinational corporations (MNCs) remained the key players in ICT development. In particular, International Business Machines (IBM) sought to increase its presence in Africa by selecting Nairobi as the location for its Research and Development (R&D) lab. The deal between IBM and the government of Kenya, signed in 2012, aimed at increasing the use of technological products in mainly the public sectors.

The government of Kenya (through the Ministry of Information, Communications and Technology) supported the IBM research lab and contributed about $2 million toward the project. The research lab would assist the country in finding information and communication technology solutions to problems like traffic congestions, water management, and other problems arising from population growth. IBM has eleven other labs located in countries as diverse as the United States, Australia, Brazil, China, Ireland, Israel, Japan, and Switzerland. Many of these labs have produced some of the best researchers in the IT areas and are well recognized for excellence in applied research. The IBM lab is the first of its kind in Africa.

In building partnerships with IBM, the government was seeking ICT solutions for its Vision 2030 Development Blueprint and find paths to sustainable development and modernization through cost-efficient means. IBM has extensive experience in providing ICT solutions in areas like cloud computing, data analytics, and management. IBM's technical solutions were also seen as one way of improving productivity and efficiency and checking fraud and abuse of offices in the public sector. With Kenya's embrace of e-government solutions, partnership with IBM was considered a step toward building human capacity in ICTs. Kenyan researchers will benefit from IBM Research Resident Scientist and other human development initiatives.

Using legislative and administrative means, MNCs were given a free hand in investing in the country. Throughout the late 1960s and early 1970s things seemed to work, and the emergent middle classes propelled Kenya to a polity that showed much promise. In fact, an African bourgeoisie had already emerged. Academics engaged in endless debates over the duality of the economy, the differentiation of the peasantry, the plight of the urban workers, and the hope for an African success. At the time of the oil crisis, and the emergent debt regime, the 1980s became a lost decade in terms of both political and economic development. Industry suffered as the state failed to ease its grip on the economic activities in the land. Industrial gains collapsed, and as a result, prospects for greater job creation and industrialization dwindled (Kaplinsky 1978; Langdon 1981; Leys 1975; Swainson 1980).

By the 1990s, Kenya had not recovered from ailments acquired during the last decade. Some of the Asian countries that had been at par with Kenya in the 1960s, namely the "Tigers," had by now emerged from the morass of poverty and traditionalism, and to a large extent, modernized. For example, in the 1950s, South Korea was poorer than a number of African countries and on the brink of a devastating civil war, and Hong Kong and Singapore were busy little ports, but not a lot more. Not only did they experience transformations in social and economic systems, they also earned the title of newly industrialized nations and provided citizens with better standards of living. We know for a fact that these Asian countries are now leaders in production and export of ICT products. On the other hand, African countries export minerals and import ICT products. Yet we must not compare these eventualities without consideration of the enabling motivations. Answers as to why Africa could not industrialize during the Industrial Revolution "spurt" are not the core subject of this chapter and are adequately addressed by Barrington Moore (1966) and others who link backwardness to lack of industrialization. As one important study posits:

> Yet it is equally true that one cannot understand the industrial development of any country, as long as it be considered in isolation. Backwardness, of course, is a relative term. It presupposes the existence of more advanced countries. Moreover, it is only by comparing industrialization processes in several countries at various levels of backwardness that one can hope to separate what is accidental in a given industrial evolution from what can be reasonably attributed to the historical lags in a country's development. (Gerschenkron, 1962, p. 42)

Gerschenkron regarded backwardness as an operational term that could be measured but acknowledged that the measurements were not always perfect. Perhaps, the tie between industrialization and eradication of poverty continues to be a major influence in explaining why Kenya and other African countries did not achieve the "Asian Tiger Miracle." A distinguished Harvard professor makes the following argument:

> The proximate cause of poverty is low productivity. Poor people are poor because their labor enables them to produce too little to adequately feed and house themselves, let alone provide for other needs such as health and education. Low productivity in turn has adverse and multiple causes. . . . It may be result of lack of access to new and better

> technologies. It may be the lack of skills, knowledge, and job opportunities. It may be the consequence of small market size, which depresses the profitability of acquiring new equipment and technologies. (Rodrik, 2011, p. 137)

Obviously, the reduction of poverty through export-driven industrialization was an important part of building a base for production and consumption of ICT artifacts. And even so, tying elimination of poverty and backwardness to the history of industrialization and productivity in South Asian countries offers some lessons for East Africa.

A Tigers' Model? Lessons to Be Learned

And what is the relevance of the late industrialization trend? The success of the Asian Tigers became a demonstration effect for the African nations. And African media became replete with editorials calling for the emulation of the Asian Tigers and industrialization. The Tigers' path to industrialization was made possible by different set of human capital conditions. Taiwan (Taipei), South Korea, Hong Kong, and Singapore realized industrialization through a dependent type of industrialization. Capital availability was linked with Japanese and Western finance. Clearly, the majority of southeast Asian countries received more aid and capital infusion than African nations, except for a few countries such as Nigeria and Egypt. Among the largest recipients of Western investment were Malaysia, Thailand, Indonesia, and Korea (Phillips, 1997, p. R6). These countries also enjoyed a larger degree of foreign investment than Kenya or Africa for that matter. As a result, an economist writing in 1985 observed:

> For the past 25 years East Asian economies [to include what we describe as Southeast Asian] have grown more than twice as fast as the average rate for the rest of the world. . . . These successes have been fostered by sound fiscal policies, low inflation, export-drives growth, and effective institutions, which in turn helped make East Asia the world's leading recipient of foreign investment. Moreover, the region's high savings rate, more than one third of gross domestic product, is six times foreign investment. These savings have made possible a high and increasing level of investment. (Wade, 1998, p. 5)

The road to Asian Tigers' great strides to industrialization was described as a *revolution* in the sense that these countries experienced the fastest growth rates seen in the twentieth century. Among the common threads in the search for industrialization was an increase in funding for high literary rates and education. Throughout the 1990s, these countries allocated substantive resources for developing a skilled manpower base. Secondly, the political establishment deliberately put in place a system that encouraged a competitive ethic and pursued strategies that encouraged local entrepreneurs to exploit market opportunities. Industrialization was also assisted by appropriate wage interventions, which supported market development. As policy, governments "evened out" wages between the public sector workers and industry and made everyone "feel they are in the same boat" (*Sunday Nation* July 3, 1994). According to *Forbes* magazine, other factors included the institution of stable macroeconomic policies, and high saving rates (Tanzer, 1998, p. 119). Out of those efforts, South Korea emerged not only as one of the Newly Industrialized Economies (NIE) but also as one of the most advanced and top twenty largest economies in the world (BBC, 1998; Shimoli, 2016). Through hosting corporations like Samsung, it became a big player in the global production of ICTs. South Korea ranked as a leader in the production of computer memory chips, ships, and automobiles. South Korea's brands, like Samsung, Kia, LG, and Daewoo, are global household names.

Asian governments also made sure that inflation and exchange rates did not discourage investors. The predictability of investment climate was a plus for countries in search of investments from the Western countries. Such indicators made it possible for investors to calculate the rate of return on investments with some degree of certainty. Another characteristic of the Tigers was that they created conditions in which food deficits were eliminated. Ample production of rice—the staple food—was ensured and provided the foundation upon which further investments could be built. In other words, factory workers did not face hunger issues as is common in Kenya.

Approaches to Understanding Comparative Industrialization

For theoretical clarity, Alexander Gerschenkron (1962) offers an explanatory approach to relative differences in industrialization across the board. He writes that for industrialization to occur certain major obstacles must be removed and certain things propitious to it must be created. He argues that the idea that industrialization may take some form of uniformity is a misinterpretation of the reality. However, we can arrive at a set of key characteristics that are embedded in the history of a given nation (Gerschenkron, 1962, p. 31). Theoretically therefore, industrialization is construed through an identifiable model or models.

In the Gerschenkron (1962) model, which to some extent approximates an ideal type, the prerequisites to industrialization are numerous. First, a polity creates the opportunities for growth. An effort is made to create an economically unified territory. The state in this case must also be able to ensure the rights of individuals and increase productivity in agriculture and institute fair redistributive mechanisms. Labor availability, protection of property rights, a store of technological lore, existence of an entrepreneurial group willing to innovate, and availability of capital for long-term investment are necessary. Also important is the removal of guild restrictions and the guarantee of wide and absorptive markets. These prerequisites can be present in various degrees and in different "mixes" before industrialization takes place. Gerschenkron also points out that some of these conditions are products of industrialization and so some flexibility is called for. These conditions are important insofar as they are the minimum conditions for creating conditions for industrialization.

According to Gerschenkron, it is the concept of original accumulation that is most important in suggesting answers to how the capitalist state triggers off the industrialization process (1962, p. 36). While Marxist thinking may shed some light in terms of the behaviors of individual capitalists, it does not go far enough. However, for the most part, most African countries experienced the phenomenon of state-directed capitalism. How they do it is different but the bottom line is that state involvement in industrialization is overwhelming. Perhaps the state filled a void created by a lack in the entrepreneurial ethic, not to mention the creation of financial resources for original accumulation. The former position brings us to yet another important theoretical perspective posited by Max Weber.

Writing on the African situation in general, Callaghy (1988, p. 68), argued that Weber emphasized the significance of attitudinal and motivational factors in societal transformations. According to Weber, industrialization occurred in a capitalist framework through a bureaucratic state mechanism. Thus, the assumption is that a rational bureaucracy is a prerequisite for industrialization. From evidence gathered so far, this is not possible in an African environment where rational permanent enterprise and industrial capitalism face huge challenges. Weber's discourse identified elements such as rational technological applications and knowledge as being vital for transformations including industrial development. He also argued that market exchanges must not be burdened by irrational restraints and that society must have calculable law in both adjudication and state administration. Also on his list is the rationalization of the monetary system and general commercialization of economic life (Callaghy 1988, p. 72; Landes 1969, pp. 22–23). Extrapolating from Weber, the modern state is vital in all transformations, including the move to modernize through industrialization and the absorption and application of ICTs.

Galbraith (1967) and Gerschenkron (1962) both noted the importance of a strong agricultural base before industrialization flourished. For example, in Britain, the "industrial spurt" followed on the heels of an agricultural one. Similarly, in the United States, the agricultural revolution preceded the industrial one. In addition, education is a major factor in development of technological capability. There is no country that can sustain industrial competitiveness in high value-added manufacturing like the ICT arena without a supply of skilled scientific workers. Together with research and development activities, the Tigers achieved great industrial success unlike anywhere in sub-Saharan Africa (Galbraith, 1967, pp. 9–10; Asian Development Outlook, 1998, p. 18).

There are also individual governance characteristics that warrant further attention. For instance, South Korea's industrialization process benefited from loans from Japan under President Chung Hee Park (1960–1979). President Park was also a champion for industrialization. Additionally, Japanese experts played an important role in imparting skills and expertise to Korean Industries. Samsung and Gold Star, for instance, learned much from successful ICTs like Sony, Sanyo, Toshiba, and NEC. One important ingredient has been the strong and assured nature of the state in South Korea. Without associated governance structures, the state would not have facilitated successful industrialization.

Indeed, the industrialization process in South Korea resembled that in the developed countries in one more way. Few major actors or conglomerates, the largest of which were Hyundai-Kia, Daewoo, Samsung, Sum Kyung (SK), and Lucky Gold (LG-Gold Star), drove it. These accounted for one third of Korea's debt crisis as well as one half of all its exports (CNN, 1998). These export-driven "Top or Big Chaebol" were the leading manufacturer of automobiles, computers, ICTs, electronic goods, and other goods. Also the Asian Tigers relied less on other traditional Western MNC's to achieve economies of scale (Gereffi &Wyman, 1987, p. 7, p. 9; Gereffi, 1990, p. 5). Several companies associated with Daewoo did not survive the Asian financial crisis and went bankrupt in 1999.

Yet, there were similarities in terms of state behavior and action. Between 1935 and 1980, South Korea and Taiwan had the most state-centered operations in areas such as banking and manufacturing. The state coordinated, directed, and collaborated with firms entering major world industries and helped them remain competitive. In some of the new industries, the state provided cheap credit, tax breaks, and other forms of subsidy to some of the new industries as a means of protecting them. One effect of this was that these firms amassed resources on the scale needed to undertake rapid upgrading and disciplining necessary for international competitiveness such as export performance. Additionally, in some dying industries, the state helped firms exit or move offshore (World Development, 1998, p. 10).

The results of state action were remarkable. A most illustrative statement on the role of the state in Korea's industrialization is by Campbell (1994) and Maxfield (1994). Campbell argued that the different regimes treated the vital matter of technology in different ways. For instance, the state directed technological innovation and ensured that innovations guided the country's industrial development. The South Korean state infrastructure was marshaled through the Office of the President (Blue House) and a number of key ministries including the Ministries of Trade,

Industry and Science and Technology. In some ways, the role of the Ministry of Trade, Industry and Science and Technology in South Korea was similar to that of the Japan's Ministry of International Trade and Industry (MITI). According to an influential research study, MITI had real power to reorganize the electronic and automobile sectors of the Japanese economy (Pempel, 1998, p. 54). Also, MITI played a cardinal role in the formulation and implementation of strategic policies. In addition, MITI employed the best graduates it would access, which ensured a high degree of bureaucratic capability. These "bureaucrats were imbued with a sense of mission and identified themselves with national goals derived from a position of leadership in society" (Onis, 1991, p. 114). In making comparisons to East Africa, the role of bureaucracy must be given emphasis. The bureaucracy in Kenya did not have the same ambitions of the developmental state identified in the East Asian case. It is also fair to say the Kenyan bureaucrats enjoyed greater autonomy and sense of unity than their African counterparts, who were mired in strong ethnic and patronage political webs. The high autonomy from political control enabled the bureaucracy to focus on the development of policies that were fairly independent from the powerful members of the political establishment in South Korea (So & Chiu, 1995, p. 15). According to Dani Rodrik, the role of the government bureaucracy in serving the needs of industry was a big piece of the road map to industrialization and economic growth.

Furthermore, Rodrik (2011) acknowledged the Asian Tigers were influenced by the Japanese model in other ways and that the South Korean bureaucracy protected the infant industries from foreign competition. Many observers of the East Asian developmental state argue that provision of subsidies was a core element in promotion of late industrialization.

There were other arms of the state bureaucracy that were supportive of the push toward industrialization. For example, state-controlled research agencies included the Korean Energy Research Institute, South Korea Standards Research Institute, and importantly the Electronics Research Institute, which all made great contributions to the effort (Campbell, 1994). As Campbell's work demonstrated, the state played a supporting role in some of the major industries in which Korea excelled. The state did this by its "strong push to develop science and technology" as well as giving the Chaeobol space to conduct product Research and Development (R and D).

The dynamic and appeal for industrialization received impetus through the Korean state's reliance on domestic banking credit (Maxfield, 1994, pp. 582–3). This did not suggest that external funding was ignored. On the contrary, the dependence of Korean industry on state-sponsored banks dates back to colonial times. President Park, in 1972, intervened on occasions to stabilize the financial markets. For example, in 1972, he decreed that a bailout for the indebted Chaebol be made. Overall, state-owned banks and the Central Bank were key players in financing industrial development (Maxfield, 1994, p. 576). In a nutshell, South Korea and other "tiger" entrepreneurs, occasionally supported by Japanese entrepreneurs, mobilized savings for proper investments to develop a transformative capacity that allowed for industrial growth to flourish in the region.

As described above, the Asian model created a transformation in which modern ICTs and other industrial products were produced locally, primarily for export. The case of Kenya's absorption of ICTs was based on structural conditions remarkably different from those in Asia. In the next section, we focus on foundations of ICT diffusions and the institutional context of industrialization. In many instances, the political environment lays the foundation for capacity building for industrialization. To account for the reliance on imported ICT products, we have to look at Kenya's government policies especially its stewardship of the labor and capital resources.

Industrialization Experimentation and Capacity for Production of ICTs

The most obvious reasons why strong industrialization did not occur in Kenya is not so much that the lack of ingredients identified the Weber-Gerschenkron-Galbraith model, but the complex nature of its politics and state capacity. Arguably, the model itself is flawed by the complicated nature of Africa's dependency on imported technologies. Careful analysis of African economies suggests that the first goal of food security is far from achieved. Galbraith, Moore and Gerschenkron, and other scholars argue that there can never be industrialization without transformations in the agricultural sector. Kenya is a food-deficit country and has multiple agrarian issues to ponder, including land tenure and consolidation questions. FAO's Household Food Security Index rated Kenya as one of the most food-insecure developing countries, placing it fifty-one out of sixty-one low-income food-deficit countries (Orvis, 1997).

At the time of Europe's industrialization, in the eighteenth century, citizens were already living above food insecurity thresholds and had some money to buy the products of industry (Landes, 1969, p. 5). As we shall discuss, based on poverty levels and cost of Internet, mobile phones and other ICT products are a huge financial drain on Kenya's poor masses. Of course, moneymaking opportunities for the vast majority of people are also based on abilities to tap into these new technologies.

Significantly also, the level of technological innovation in Africa is extremely low or completely lacking across the board. By twenty-first-century standards, Africa's capacity to produce ICT products remains weak or unexplored. Therefore, the dependency on particularly European and Asian manufacturing technologies is evident. Reliance on inputs made in Europe and Asia was previously buttressed within a failed import substitution industrialization strategy adapted in Kenya at independence. At independence, in a few Asian countries, the dependency existed but foreign investors were discouraged from retaining monopoly in the supply of external inputs.

For its part, Kenya failed to establish appropriate scientific and technological infrastructures needed for sustainable industrialization and technological production. Considering the amounts spent on political conflict and general administration, industrialization does not seem to be a top priority for African governments. Misdirected politics takes center stage even after attempting to draw public attention to the need for industrialization. For example, Kenya attempted to make its own car, Nyayo Pioneer, but the whole project collapsed due to corruption. The Nyayo, named after former President Moi's popular slogan, was a state-funded project that sought to emulate the South Korean Hyundai, Malaysian Proton, and India's Tata automobile manufacturing approach. However, embezzlement of funds allocated for the development of the car led to its abrupt dissolution. Additionally, the Asian vehicle manufacturers moved quickly to station dealers in African states and easily influenced African political leaders out of the idea of manufacturing a homegrown automobile. It is instructive that the failed Nyayo Pioneer car project was associated with the University of Nairobi. Education and technological progress go hand in hand. This brings us to the role of education and institutions in industrialization.

Labor, Education, Skills, and Ministerial Capacity

Writing about domestic capitalists and the state in Kenya, Himbara (1994), posited that at one time Kenya had great promise. However, its nascent industrialization success was problematic (Himbara, 1994, pp. 69–81). The reason for this was that the state apparatus failed to marshal the country's entrepreneurial skills. Neither the Ministry of Education nor that of Commerce and Industry (and its successor institutions) was successful at inculcating values that would trigger a wave of industrialization. Affiliated state-owned research organizations such as the Kenya Industrial Research Institute were perpetually underfunded and run by inept personalities. Moreover, there was no link between research and industry within Kenya's educational system. Instead of appointment of competent individuals, the system promoted patronage whereby appointment of political figures—nontechnical persons—to oversee the operations of industrial research was the norm.

Significantly, many of the state-owned enterprises that conduct research were perennially placed under the aegis of a nonperforming former Ministry of Science, Research and Technology or associated government departments. For the most part, program uncertainties prevailed in the overcentralized Kenya state. And until after 2013, ministries were created and wound up the following year discouraging program stability in rendering scientific and technical endeavors. The Ministry of Industrialization and Enterprise Development established in 2013 continued patronage practices and firefighting. To illustrate, for example, in 2015, Cabinet Secretary Adan Mohamed had to defend the Chinese investors involved in the construction of the 487-kilometer Mombasa-Nairobi Railway line for not providing employment to Kenyans. Mohamed acknowledged that even in 2013, Kenya lacked the "technology to produce the quality of cement required for the project, so China was forced to import 6,000 metric tons of cement" (Liqiang, 2015, p. 2). The Chinese authorities have mastered the art of managing criticism and published contrary views that claimed China has already transferred skills to the local cement industry, enabling local suppliers to supply cement for roads and railway construction. Previous evidence suggests that older factories like Bamburi Cement had all the requisite skills and products. However, the capacity of Kenyan authorities to shed light on quality matters is itself questioned.

Arguably, the Kenya Bureau of Standards (KBS), which is functionally similar to the South Korean Standards Research Institute, produced little capacity for development toward industrialization. Several reasons may explain this disconnect. First, few or no funds are allocated for meaningful research. Second, the agency is inadequately staffed and lacked the physical resources needed for project development. Third, due to leadership issues, Kenya is ill equipped to handle its strategic management and critical operating tasks. Several Kenyan industrial ventures that include the small-scale *Jua Kali* (informal) enterprises as a consequence "bought beforehand" the routine KBS stamps. In other words, KBS quality control inspectors were powerless.

It might be suggested that, to some extent, the ministry overseeing industrialization, as well as the treasury, which supervised state corporations, was ill prepared to serve as lead agency for industrial development. In the case of the treasury, evidence of its failure to collect taxes on cheap imported goods to the detriment of local firms is part proof of Kenya's undercapacity. In June 2014, a conference on devolution pointed out that over two thousand acres of land would be set aside in county governments to support *Jua Kali* entrepreneurs. The county governors also identified lack of support for the sector as a barrier for industrial development in the country and recommended establishment of SACCOS.

By contrast, as alluded, lead and anchor departments in Asia served the cause of national industrialization. The Ministry of International Trade and Industry (MITI) in Japan is an example. Then, Ministry of Trade, Industry and Energy (MOTIE) led the policy initiatives that guaranteed the Republic of Korea's industrialization spurt and rise to a global powerhouse in the manufacturing of ICTs and other industrial products.

In 1989, the country established Korea Institute of Industrial Technology (KITECH) to develop advanced technologies. In addition, the Korea Academy of Industrial Technology (KAITEC) was established and later reorganized to be a part of the Korea Research Council for Industrial Science and Technology to lead the drive to a Knowledge Economy. And today, Korea is one of the few countries with a Ministry of Knowledge Economy whose oversight includes KRCIST.

There are many other examples of a country's lead agency providing leadership in development of a strong industrialization and technology base. Germany's *Bundeswirtschaftsministerium* (Ministry of Economics) played key roles in the industrialization processes by directing investment toward basic material and capital goods industries (Campbell, 1994; Evans, 1995; Schneider, 1998; Silva, 1996; Weiss, 1998, p. 127). Intervening by way of sponsoring mergers and cartels and subsidizing key industries, the state was in charge of the broader planning of industrialization not only in Japan and Germany but also in the Asian Tigers. Evans (1995) contends that state husbanding of the firms is vital in securing industrialization and technological development. Following Gerschenkron and Weber, Evans adds that bureaucratic competence is a vital element in the search for late industrialization. According to Evans (1995, p. 12) there is no substitution for a meritocratic bureaucracy, if it has to serve as a capacity builder for industrialization. Weiss (1998, pp. 50–51), on the other hand, posits that high-quality bureaucrats are essential and that this was an important resource for successful industrialization in states like Japan and Korea.

In comparison, state intervention in Kenya's industrialization is direct. Earlier explanations for failure to "take off" and industrialize were explained by the argument that Kenya and other African countries are relatively young nations, emerging from colonialism. Colonialism, it is argued, denied Africans a chance to own capital. By the end of colonialism, very few Africans had the ability to manufacture anything major. The state entered the production fray with a bang and every sector was invaded by state-owned enterprises to fill in the gap left by the lack of an African business and manufacturing class. Later this class emerged as an appendage of the multinational corporations. The undoing of the state-owned enterprises was poor management and the over domineering role of the state in the economy.

Perhaps due to the proliferation of the state-owned enterprises the state in Kenya is sometimes described as an "overdeveloped," or "over swollen," or "vampire "(Callaghy, 1988, p. 78; Diamond, 1987; Ngethe 1995, p. 261; Villalon, 1998, p. 11). The number of adjectives that describes the African state is long and includes "inefficient, rentier, corrupt, personalistic and authoritarian" (Callaghy, 1988, pp. 80–81). Not surprisingly, some of Kenya's SOE's failed because of serving the patron client relationships among ruling elites. Supervision of these enterprises was found wanting (Grosh 1991). Grosh, in particular, emphasized that the majority of these ventures were technically undercapitalized and unable to perform at the optimum levels necessary for sustainable outcomes.

It follows that skeptics viewed Africa's hope for industrialization as a pipe dream because Kenya and other African countries became increasingly dependent on imports of small items like clothes and matchsticks from countries such as China. Journalist Otula Owuor wrote:

> The continent is even losing its capacity to clothe its people. Although people will always wear clothes, there are few African nations, which have the technology to fully process and manufacture clothes. Indeed, nowadays most of the famous traditional West African cloths are actually made in Asia. (Owuor, 1994)

The fact is that with the massive importation of cheap clothing especially from Asia, and *Mitumba,* that is, used clothing from the West, undermined the productive capacity of Kenya and other African countries. Essentially, Africa remains a source of raw materials for industrialization elsewhere. In some cases, African firms import raw materials like palm oil from Malaysia and other parts of Asia, even though the continent is endowed with similar materials.

There was previous optimism that Kenya's indigenous technological sector, otherwise known as the *Jua Kali* informal sector, would propel the country to a stronger industrialization base. That did not occur. Instead, the sector became a major provider of employment but not a source for major research and development initiatives for producing ICTs or other products of industrialization. The sector employed close to 11.8 million in 2015 and accounted for 20 percent of the GDP. The *Jua Kali* sector received little support from the state, which instead, subsidized foreign multinational corporations.

We can speculate Himbara's (1994) bold assertion that the *Jua Kali* was the bourgeoisie-in-formation was not sustainable and dismissible for several reasons. First, while the skills level in the *Jua Kali* sector appeared to be *reasonably good,* it was not based on intensive scientific research. *Jua Kali* artisans employed rudimentary recycling techniques. Secondly, the products are mainly targeted to the poorest in society and cannot pass quality-control tests required in world markets. Third, the *Jua Kali* enterprises are essentially for local consumption and are extremely underfunded and undercapitalized. The sector is not well integrated into the mainstream areas of banking/markets infrastructure. Therefore, *Jua Kali* cannot be relied upon as "the real training ground for potential African Industrialists" to quote an influential scholar (Himbara, 1994, p. 69). Fourth, members of the industrial class associated with ruling elites undermined the sector.

Arguably, in some ways, smaller firms owned by indigenous Asian industrialists borrowed some of India's alternative-technology strategies to manufacture cheap substitutes. Following this logic, Michael Darkoh (2015) rejected the claim that small-scale industries in Anglophone African countries were not properly integrated in national economies and would not offer a path to sustained development. *Jua Kali* is, therefore, an auxiliary vent for utilizing indigenous low-level technology, known mainly for recycling and repairing ICT and other products and not a venue that would usher a wave toward a late industrialization spurt.

Authoritarianism and the Captured Corrupt State

Perhaps the interaction between authoritarianism, corruption, and the African state's failure to achieve industrialization and technological progress is an important part of the puzzle. Granted that the Asian Tigers had high levels of corruption, the ruling elite was able to weather economic problems associated with ensuing externalities. In many instances, Korea confined corruption to limits that did not disrupt the path to industrialization. South Korea jailed former Presidents Roh Tae Woo and Chun Doo Hwan following disclosures that they received enormous bribes from companies doing business for the public (Brademas & Heimann 1998, p. 18). Although the move toward greater accountability and intolerance of corruption was a recent phenomenon, it gave confidence to investors and the business sector. On the contrary, Kenya is regarded as one of the most corrupt nations in the world.

Corruption and poor governance in several ways affect industrialization and investments in related ICTs. Corruption undermines investor confidence and leads to poor planning and investment regimes. It also results in using scarce public resources to support nonessential projects rather than the important ones and encourages the purchase of shoddy materials leading to break down in state infrastructure like roads, ports, and telecommunications. This is expensive for potential industries, which have to cope with huge maintenance costs. George Ayittei (1992, pp. 182–239), and Jonah Anguka (1998, part 3), provided vivid evidence on Kenya. Ayittei stated that due to corruption, U.S. firms pulled out of Kenya from 1982 to 1989. The number fell from 140 to 115.

Besides, several state-owned firms were looted. Anguka, a former official in the government of Kenya, explained corruption was the reason why a former Minister for Industrial Development in Kenya, Robert J. Ouko was murdered in 1991. He claimed Ouko attempted to present a report on corruption to U.S state officials that involved the dysfunctional Kenya Chemical and Food Corporation (Kisumu Molasses Plant). This plant would have been one of the largest manufacturers of ethanol in the region. According to Anguka, the project was subverted through infighting between Kenyan state officials and some foreign interests, including the Italian companies, Bak Group, and Texnomasio Italiano Brown, a subsidiary of Asea Brown Boveri. What transpired was that millions of dollars were invested in a nonfunctioning project, most of which were taken in as bribes. A government statement later denied involvement in the murder of the minister (*Daily Nation*, November 28, 1998). In his memoir, Smith Hempstone, former U.S. ambassador to Kenya, suspected the government of involvement in and cover up of the murder and lamented the truth will never be known (Hempstone, 1997, p. 66).

Corruption inhibits state autonomy, which is essential for growth and development (Nordliger, 1981, p. 361). Toward the end of President Moi's regime in 2002, the World Bank and International Monetary Fund withdrew important financial support, citing endemic corruption in Kenya.

Even if the World Bank had not withdrawn funds, poor governance and bureaucratic inefficiency resulting from "strongmen" and negative ethnicity is a key feature of politics in Kenya (Throup & Hornsby, 1998, p. 37; Villalon, 1998, p. 12). President Moi's strongman rule prevented the country from achieving political efficiencies and accountability in public affairs.

With regard to state capacity under an authoritarian ruler, Migdal (1988, p. 427), Ngethe (1995, p. 261), Roseberg and Jackson (1994, pp. 300–4) refer to states misallocating resources and failing to provide for the masses. Migdal's argument is that strongmen, in proffering their strategies of survival, use a share of the state resources at their disposal to bind the population to them. The state leaders view the state as a mechanism to "create a single jurisdiction," a rule of law in which they are the dominant players. For Migdal, this is a desideratum of the modern state (Migdal 1988, pp. 426–27). An appropriated state is very vulnerable and lacks a transformational capacity. So vulnerable is this state that it is itself attacked by the person of the head of state (Villalon 1998, p. 9). A state so shaped is likely to be embedded in corruption so that quite often the president, by his behavior, appears to own state firms and uses his position to provide jobs to his cronies. Using market controls and other interventions, private firms owned by the president or his cronies become the major beneficiaries of state largesse and contracts, often at nonmarket rates. De Leon (1993, p. 21) argues that corruption cases increase when resources are scarce, and this was evidenced in Kenya throughout its history as an independent country. Corruption is a regime issue sustained throughout the Daniel arap Moi, Mwai Kibaki, and Uhuru Kenyatta administrations. The point is; the level of corruption in Kenya reached a threshold in which it threatened state capacity to sustain an environment conducive for investments and creativity necessary for innovations to occur on a sustainable basis.

Also important was the fact that the Kenyan elite was outward looking, as opposed to the Asian crony capitalists, who invested locally. Ghanaian economist George Ayittey, while recognizing that industrialization was the key to Africa's growth, further argued that the perils of "looting of Africa" through conspicuous consumption and transfer of resources to Swiss and other Western banks was a disincentive to absorption of new industries (Ayittey, 1991, pp. 158–244). Further, the one-man and ethnic-driven rule stifled competition, which was important for entrepreneurial success in Kenya (Otenyo, 1998).

Kenya's vital finance and banking infrastructures were also linked to corruption practices. The establishment of ethnic "political banks" served to channel funds to regime consolidation schemes. The explanation provided in the literature merits consideration. For example, Scott observed that this ethic of loyalty to the tribe rather than the state in Africa and Asia was an aspect of corruption that ran afoul of modern bureaucratic standards (Scott, 1972, p. 12). German scholar Dirk Berg-Scholsser (1992) made this point in a different way. According to him, Kenyan capitalists or the "state class" were drawn along race and ethnic lines. Consequently, conflicts over state resources and patronage took an identity tone (Berg-Scholsser, 1992, pp. 258–59).

An excellent discussion on the dynamics of interest groups and industrialization in the Tiger nations is contained in Smith (1998). While focusing on Taiwan, Smith observed that the state, in pursuing an industrialization strategy, had its own logic. For Taiwan, the "national interest" included promoting economic growth, national security, protecting and nurturing infant industries, ensuring price stability, and promoting some equity in resource allocation. While the state in Taiwan was authoritarian, it had imbibed the notion of equity in promoting industrialization so long as the industrialization fitted into the broad national planning regime.

As a result, the state gave support to industrialization by making sector-specific interventions such as having a well-trained bureaucracy, and planning alongside the industrial class to promote the ideology of growth. In terms of groups, Taiwan and other then newly industrializing economies did not fall prey to the rent-seeking proclivities of societal groups by insulating the state from the same groups. Argued differently, state autonomy helped it promote industrialization regardless of cleavages. This was not the same in Kenya, where, as demonstrated above, the state is controlled and secludes rival and competing groups regardless of their contribution to the overall growth objectives. While borrowing from Robert Wade (1988), one may discern Smith as arguing that in Korea, unlike Kenya, the state sees public policy as the vector of particular interests in which government agencies serve as the fiefdoms of particular private interests (Smith, 1998, pp. 158–59).

Another lesson common in Asia's industrialization was to welcome investments form outside. This is not unusual. But there is a huge difference in state ability to handle foreign investments. While Kenya called for investments from outside, the state capacity to nurture these remains weak, and captured by political cartels. Peter Anyang Nyongo (1996) summed up the problem thus:

> Thus it is not enough just to remove restrictions on sectoral investments, do away with screening procedures, abolish import licensing and so on. More is required and in Africa, the missing link is in the area of physical and social infrastructure, human resources development and availability, and good governance.
>
> Investors will always be discouraged where one or two of them enjoy unfair advantages over the other, either through political connections or other means. They want to compete on a level playing field. Bribery, political intimidation, lack of access to information, political favoritism all scare off potential investors. (Nyongo, 1996)

While industrialization via the MNCs was one of the main policy options for Kenya, the record shows this strategy did not guarantee self-sustaining industrialization. Why was this so? Muller (1973), Colin Leys (1975), Nicola Swainson (1980), and Maria Nzomo (1992), among others noted that MNCs are not a panacea to Africa's search for industrialization because they are essentially extractive. In addition, because of the risk factor many MNCs want to make quick profits and seldom wish to be integrated in the mainstream economies of Africa. Nzomo (1992, pp. 442–44), explained that MNCs do not earn their host nation large amounts of foreign exchange. Besides, MNCs participate in transfer pricing and benefit from protectionalism.

At the same time, they lead to the marginalization of indigenous local capacity for industrialization.

Michael Todaro (1992, pp. 397–400) added to the list of problems associated with MNC-led industrialization. He identified that MNCs do not provide much support by way of transfer of entrepreneurial skills, technology, and overseas contacts. According to Todaro, MNCs may have little impact on developing local sources of these scarce skills and resources and may in fact inhibit their development by stifling the growth of indigenous entrepreneurship as a result of the MNCs dominance of local markets (1992, p. 398). In some cases, MNCs produce inappropriate products for the African economies and frequently are responsible for introducing inappropriate patterns of consumption through elite orientation, "advertising of superior marketing techniques, and consumption of products that were not a priority for local needs (Todaro, 1992, p. 399). In terms of labor relations, MNCs developed allies with local groups and created a class of high wage earners, thereby displacing local entrepreneurs "and fostering elite loyalty and socialization through pressures or conformity." In addition, MNCs "foster allies values, images, and lifestyles in compatible with local customs and beliefs" (Todaro, 1992, p. 399).

MNCs do not transfer critical technology to host countries in Africa. In addition, MNCs retain monopoly power over their technology and utilize capital-intensive technologies most of the time. Other negative attributes identified in Todaro's work include the association between MNCs and the promotion of urban bias.

Kaplinsky (1978, p. 201), notes that it is one thing to blame the MNCs but the question is whether the state or indigenous bourgeoisie would have undertaken similar or equivalent investments. The MNCs in Kenya did not add to the supply of available local savings. Instead they used local finance for short-term liquidity. Obviously this restricts the ability of the local entrepreneurs to access the same financial resources. Former U.S. Treasury Secretary Robert Rubin supported the same argument by stating that Africans "need to mobilize domestic savings and bring them into the mainstream economy and keep the capital at home. . . . An estimated 39 percent of private wealth in Africa is held overseas" (Rubin, 1998).

Throughout Kenya's history, the state was always vulnerable and is easily manipulated. For example, American fruit manufacturing giant Del Monte's (J.R. Reynolds) investment in Kenya in the 1960s was a clear exhibit for MNC manipulation. Prior to 1965, in several areas of Kenya, pineapple was grown. In the same year, the government signed an agreement with the Kenya Canners Limited—a subsidiary of the California-based Del Monte. The agreement granted Del Monte a monopoly over the production of all processed pineapples in the country. It fixed prices, did all the quality controls, and prohibited small-scale African farmers from setting up a rival firm. As a result, competitors would not emerge. Any exports of fresh pineapples had to be sanctioned by the MNC. Also, the company, like many MNCs, had tax issues and declared losses in questionable ways (Gutto, 1980; Munyakho & Kareithi, 1982, pp. 11–13; Nzomo 1992, p. 444). It took many years before this agreement was found inapplicable and unrealistic.

Therefore, arguably the MNCs wanted the state to treat them in the same manner they did the state-owned enterprises. In fact, the state and the MNCs maintained a symbiotic relationship much like prevailed in advanced industrial countries (Galbraith, 1972). Yet state capacity in Kenya was much weaker, as were civil society and trade unions, which failed to prevent workers against exploitation. State protection of MNCs through legal interventions such as Investment Protection Act (1964) is strong evidence of this reality.

An Emerging Deindustrialization Regime?

Even before the anticipated child was born, already the industrialization process recorded a retrogressive trend. Why was this the case? Evidently, the new push toward globalization changed the landscape of the country's stride toward industrialization. Kenyan policy makers had hoped the country would industrialize by the year 2000. After this date was reached, the rhetoric shifted the goal and announced the year to be 2020 (*Daily Nation*, July 27, 1998). And in 2014, the dominant policy discourse revolves around Vision 2030s, which also tilts toward an ICT-driven economy.

From all available data, the export-led industrialization was not realized. The state-sponsored Export Processing Zones (EPZs) failed to attract large-scale industrialization due to loss of investor confidence resulting from bad governance. What is clear is that the emergent globalization and trading pattern is replete with quotas that make it impossible for the already disadvantaged industries in Africa to compete. As an example, Kenya grappled with the impact of factory closures that created massive unemployment. For example, globalization exacerbated the introduction of quotas in the textile industries, forcing the closure of several factories in Kenya. According to the Kenya Tailoring and Textile Workers Union, a total of eighty-seven textile factories in Kenya collapsed. Forty-four of these firms were in Nairobi; twenty-five in Mombasa; five in Kisumu; two each in Nakuru, Nanyuki, Machakos, and Thika; and one each in Eldoret, Siaya, and Kitale (*Daily Nation*, November 24, 1998).

Thika, one of Kenya's leading industrial towns, experienced closures in several other factories as well. In addition to the Thika Textile Mills, and the Thika Cloth Mills, other firms affected negatively included the Kenya Nut Company, Leather Industries of Kenya, Bulleys Tanneries, and numerous sugar-producing ventures. Yet downsizing of operations was experienced in most factories such as Del Monte, Macademia (Kenya Nut Company), Metal Box, and several others. The main reason for this deindustrialization was the proliferation of cheap imports from Asian countries including, Singapore, Hong Kong, Taiwan and China, South Korea, and Malaysia. Cheap imports that include *Mitumba* (secondhand clothes) imported from developed countries contributed immensely to the decline in the manufacturing of domestic textile industries.

Another factor contributing to this deindustrialization is the fact that "liberalization of the sector caught many of the African industries unprepared" (*Daily Nation*, November 23, 1998). Excellent examples of the effect of cheap imports are evident in iron and steel mill, leather, paper, and sugar industries. The Pan African Paper Mills located in Webuye (Bungoma East) closed in February 2009 after being in service since 1974. The plant was run down and unable to pay its electricity bills. More than one thousand employees, mostly temporary workers (casual laborers) were rendered jobless. Subsequently, creditors including Total Kenya, Kenya Commercial Bank, PTA BANK, and the Kenya Power and Lighting Company placed the factory under receivership. In 2013, the government, through cabinet secretary for industrialization Adan Muhammad, announced the intention to privatize the factory.

Deindustrialization (better still de-manufacturing) continued to manifest in the sugar industry well into 2014. The sugar sector was on the verge of collapse because the government, through corrupt deals, allowed the importation of cheap substitutes into the country. Senator Peter Nyong'o opined that "influential people in government illegally shipped duty free sugar into the country" thereby affecting the cost of sugar production in mostly state-owned local industries such as at Muhoroni and Chemelil. The factories were on the verge of collapse and in huge debts because they would not sell produce (Standard, 2014).

Mumias Sugar Factory, the largest sugar producer, faced greater competition as well. With cheaper imports flooding the market, farmers in the Mumias area also experienced poor returns to their labor. Kenya previously imposed a tariff that protected domestic producers against foreign imports. The globalized nature of the business now demanded firms to produce efficiently to lower costs. And competition from the Common Market for Eastern and Southern Africa (COMESA) required greater attention to this reality.

Deindustrialization was accompanied by restructure of most multinational corporations operating in Kenya. Corporations like Coca Cola, Tata Chemicals Magadi, Karuturi, Standard Chartered, Nestlé, and Cadbury laid off employees to respond to the reduced demand for their products following the economic recession and economic downturn for (Nyabiage, 2015).

European corporations sought to restructure and be present only in cities that potential for significant economic growth. Ironically, downsizing was recommended because of the growth in digital services. Corporations can transact their services with minimal staff in African countries. Other companies planned to exit from Kenya, blaming high production costs, especially labor and bureaucratic inefficiency.

Arguably, the loss of manufacturing is not just an unintended consequence of globalization but a failure in development policy. At independence, planners envisioned development "take-off" driven by growth in manufacturing and agriculture. Agriculture, touted as the "engine" of the economy, was to provide food and raw materials for agro-processing activities. Manufacture of food and beverage products, leather, textiles, and furniture would be boosted. In addition, the emerging expansion of Kenya and East Africa's mineral profile was expected to boost manufacturing activities in areas like electrical and machinery components.

Surveys supported by African Development Bank studies show that the role of manufacturing in Kenya and other East African Economies is too low as a percentage of the region's Gross Domestic Product. In 2014, manufacturing contributed 10 percent of East Africa's regional GDP. By comparison, Vietnam's manufacturing as percentage of GDP was 20 percent. Low levels of manufacturing mean limited opportunities for creation of employment opportunities.

With increased manufacturing, the possibility of establishing greater diversification in the economy was possible. And with industrialization, potential for technological development would be enhanced. But the forces for deindustrialization had to be addressed. Kenya's economy suffers from structural problems to the extent that manufacturing continues to be a smaller segment of the industrial sector. According to World Bank Country Director Diarietou Gaye, new manufacturing ventures have a 35 percent chance of surviving in the market (Gisesa, 2015). World Bank data suggests that the value added per worker has declined steadily in the last thirty years, and the manufacturing sector has for the most part been stagnant (Gisesa, 2015). Between 2010 and 2013, manufacturing in Kenya trailed economic growth, and the sector contributed only 11 percent of the GDP in 2013. In 2013, manufacturing employed only 12 percent of the 2.3 million in the formal labor force (Gisesa, 2015). Further, Kenya's manufacturing sector contributed 26 percent of the country's exports, 40 percent of which were sold in the east African region. Kenya's top export destinations include the United States, Germany, France, Canada, Italy, China, Rwanda, Tanzania, Mauritius, and Uganda. The World Bank recommended that the country invest in infrastructure and also develop a strong manufacturing sector to create jobs for the youth (World Bank, 2015).

Deindustrialization notwithstanding, overall infrastructure remained problematic. In 2003 Kibaki's government shifted considerable resources to rehabilitation of the nation's infrastructure. Under Daniel Moi, the economy was in rapid decline due to, among other reasons, incompetence and corruption in the management of the economy and reduced foreign aid and decline in export earnings. Kibaki responded by expanding education through providing partial free education, investing in infrastructure and supporting monetary policy that increased support for private sector activities.

Infrastructural expansions received greater attention in Kibaki's government than in previous Moi administrations. Notable was the Thika Superhighway, which cost over 34 million shillings and helped provide links on the Trans-African Highway, which was envisioned to connect Cairo to Cape Town. Before leaving office in 2013, Kibaki had also inaugurated construction of the Turbi-Moyale road, Arusha-Namanga, and the Taita Taveta-Voi Road, and laid groundwork for improving railways from Mombasa to Kisumu among other projects.

Through loans, China promised Sh. 6 billion to provide fiber optic cables to connect e-services in 36 districts. The fiber optic cables provided the backbone of the emerging national e-government infrastructure, leading to the provision of inexpensive bandwidth and allowing open access to millions of Kenyans. The government signaled its move toward construction of undersea cable networks. It was also on Kibaki's watch that the country's ICT infrastructure made great strides. Through Safaricom's M-PESA, Kenya became the leader in Mobile money transfers. M-PESA transferred more than 3 billion shillings a day. Internet use expanded to make Kenya the most wired country in the region, with over 14 million users.

In addition to the massive infrastructural developments, the country continued to pursue policy reforms. Policy reforms targeted state-owned enterprises and opened up possibilities of additional actors in areas such as provision of electric power. As a result, the Olkaria geothermal project added to KenGen's electric capacity. The production of electricity in the country is now liberalized, with KenGen competing with other minor producers. The state-owned enterprise Kenya Power and Lighting Company (KPLC) distributes most of the country's generated power.

Through Western support, attempts were made to privatize some of the state-owned enterprises to make them viable but not much remained to be accomplished. In particular, banking and financial markets required much liberalization and oversight. Further, necessary state interventions in ensuring currency stability and organization of capital markets remained narrow and riddled with ineptitude and political cronyism. Functioning capital markets are key to financing industrialization and must be streamlined to control fraud and other corrupt monetary schemes. The establishment of bureaucratic organizations complicated Kenya's investment infrastructure. Besides the Kenya Investment Authority (KenInvest) the parastatal that promotes the country as a preferred destination for investments, the Kenya Markets Capital Authority had a wider responsibility of managing capital markets. The Authority established a Capital Markets Master Plan that included addressing the diaspora investment and Islamic Banking concerns. Thus far, the regulatory mechanism and opportunities for foreign investments are still being refined to meet the goals set in the national Vision 2030 blueprint.

Although Kenya's dream to achieve an "industrialization revolution" remains a work in progress, there are lessons from the late-industrializing Tigers. The first was to avoid political instability and corruption. Next, the efficacy of industrializing via exports as opposed to import substitutions is very much a subject of prudent economic management. The 1998 Asian economic "hiccup," while attributed to numerous reasons including currency speculations, was also a failure of the state to intervene *optimally* in terms of economic management. Commentators including former Prime Minister of Singapore Lee Kuan Yew viewed the Asian crisis as a temporary event and a lesson for other countries (Tanzer, 1998).

In the case of Kenya, exported goods suffer from overreliance on imported contents, the country faces balance-of-payments problems, and the cost of doing business remains a challenge. For instance, the country planned several infrastructure solutions to improve competitiveness. International trunk roads to link Kenya with its neighbors, a standard-gauge railway from Mombasa to Kigali, Rwanda, and a new port in Lamu are among the flagship projects that were touted to set the country on a better route to industrial prosperity. The US$25.5 billion Lamu Port-South Sudan-Ethiopia Transport (LAPSSET) transport project was a collaboration of the South Sudan, Ethiopia, and Kenya governments. Although the railway line component had originally been designed to include Rwanda, the government in Kigali opted out and chose to transport its goods through Tanzania's emerging corridor.

Experts believed the Rwandan government preferred the Dar-es Salaam-Isaka-Kigali/Keza-Musongati Standard Gauge Railway route because it was cheaper than going through the Kenya route. There were claims that Kenya's bureaucracy was too corrupt and had created a business environment that discouraged investors. Moreover, policy implementation, especially in the critical infrastructures, was erratic and lacked coordination.

Some experts went further to note that Kenya's failure to identify its competitive advantages in areas like tourism, horticulture, and IT must be addressed (Charles Robertson, 2014 quoted in *Daily Nation*, June 11, 2014 article: "Ready for takeoff? Politics, infrastructure remain challenges for Kenya"). In addition, the country spends only three percent of its GDP on infrastructure. For any meaningful development to occur, the World Bank recommended a much higher expenditure. An example of how politics manifested itself was in the failed partnership between Kenya's parastatal Telkom and French Orange Telekom. In 2007, 51 percent of Telkom Kenya was sold to Orange for about $390 million. The government also spent additional funds in tax benefits.

Initially, France Telekom complained that the regulatory body, the Communications Authority of Kenya, did not provide a level playing field and favored the growth of Safaricom, a subsidiary of Vodafone. In 2014, a customer center, the Information Communication Technology of Kenya (ICTAK) even wrote to the government accusing Safaricom for failure to comply with several laws. Cabinet Secretary Fred Matiangi canceled Orange's contract under which it managed the National Optic Fibre Backbone Infrastructure (NOFBI). Orange also faced enormous legal disputes over retirement benefits owed by more than 15,000 employees of the defunct Telekom Kenya (Kisero, 2014).

Besides, economic reforms are vital for sustainable industrialization and absorption of new technologies to be achieved. Commenting on the reforms that are required before industrialization is achieved in Kenya, then Director General of the United Nations Industrial Development Organization (UNIDO), Carlos Magarinos (1998) while addressing a Steering Committee of the Alliance for Africa's Industrialization in Abidjan, Cote D'Ivorie, observed:

> Africa should not reverse liberalization and return to controls when it still accounts for two percent of the world trade and most of the countries are among the poorest in the world . . . it was futile for Africa to start debating over again the fundamentals of economic development because of the Asian crisis or to use old methods to solve new problems. Instead they should learn from the crisis and strengthen the economic reform programs. (Magarinos, 1998)

The import of this statement is African countries might follow the path taken by Asia. Except that the African state should manage its macroeconomic environment in a more cautious manner than the Asian states did. Kenya and other African countries must confront inflation, and manage huge debts that undermine savings and lower potential for investments. In addition, good governance and security will assure investors that their money is safe in Kenya. Without transparency, strategic planning, and prudent management of liberalization policies, the ecological conditions for expanding industries and enabling a robust IT-driven agenda are a mere dream.

A technologically advanced economy will not be one that just produces raw materials or is a dumping ground for computer waste products but one in which ICT products, which include computers, mobile phones, and CDs and other data storage devices form a part of the daily culture. To change culture and be a producer and consumer of modern technologies, leadership matters. Of course, the Kenya government's stated wish is to promote industrialization. The intent is expressed in most policy speeches by the political elites. But their actions don't necessarily match their political and policy actions. As Poggi (1978) argued the path to industrialization may not so much be dependent on a liberal or democratic nature of the state. Since industrialization is the most important feature in modernization, the role of leadership must not be minimized. Poggi (1978, p. 146) emphasized the importance of statesmanship.

Leadership can marshal resources for growing an industrially and technologically inclined society. President Moi was not off the mark when he stated: "Kenya must industrialize by generating its own resources if the country was to maintain its dignity as a nation" (Moi, 1998).

Likewise, speaking at a conference of economists, businesspersons, and technocrats, President Uhuru Kenyatta commented that his government aimed to bring about an "industrial revolution" and turn Kenya into a middle-income country by 2030.

> My Administration intends to set off an industrial revolution to power our ambition of becoming a middle income country by 2030. As a starting point, we shall concentrate on infrastructure through expanding the road and rail network while expanding power supply. The Jubilee Vision dovetails nicely with the essence of Kenya National Vision 2013. (Kenyatta, September 17, 2013)

In the same speech, Uhuru Kenyatta touted the example of Singapore's success story as a model for Kenyan planners. Indeed, Uhuru Kenyatta's Jubilee Coalition's stated manifesto touted unity, economic growth, and openness as key pillars.

Uhuru Kenyatta's vision included strengthening the country's traditional sectors and pursuing manufacturing and telecommunications. His vision was to "make Kenya Africa's gateway, manufacturing and technology hub and a home to millions of entrepreneurs" (Uhuru Kenyatta September 17, 2013). For Kenyatta, the attainment of a "take off" involved harnessing the "youth dividend" by increasing skills for the youth and providing empowerment projects, through Uwezo Fund. Importantly, in addition to exploitation of oil and other mineral resources, financial intermediation and ICT were identified as priority areas for the administration's plans.

In the area of ICTs, the government created conditions in which over 30 million telephone handsets were in use. Foreign investors, notably IBM, were in the process of establishing their only research lab in Kenya. Other global mega companies like Google also established their regional headquarters in Kenya. Kenya also planned to establish a regional techno city at Konza to serve as the Silicon Savannah. Kenya's ruling elites made no secret about making the country the region's technology hub.

Although these initiatives are remarkable, Kenya's industrialization was still similar to previous MNC-led import substitution models that were adopted in Latin America and Africa (Gereffi, 1990, p. 6). It is through collaboration with MNCs that Kenya welcomed global business corporations like General Electric, Google, IBM, Vista International, Pepsi, Foton Automobiles, IFC, Chase Morgan, HSBC Bank, Nestlé, Tullow Oil Group, the BP Group, and British telecommunication Vodafone Group. These MNCs made Kenya their regional operational bases. This open-door policy resulted in Kenya being ranked as a leading investment hub for global firms. Frontier Strategy Group placed Kenya at number two in its 2014 Africa-wide rankings behind Nigeria. The index was developed from data gathered from operations of at least two hundred multinationals. Similar accolades have come from Business Monitor International (BMI), an independent provider of business data.

And to further illustrate the power of global corporations, the dominant players in the service industries are also MNCs. For instance, Kenya relies on Maersk and Lloyds for shipment, and several Banking and Financial Service institutions like Barclays Bank, Visa, and MasterCard for international money transactions. The Kenya government sought expertise support from IBM to develop the country's electronic master plan. These collaborate with the merging ICT providers to form intertwined networks. Among the new IT actors in Kenya's emerging telecommunications sector are global corporations like IBM, Microsoft, Accenture and Cisco. The next section focuses on Vision 2030, the economic and political blueprint shaping the emerging information and telecommunication sector.

Telecommunications and Vision 2030

In line with Kenya's Vision 2030, the ICT sector was expected to catapult the economy to a new economy. Although the ICT sector's contribution to the GDP was between 3–4 percent of the GDP, the government aimed to make it a lead contributor. The sector was allocated over KSh. 7.2 billion in the 2012 budget (Shahonya, 2012). Monetary policies to support the sector included reduction of duty on imported software to enable greater affordability for a majority of end users. The government also removed taxes in importation of equipment to support migration to Digital TV platforms. Efforts to create viable ICT frameworks also received funds for rural electrification programs.

For the 2014 year, the government's allocation to the development of ICT sector included development of e-procurement platforms to enhance efficiency and economy in supply management practices (Musambi, 2014). The government also funded the Digital Payment Gateway and Treasury Single Account portals to track expenditures at all levels of government.

The 2014 budget provided Sh. 17.4 billion to build computer laboratories, development of digital content, capacity building through teacher development initiatives, and supply of laptops to schools.

Policies and investments in ICTs were calculated to recalibrate Kenya's industrialization to minimize the factory-based manufacturing model that dominated the previous decades. Like in most twenty-first century economies, ICTs are expected to accelerate wealth production and job creation. Corporations like Vodafone—which owns over 40 percent of Safaricom—the largest ICT business enterprise in Kenya, established themselves as pivotal players in the national psyche and economy. Safaricom controlled 68 percent of Kenya's over 31 million mobile phone users' market. According to the Kenya Revenue Authority, for the seventh consecutive year, in 2014, Safaricom was Kenya's highest taxpayer, outdoing government bureaucracies like the Teachers Service Commission, Ministry of Interior, Kenya Commercial Bank (KCB), Kenya Breweries, Equity Group, Standard Chartered Bank, Barclays Bank, Kenya Pipeline Company, and the Ministry of Health. The profitability of Safaricom signified the significant contributions to Kenya's economy of the Information and Communication Technology (ICT) sector (Okoth, 2014).

Another initial player in Kenya's mobile phone industry was Kencell. In 2000, Safaricom and Kencell were the two dominant business firms in the telecommunications market, which replaced the country's 200,000 dysfunctional landline telephone systems. Kencell was associated with Kenyan business leader Naushad Merali of the Sameer Investments. His initial equity shares amounted to 40 percent. French corporation Vivendi owned the majority shares in Kencell but sold to Celtel International. The company was renamed Celtel Kenya. With 31.3 million mobile telephone lines in 2013, Kenya achieved remarkable connectivity and created a truly wired society.

Kenya's telecommunication industry is highly lucrative and has witnessed several mergers and realignments. Celtel merged with Kuwait-based Zain Corporation. In 2010, Zain had a change of guard and was rebranded Airtel, a subsidiary of India's Bharti Airtel Limited. Zain is the second largest network with over two million subscribers, or 17 percent of the market. With Essar's YuMobile (about 9 percent) and Orange Mobile (Telkom Kenya Limited, about 7.7 percent), the four corporations dominate the mobile phone industry in East Africa. Essar-YuMobile (Essar Capital), which has its headquarters in Mumbai, India, started operating in Kenya in 2008 but failed to keep up with the stiff competition. Essar sold its "Yu" brand business to Sarfaricom and Airtel for around US$120 million. Orange Mobile is a joint venture between former parastatal Kenya Government's Telcom and France Telecom (now majority shareholder).

Although impressive, mobile phone coverage has not reached all corners of the country. The vast desert and semi-arid lands of the northeastern and eastern provinces are not well covered. Approximately 51 percent of the country has mobile penetration and with increased competition, rates became affordable to most middle-class families. But these numbers change by the day as more residents acquire mobile phones and networks expand.

Outside of the mobile voice and text message industry, the ICT world also provides money transfer services. Considered as a Kenyan invention, the mobile money transfer services cover all the key towns in the country. The transfer process is simple; individual senders use their mobile phones to make payments from bank accounts or special accounts established with the mobile phone company. An SMS is sent to the recipient with a notification code to be used for money retrieval. The retrieval code must be presented to authorized agents spread across the country. Kenya was the first country in the world to pioneer the use of mobile phones to make instant cash transfers between individuals.

Launched in 2007, Safaricom's Mobile phone banking SMS-based service platform, M-PESA changed Kenya's financial landscape and culture. As did the mobile phone culture, which became an important contributor to emerging M-government services like using short message services (SMS) to inform the public of government programs and projects. In 2014, Airtel, yuMobile, and Orange petitioned the Communication Authority of Kenya (CAK) to compete in the lucrative mobile money transfer market. M-PESA, with 18.1 million customers, became East Africa's most successful money transfer company. In 2013 M-PESA generated over 26.6 billion shillings (US$303 million) in revenue (Wachira, 2014).

Safaricom's Market Domination Challenged

However, other operators deemed its dominant position problematic and demanded new interoperability rules. Airtel, yuMobile, and Orange petitioned Kenyan authorities to compel Safaricom to allow their users to send money freely across a common network. Airtel teamed with Equity Bank, the largest lender by market value, to compete aggressively with Safaricom's M-PESA System. It is envisioned that Equity Bank (through FINSERVE) will in the near future roll out its Mobile Virtual Network Operator (MVNO) to compete with Safaricom. Also, entry of more international corporations may take place. For example, Vittel, a Vietnamese corporation, and MTN (South Africa) are known to be interested in doing business in Kenya. The Communications Authority of Kenya (CAK) has licensed those three mobile Virtual Network Operators (MVNO) to use infrastructure built by Safaricom and other existing operators, on a commercial basis, to provide telephony services. The three, Zioncell (operated by MoDe), Finserve Africa Limited, and Tangaza Pesa offer mobile phone services on infrastructure built by others. Although Telkom Kenya applied for the same facility to host MVNOs their application was pending. In addition to Equity, Vittel, and MTN, CAK has received applications from Kenya Airways to tap into the mobile money services.

Safaricom continued to be the most profitable business in the East and Central African region, earning over KSh 31.9 billion in profits, the year ending March 2015. Safaricom's control of the telecommunication sector was also evident in its domination of the SMS market, in many instances, securing market shares above the 50 percent mark. Safaricom controlled 93 percent of the SMS market, 70 percent of the mobile data, and 75.6 percent of the voice telephony (Ochieng, 2015). By mid-2015, members of Kenya's parliament also sought to place further restrictions to Safaricom's dominance in areas of infrastructure, mobile phones, and M-PESA.

Siding with the parliament, the Cabinet Secretary in charge of Information and Communications, Matiangi, joined the call for further deregulation of the sector to provide greater competition. Among the proposals was to have Safaricom maintain separate book accounts for its various services.

Konza Technology City ("Africa's Silicon Savannah")

If the Konza Technology City is completed, it will be expected to create thousands of jobs. Konza City is part of the government's Vision 2030 Special Economic Zones (SEZ) flagship projects for the twenty-first century. Launched in July 2013 and touted as Africa's silicon savannah,

Konza City technopolis sits on five thousand acres of land in Malili, about 60 kilometers outside Nairobi. Built in different phases, Konza Technology City's completion date is scheduled for 2038. Although the completion date has been set, media reports show that government's preparation is shaky. For example, Konza Technopolis Development Authority (KOTDA) reported personnel problems especially related with nonappointment of a substantive chief executive. The Authority had relied on secondment of officials from the Ministry of Communication and Technology.

The ministry also contracted a U.S. company, Tetra Tech, to oversee the planning and construction of phase one of the project. Phase one was expected to create 16,200 jobs in construction, residential, university and other facilities.

The project entails construction of houses, malls, business and science parks, and a university. The city is grounded on the notion that ICTs are the future drivers of the economy and, therefore, emphasis on investments. In 2013 alone, at least 345 investors, including light manufacturing and research interests, had expressed interest in establishing firms on the land.

Although the Konza project initially attracted more than three hundred investors, there were concerns about corruption and fraud on the part of government officials. The first scandal involved the purchase of land from Malili Ranch Company. Reports indicated that some of the shareholders were duped into selling the property to the techno city. There were also reports that Chinese investors planned a nearby New Machakos city to be modeled after the United Arab Emirates' Dubai City and threaten the viability of Konza (Mumo, 2014). The involvement of Chinese investors, especially if designed to compete with Konza, would challenge the capacity of Kenya's business community to absorb debt and manage infrastructures. Yet, the bigger picture was that the Konza City project implied a shift from an agriculture-based to a service-dominant economy. There will be multiplier effects from projects like that in Konza City. The government ambitiously projected that by 2030, the emerging new ICT products will immensely drive Kenya's economy. Also an important SEZ is the Lamu Port (LAPSET) project that involves the construction of a new port facility to serve Kenya, Uganda, South Sudan, and Ethiopia. SEZs are touted to be main providers of job opportunities, especially among the youth.

Another important pillar to drive the government's Vision 2030 is to establish Kenya as a leading Business Process Outsourcing (BPO) site. The goal for 2012 was to create at least 7,500 direct BPO jobs and contribute KSh 10 billion in the national economy. The goal was to create jobs through investments from multinational corporations (Republic of Kenya, 2007, p. 9). At least five major IT suppliers would be invited to participate as BPO players. Kenya wants to emulate India's success as the world's leading BPO country. In order to be a leading sourcing destination, developing countries have opted to lower labor costs, develop infrastructures, provide data security and legal protections, and improve education opportunities. Kenya has marketed itself as having a tech-savvy youthful population with the advantage of being an English-speaking nation. In addition, policy implementers promote Kenya's incentive structure, which includes a liberalized telecommunication industry and availability of cheap labor. According to government planners, the BPO will provide infrastructure and support services for enterprises and will encourage transfer of ICT skills and resources. Kenya is said to have an advantage over many of its African rivals because the country has strategic location advantages and has a higher level of global integration than all its neighbors and most of Africa. Africa's integration index ranked it behind South Africa as most integrated country on the African continent (Wokabi, 2014).

Moreover, Kenya's BPO Park will benefit from economies of scale occasioned by an existing mobile Internet infrastructure and cheap labor. Kenya also has a time zone that is close to the European landmass and has a vibrant banking and tech-savvy youthful labor force. One unique advantage of Kenya's youth is their readiness to adopt and use new information technologies. Already Nakuru and other inland cities have begun launching free Wi-Fi facilities for residents. Business Monitor International (BMI) recognized this potential and added that Kenya's potential for further investments was boosted through discoveries of oil resources in the northern counties.

Since 2004, when Kenya established its first BPO, it has licensed at least eighteen call centers. In accordance with World Bank recommendations, in order to expand opportunities for ICT-led economic growth, government had to provide additional incentives to investors. The Bank argued that further liberalization of the telecommunication industry would attract Foreign Direct Investment (FDI) flows. Many industry observers argue that the liberalization is one of the reasons for the growing presence of giant international ICT firms like Cisco, IBM, Microsoft, and Accenture. It was also envisioned that direct investment by the government through the establishment of the 7,500-seat BPO Park in Nairobi will help catapult the ICT sector.

Although the goal is to expand use of ICTs, the enabling political climate directly challenges the realization of the full potential of these new technologies. Kenya's entry into the digital era did not change much concerning development of a strong culture of competition and free enterprise. The rollout of most ICT projects was riddled with allegations of either incompetence or straight corruption. For instance, several officials involved with Konza Techno City were investigated. Moreover, the laptop project did not sail smoothly, nor did other ICT related programs like the opening up of mobile money infrastructures for competition. The ruling elite sought to retain past symbiotic relationships with MNCs in the expanding ICT sector. For instance, at the government's request, Vodafone allowed the state to eavesdrop on phone calls. Although the Consumer Federation of Kenya (COFEK) protested against the state's wiretapping demands, the government maintained the practice, citing "security concerns." This was made possible through legal frameworks such as the Official Secrets Act, the Prevention of Terrorism Act, and the National Intelligence Service Act. And although consumers' agencies advocated for greater data protection, the government delayed enacting the Data Protection Bill.

In addition to state continuation of symbiotic relationships with MNCs, the leadership of the Communication Commission of Kenya (CCK) remained a patronage agency. Kenya has a long history of politicizing state positions and, in strategic agencies, the president appoints officials likely to perpetuate authoritarian tendencies. Evidence of patronage and lack of insulation from politics can be found in the content analysis of appointments to various state commissions and governing boards and managerial government ministry positions. Ministerial efforts aimed at promoting micro-level enterprises, establishing industrial parks, and economic zones have not transcended narrow spoils politics.

The Ministry of Information and Communication retained policy oversight. After the 2013 elections, there were further ministerial restructuring culminating in refining the nations's ICT policy. Part of the reason for the reorganization was to help develop a strategic ICT plan and help attract investors in the sector. The ICT Board reported to the Minister of Information and Communication. Following a Pricewaterhouse Coopers (PwC) study, there was call for consolidation of the Government Information Technology Services (GITS), the ICT Board, and the Directorate of e-Government into one advisory body. In the previous structure, GITS operated under the aegis of the Ministry of Finance. The Directorate of e-Government was answerable to the Office of the President, Harambee House. Consolidation of ICT agencies was to ensure program cohesion and standardization of operations throughout the public sector.

If that is the chosen philosophy, investor-confidence-boosting initiatives are essential. Leadership, in the management of the emerging knowledge economy, would still have to deal with providing appropriate state interventions in core areas of governance, directing appropriate education, nurturing technological culture, planning, providing infrastructure, and financing capital projects and macroeconomic management.

With the gazettement of members of the Universal Service Advisory Council (USAC), the business climate will have to grapple with a wide range of governance issues. USAC stems from the Kenya Information and Communication administration of the Universal Service Fund (USF). The fund is designed to support access to ICT, support capacity building, and help build a strong base for innovation in the ICT sector. Among the expectation is the levy of taxes or fees for industries in the ICT sector. Because of Kenya's history of corruption, in managing funds such as the NHIF and NSSF, the expectation should be that funds raised would support development of ICT infrastructure in an equitable manner. Importantly, the administration of the levy should not be a disincentive to investments in the ICT sector. If the fund works as is planned, it will provide the desired link between capacity building and investments. In other words, efforts aimed at building local capacity to harness ICTs are steps in the direction of indigenization of the emerging knowledge society.

CONCLUSIONS

In conclusion, Kenyan authorities continue to further integrate the country into the changing global markets. A major shift has already occurred; Kenya's ICT sector is now firmly established within the national industrialization and technological mosaic. Although the roles of MNCs are prominent, the emergence of China's industrialization machine changes the partnership equation. Critics argue that China has not done enough to transfer technology to Africa and it still exports labor, in Africa, with disastrous effects on unemployment. Labor unions are beginning to take note of the possibility that China's own labor transfers raise challenges to policy makers. Yet, on the positive side, China's study-work programs and other skill transfer models may, in the long run, benefit Africans, especially in the ICT sectors. The ICT components in Vision 2030 signify possibilities for changing Kenya's economic landscapes. Through organizational learning and technology transfers, it is possible that Africa may follow the paths of the more advanced economies, if they have the skills, knowledge, abilities, will, and discipline observed in cases where transfers were successful.

Liqiang (2015, p. 7) writes that it is possible for Africa to experience large-scale industrial transfers, as was in the case of United States to Japan; Japan to the four Asian Tigers (China-Hong Kong and Taiwan, Singapore and South Korea), then to mainland China. Africans are persuaded that Western-style development aid did not succeed in creating growth patterns that were satisfactory. ICT development is a key component of the public-private partnerships (PPP) that guide the policy discourses between Kenya and its development partners. Today, ICTs infrastructures are not separable from roads and railways. With massive infrastructural development taking place, labor must be organized to play its part, especially in localizing talent for the emerging economy.

FOUR

Unions

Education, Laptops, and Shrinking of the Digital Divide

INTRODUCTION

The crisis in Kenya's education system is one of the most debated public policy issues of the twenty-first century. Concerns about declining standards and also irrelevance of education to national development are widely debated in public arenas. Not a single day passes without a national leader mentioning problems in the country's education sector. This is, in part, because public education fulfills some of the most important functions in the continuation of nationhood and survival of political institutions. Without an educated people, society's economic potential cannot be realized. Also, the founders of the nation regarded education as offering the best hope for bringing different communities together. This was to be achieved through promotion of literacy in math, Kiswahili, and English. Another strategy was to create national schools and post teachers to any part of the country without privileging ethnic affiliations. Like other governments, public investment in education is both a political and moral issue. For Kenya, investments in education meant equipping the population with skills and knowledge for nation building and to empower individuals to better themselves. In the 1970s, considerable progress was achieved, and Kenya's education policy evolved to be among the most remarkable ones in the east and central African region.

At the core of policy was elimination of illiteracy and increase in access, especially at the primary school level. However, by the 1990s, it was quite obvious that some of the goals established in development plans had not been realized. And in some instances, school administration suffered from enormous issues of accountability. Academic standards were declining at a rapid rate. At the same time, instances of cheating on national exams and corruption in school management were widely reported. Without sound administrative practices, it became much harder for government to attain the larger goals of equipping students with knowledge in critical subjects necessary for the country's development.

By 2008, even the simple objectives of national literacy and basic civic education had not been met. Primary schools, especially in rural communities, lacked basic facilities including safe buildings, water, bathrooms, adequate sports grounds, and basic instructional resources like books. Moreover, even though the government declared that it would offer free education, it lacked the capacity to administer the policies that were enshrined in law and policy documents. The crisis is captured in statistical data from the Institute of Economic Affairs, which reported that in 2015, 58 percent of students did not sit for their form four national standardized Kenya Certificate of Secondary Examinations (KCSE) (Ngethe, 2016). In raw numbers, in 2015, 525,802 candidates who took the KCSE were 42 percent of the 1,252, 400 who had enrolled in elementary school in 2004 (Ngethe, 2016). This means the subsidized secondary school system failed to meet its targets. The dropout rates were, therefore, a huge indictment on the quality of school administration in the country.

Another finding was that teacher training appeared to be based on outdated technologies and poorly designed for the needs of the information age. A *Daily Nation* editorial opined that successful implementation of free primary education was an incomplete picture of the sector's problems. The newspaper instead brought to the attention of its readers that close to half of Kenya's 33 million people in 2008 were illiterate (*Daily Nation*, 2008). The editorial piece remarked;

> "An illiterate population in the twenty-first century is an abomination. It is an indictment of our value system as a society, and our education system." It is now over ten years since Kenyans started agitating for an overhaul of the education system to update the syllabus in keeping up with the market needs and social development. This has not happened. (*Daily Nation*, 2008)

Then, Education Cabinet Secretary, Jacob Kaimenyi further reported that 2 million children, especially in urban slums, arid and semi-arid regions of Kenya were not even attending school (Wanzala, 2015a). The alarming statistics revealed that 39 percent of youths aged between fifteen and twenty-five were most affected, thereby frustrating the country's goals of meeting the Millennium Development Goals (MDG) for 2015.

Similar concerns were reported in a World Bank (2015) study report titled *Kenya's Education Achievement and Challenges*, which confirmed fears that Kenya's education system was failing to produce graduates with relevant knowledge, abilities, and skills required for achievement of Vision 2030 development goals. The report noted the country's educational institutions were dysfunctional and lacking in coordination. In addition, the education sector had weaknesses in the areas of governance especially lack of accountability in operations. Further, the World Bank identified wastefulness, through duplication and inefficiencies in service delivery efforts. Importantly, the World Bank identified lack of data as a concern for proper planning, management, and monitoring of education projects. These problems seem to persist in spite of visible but insufficient political attention to the matter. In most cases, reforms have been symbolic but not based on data.

Although reforms attempted to streamline the problems of access, problems persisted. For some, the government instituted an eight-year mandatory elementary schooling known as the 8–4–4 systems, which replaced an earlier system in which students spent seven years in primary school. Students spent next four years in secondary and university institutions respectively. Although much has been written about this system's weaknesses, it must also be recognized that Kenya outperformed most African countries in terms of student completion rates at the secondary level. There may be issues of quality and relevance but by mere investments, the country's attention to education is remarkable.

Still, the system faced serious challenges and has, for the most part, focused on quantity rather than quality. A lecturer at Kenyatta University and advisor for the German Academic Exchange (DAAD) program captured the crisis thus:

> Many children drop out of the free, public elementary schools before reaching eighth grade because of unmet needs for school uniforms and shoes, books, pencils and notebooks. Many families cannot afford to provide their children with the necessities for school (Verweyen (2012). Public classrooms are overflowing, and one poorly paid teacher must often handle a class with 40 pupils or more. There may not be enough desks for all of the students, books and maps may be scarce, and many schools have dirt floors. (Verweyen, 2012)

Most Kenyan officials know that there is something amiss with the prevailing status of education. Yet, the political elite has not acted, with resolve, to correct the problems of access and quality of education in the country. Instead, the country has expanded the number of universities to levels that are unsustainable. Over fifty universities have been registered in the country. And some of the universities do not offer the "right" qualifications for the job markets and needs of local industry (Gekera & Kumba, 2009; Nyanchama, 2015). Others see Kenya's education system as elitist to the core and serving to perpetuate inequalities in the polity (Kigotho, 2009; Otenyo, 2000, p. 37). Wachira Kigotho, a Standard Media journalist, commented:

> The legacy of colonial education and the political economy of post-independence Kenya have led to an education system that favors the most advantaged students. Subsequently, the aim of the Ministry of Education to enroll most of primary school leavers is still-born, taking into account that there are only 4,250 secondary schools compared to 18,900 primary schools in the country. (Kigotho, 2009)

At the root of the "education crisis" are resource limitations, poor planning, and misplaced political priorities. Structural weaknesses are evident from the fact that each year over 93,000 elementary school students do not receive admission to secondary schools and have no other opportunities after the Kenya Certificate of Primary Education (KCPE). Moreover, the scourge of illiteracy has not been eliminated in marginalized communities such as along the Pokot-Baringo areas (Mbatiah, 2015).

Admittedly, over the years, there has been concern that the education system faced difficult challenges and does not meet the needs of a modernizing society. Critics argue that technical education in the country is not aligned to industry needs (Kahihu, 2015). In recent years, several Technical and Vocational Education Training Institutions (TVET) that previously absorbed elementary school students have either been transformed into university colleges or are facing structural challenges and are unable to offer quality training in areas like computer and information technologies. In this chapter, we examine and describe the place of information and communication technologies (ICTs) in the search for reforms in Kenya's education system. We discuss some of the challenges experienced in the efforts by unions and other stakeholders to navigate through the new world of digitized education platforms.

IMPORTANCE OF ICTS IN KENYA'S EDUCATION SECTOR

At the outset, one must note that recognition of the importance of ICTs in education predates the Jubilee Government's platform to be the digital government. In 2007, Kenya joined South Africa and Nigeria to become the third African country to launch e-learning facilities in secondary schools. The initiative by Intel was launched at Kamiti Secondary School through collaboration between the Ministry of Educations and local companies and multinational corporations. The project, entailed teachers using laptops connected with low-cost student laptops known as "classmates" and linked to touch screen classroom blackboards connected through wireless platforms.

The program was small, but it symbolized the country's "commitment to empowering Kenyans with ICT capabilities." Although these partnerships between government and the private sector have been encouraged, huge structural problems continue to cause challenges to the road to building a robust ICT framework for the education sector.

Among the contemporary challenges is the disparity in education opportunities between rural and urban households. Especially disadvantaged are rural marginalized areas such as in the arid and semi-arid regions of Northern Kenya. Disparities between girls and boys have also been reported in various United Nations Educational, Scientific and Cultural Organization (UNESCO) studies. Accesses to technological disparities compound these structural difficulties.

Several stakeholders, including international donors confirm that equalizing access to technological resources could be one way of improving educational opportunities in rural and poor urban households. The question would then be, how so? One sure way to removing the barriers to access would be to provide ICT platforms to the marginalized communities. Examples of such activities are receiving media attention. Among the most publicized initiatives was the iMlango (Kiswahili word for door or portal) Project. iMlango was designed to improve educational outcomes for over 25,000 girls attending close to 195 primary schools in Kenya. The first ninety-five schools would be equipped by end of 2014, with the remaining one hundred serviced by end of 2015 (iMlango, 2016).

iMlango, was supported by funds provided through the United Kingdom's Department for International Development (DFID), private sector firms such as Avanti Communications, a satellite operator, and Kenya's Ministry of Education. The key element of iMlango is provision of high-speed Internet access supported though satellite broadband connectivity to predetermined schools. In addition, funds would be allocated for providing online educational content for subject areas such as math, reading, and life skills. It is envisioned that monetary incentives would be available to ensure participation and reduce dropout rates. The project is among the first to measure in real-time daily attention rates. Schoolteachers would also be trained in ICT applications.

The projects reinforced the need to improve ICT education as a key component in achievement of Kenya's development goals. Still, the perennial challenges to ensure sustainability persist. Critics argued that Kenya's education suffered from lack of funds, especially in utilization of information technology. Use of ICTs in education has been low, mostly due to lack of funding for hardware and software, network maintenance, and unavailability of sufficient trainers. To make matters worse, the cost of electricity is beyond the reach of most rural schools, which have to pay more than their contemporaries in the developed world.

Wabuyele (2003) identified some of the reasons why the education sector lagged behind banking, and medical sectors in embracing ICTs. Mobile phones make banking relatively easy, as is evidenced by the growth of M-PESA applications. Likewise, apps facilitated disease surveillance and cut short time for delivery in areas such as maternity and emergency services. Increased uses of various applications also support the farming community by reducing travel time and expenses. Farmers can call into new services to access market information. The education sector in Kenya is a latecomer in application of various e-platforms and apps. Wabuyele's (2003) research found that use of ICTs in schools was hampered by teacher attitudes, lack of pre-service training, and failure of government to provide adequate development infrastructures for those in the education sector.

Leading ICT and public administration scholar David Garson (2006) identified skills deficiency as a major barrier to use and absorption of ICTs in the government sector. Way back in 2003, Arun Devani, Chairman of the Kenya Association of Manufacturers (KAM), told a conference in Nyeri that the country's education system created incompetent graduates without relevant competency in technical fields (Devani, 2003). This leads to the discussion about literacy and technical skills. Indeed, government websites should ideally be written in language that is simple enough for the majority of the population to comprehend. It follows, therefore, that the quality of primary education should be sound enough to impart strong reading and writing competencies. Observers at that level have recently raised questions about the literacy skills in East Africa. A 2012 study by Uwezo placed Kenyan elementary students ahead of their counterparts in Uganda and Tanzania but still ranked the country poorly in terms of overall academic competencies.

The report found that 20 percent of students enrolled in Standard Seven did not have Standard Two-level literacy in reading and math skills. Although many in the education sector were sympathetic to the findings of the Uwezo study, the Kenya National Union of Teachers (KNUT) rejected the report on the grounds that it was not involved in the research (Omollo, 2014). Without literacy and numeracy competencies at the primary school level, it is hard to move forward with an ICT development agenda.

In 2011, professional associations like the Engineers Registration Board, the Kenya Medical Laboratory and Technicians Board, and the Council of Legal Education rejected curriculums offered in local universities and refused to recognize degrees from several local institutions. Another revealing commentary on graduate education came from the Inter-University Council for East Africa (IUCEA). IUCEA was created to provide regulatory oversight of skills learned in regional centers of higher education.

A 2014 IUCEA report showed that over 50 percent of students graduating from universities in East Africa were "half-baked." Although Kenya was slightly ahead of Uganda and Tanzania in providing employment skills, 51 percent of graduates from its universities were perceived to be incompetent. Employers found graduates to be deficient in the technical mastery necessary for new economies (Ernest, 2014).

One of the key specific areas where critical skills are lacking is in the area of information technology. The deficit in skilled ICT resources will certainly hamper efforts to build a robust knowledge-based economy. Part of the problem stems from a weak training regime. In other words, providers of higher education need to be leaders in enabling ICT training to flourish throughout the schools' system. Mwenda and Muuka (2009) identify curricula and teacher training as vital ingredients in integration of ICTs.

Research also shows that successful implementation of ICTs in all schools is a function of, among other variables, teacher training. It is argued that school administrators and teacher trainers who use ICTs provide examples to others in the learning communities. Beyond that, confident teachers offer the best chance for innovative uses of ICTs in school settings (Lundall & Howell, 2000). Lundall and Howell (2000) also emphasize that teachers who are pessimists with regard to ICT applications are not likely to encourage students to benefit from the resources enabled by ICTs. In most African countries, even when ICT education is offered, it is not good quality, compared to that offered in developed nations. A survey conducted by the Kenya ICT Board revealed that 25 percent of companies were not satisfied with the quality of ICT professionals produced from Kenyan institutions of higher education.

To remedy the situation, a number of interventions have been suggested. Key partnerships between business corporations and universities have to be forged. Stakeholder involvement is necessary for goal realization. Strathmore University and Safaricom entered into a partnership that supports students in the Master of Science program. Similarly, the Federation of Kenya Employers (FKE) supported apprenticeship programs for university students with an aim of increasing industrial skills.

Unions in the education sector will be expected to take a lead role in promoting policies that will advance the use of ICTs for achievement of better learning outcomes. Schoolchildren in Kenya are a part of a globalized world. This argument is not new. In a paper to the International Labor Organization (ILO), Mwamadzigo (2003) suggested that trade unions had a major role to play in the design and coordination of the ICT agenda in Africa. Without trade unions embracing technology in the workforce, the digital divide would be hard to reduce. In most countries, teachers are a huge cohort in the labor movement, which therefore places a special charge to unions like KNUT.

Unions must promote effective good governance to ensure progressive ICT policy is implemented. As has been demonstrated in Cheol-Sung Lee's work (2007), unions, as members of civic associations, are a core part of the governance networks. Through mobilization and policy engagement, union power helps shape reform agendas in various countries. Unions' policy mobilization can make policy makers privilege approaches that encourage efficiency in production of good and services. Such policies include policies that promote sustainable ICT solutions.

Indeed, for the country to be a player in the new economy, modern classrooms must be able to use new technologies. The old technologies like print media and radio and indigenous forms of conveying knowledge and sharing information like oral storytelling and village theaters are considered less exciting for millennial generations.

All over the world, the pace of technological change has forced governments to reconsider traditional schooling approaches. Digital economies require teachers to have new skills and tools to navigate through information technologies. Old mind-sets of reliance on brick-and-mortar delivery platforms have increasingly been replaced with computer networks reinforced by cellular and Wi-Fi connections.

The world economy has moved from mere production of commodities and services to knowledge production. Perhaps, because of its ability to reproduce information, the Internet is a symbol of the emerging knowledge economy. Scholars now argue that some regions have an abundance of world knowledge thanks to the Internet. Those regions with greater ability to tap into the vast ocean of Internet resources stand the best chance to dominate intellectual and digital power.

A blogger observed that a university education is the new global currency and that national borders are increasingly permeable, making it possible for graduates to compete in international job markets (Morrison, 2014). It is precisely one of the motivations for governments to allocate funds to empower schools and other education institutions to acquire digital technologies. Therefore, access to computers and relevant software and training are tools that modern students need for successful careers.

The classroom, as a modern workplace, is where you will find increasing use of new technologies. The forces driving the changes are complex and cannot be narrowed down to a few variables. First, in developing countries, students, especially those from urban and middle- and upper-class schools desire to be competitive and be a part of the globalized, tech-saturated world. They have mobile phones, which link them up with their peers in the developed countries. In this day, the Kenyan diaspora numbers into the millions. Students and educators favor the new technologies as a motivational tool.

Another reason for the move toward online texts and adoption of educational digital context is the national elite's desire to control the learning processes. More important, the ruling elite recognizes the old adage that information resources translate into more power. New ICTs are also known to be lucrative businesses that attract the ruling elite, working in conjunction with multinational corporations. In the long run, hardware, software, and digital infrastructures are investments waiting to be tapped into.

Countries that fail to embrace new classroom technologies are not likely to be integrated fully in new economies. The modern classroom is wired, and students use technologies to enhance learning experiences. They use mobile (cell) phones (smartphones and mobile apps), teleconferencing, online textbooks (e-books), iPods and iPads for assignments, Chromebooks, e-readers and tablets, and interactive digital whiteboards, and participate in various chat forums. In many instances, students use iPads to load lessons on mathematical problem solving and for enhanced learning. At the same time, teachers use new technologies to bring to life materials taught in class curriculums. In advanced classroom settings, it is not unusual for students to be treated to "game-based learning," whereby teachers use electronic apps, games, and other interactive devices to explore the world. A new version of gaming is the increased use of simulations and drones that are enriching learning experiences.

Furthermore, virtual worlds are suitable for immersive learning, especially in disciplines like engineering and nursing. Using video screens, students can attend classes while on the road. Without modern information technologies, it is difficult to learn about key concepts in the vital Science, Technology, Mathematics, and Engineering, (STEM) fields. These are fields in which Kenya's education system remains comparatively weak in terms of student enrollments and investments (Matiangi, 2016).

New technologies also involve upgrades to library media centers and providing online tutoring services. In many advanced economies, schools have hired technology directors to help learn how to unleash the potential of these instructional devices. In fact, old-style textbooks are considered "old-school" methods. Instead e-books and e-portfolio systems are preferred. E-portfolios may include syllabi, package of readings, and inbuilt communication and assignment submission pages and devices. The same logic applies to student record keeping through devices like online grade books. There are numerous advanced apps that are increasingly popular, examples such as registration portals, financial aid tools, bill pay devices, and campus information tools, among others.

In some instances, the desire is to achieve some measure of a paperless classroom. A paperless classroom is said to have advantages in terms of creating an electronic trail, which helps in accountability and more effective teaching. Substantial resources have therefore been put in place to keep the costs of education down. Linked to the idea of electronic trails is "personalized learning education." Developments in ICTs and especially online learning platforms have contributed significantly to the growth of personalized education, thereby providing students with diverse opportunities.

Personalized learning adds value to student success in more than one way. It entails application of learning analytics whereby stakeholders can leverage technology for testing, tracking, and reporting student activities. Tracking data can inform instruction as it allows teachers to get closer to providing personalized interventions, identifying areas of strengths and weaknesses. Class reports and progress over the years can be factored into administrative decision-making. Integrating analytics is a huge tool for early alert, interventions, and collaboration. Through these evaluative systems, at-risk students are assisted and given the needed support. Countries that have embraced new ICTs for personalized learning solutions will, in the end, provide the best education for their citizens.

Virtual academies are not confined to higher education. In many private elementary schools, students at the lowest levels are exposed to new technologies and other next-generation learning opportunities. Virtual schools are also known to provide avenues whereby students take a fresh look at real-world experiences. One may note that ICTs have made it easier for self-directed learning in some situations. Online schools also have provided opportunities for students to take courses from other school districts, especially at high school levels.

Blended learning approaches are increasingly popular. Blended learning refers to the combination of online and face-to-face learning. One simple plan has been to apply a Flex model, which allows students to go online for given assignments and also receive instruction from teachers at on-site brick-and-mortar buildings, as need arises. Educators may apportion a percentage of time for online learning while the remaining time may be applied to small-group instruction. It is also possible to embrace models that require students to attend traditional schools and take courses or classes that are not offered in the traditional schools. And still there is room for online teachers to be the same as the in-person instructors. Many experts consider the latter as a highly enriching approach to blended learning.

In blended learning, students are likely to achieve greater competency through tapping into the advantages of offline and online approaches. An obvious advantage of blended learning is that it allows schools to individualize each student's education experience. Online assessments are helpful when a student prefers to work at their own pace. In addition, online content is more modular, allowing for students to learn in ways that work best for each of them. Studies also show that blended learning promotes the use of time-based practices and can make learning more effective and efficient.

Digital Divide as Major Barrier

Statistics reported in a McKinsey Consultants study (2013) show that the Internet penetration in Kenya was at 28 percent, the majority of which is in urban areas. Only 24 percent of government departments were online and less than a quarter have well-established information systems online (McKinsey, 2013, p. 4). Further, the use of tablet computers was also quite low. Only 1 percent of Kenyans owned tablet computers in 2012 (Sunday, 2012). Although Apple iPads were introduced in mid-2010, most Kenyans considered tablets out of reach. The one area where ICT growth is outstanding is in mobile phone penetration, where over half of the adult population owns a mobile phone with Internet capability. In another statistic from the Internet World Statistics Organization's 2015 ranking, Kenya had the best performer in terms of Internet penetration, at 70 percent, which was higher than Morocco and Nigeria (De Argaez, 2016). About 31.8 million users in Kenya accessed the Internet compared to Nigeria's 92.5 million between 2000 and 2016. Going by those data, Kenya is ranked well by African standards in its use of ICT platforms (De Argaez, 2016). Yet, amid such progress, use of digital devices remains low in comparison to global standards, especially in terms of access to fixed-wire broadband penetration. Evidence suggests fixed-wire broadband is most suitable for functions such as downloading and uploading files, videoconferencing, and streaming services that are vital for e-commerce and running of a modern economy. Moreover, according to the country's *Economic Survey*, only 111,130 fixed-wire broadband connections for office and homes were provided for in 2015 (Otieno & Ngethe, 2016). And according to the World Bank's 2014 figures, with Kenya's subscription rates of fixed broadband as low as 0.2 per 100 people, a real digital divide exists among the country's residents (Otieno & Ngethe, 2016).

Consequently, the first barrier to experiencing benefits of ICTs is to narrow the digital divide. The divide threatens to multiply Africa's educational gaps by leaving out the disadvantaged poor and hinders their prospects for socioeconomic development. Workers in the twenty-first century who lack sufficient ICT skills are likely to be severely disadvantaged in the new economy. Although the digital divide captures much of the complexity in understanding country readiness in use of ICT platforms, a more robust framework accounts for the fact that differences in access opportunities mirror income disparities among the nations.

In other words, richer nations will always have an advantage over access, exploitation, and innovation of ICTs. Expenditures on ICTs correspond with national incomes and developing countries have not necessarily translated ICT acquisition into economic advantage. This brings to the fore the importance of digital effectiveness as a means to leverage ICTs to solve societal problems (Barclay & Duggan, 2008). Developed countries are also known to have higher levels of innovation and derive greater benefits from ICTs.

Barclay and Duggan (2008) argue that policy makers should go beyond notions of the digital divide, conceptualized as a "bipolar division between the haves and the have-nots and the connected and the disconnected," and instead focus on the effectiveness of harnessing the digital capabilities and creation of relevant knowledge for the benefit of social and economic development. They contend that developing countries must think beyond mere acquisition of ICT infrastructures and develop capabilities to use these ICTs.

Since ICTs provide a path toward gaining opportunities in an increasingly competitive and globalized world, it is important that countries like Kenya go beyond acquisition and embrace discourse that highlights the effectiveness of digital solutions. Of relevance to the modern workplace is that increasingly many job advertisements are only available in the Internet. It is also through the Internet that various job-related information and transactions are carried out. In addition, the Internet provides workers with much transformative power because it is a means of e-commerce allowing users to acquire tools needed for advancements and productivity enhancement. Without doubt, the Internet allows workers to move around huge quantities of data over long distances at low cost.

Furthermore, voice and video properties make it easy to communicate across long distances. Cost savings through ICTs may come from elimination of traveling and parking, as more and more work is conducted online. For these and other reasons, closing the digital divide is an important matter for workers all over the world. The digital divide is a complex idea but mostly refers to disparities among those who have access to Information and Communication Technologies (ICTs) and those who do not. Public administration scholar Christopher Reddick captures the divide thus:

> This digital access divide is the result of social, environmental, and organizational factors that prevent use of technology. The multidimensional perspective treats not only access to technology as a problem, but race, ethnicity, income, skills, geography, cultural content and education as well. (Reddick, 2012, p. 56)

The digital divide is a huge challenge for Kenya because not everyone is literate or *rich* enough to own computers with up-to-date software. The digital divide affects mostly rural and urban poor, people with disabilities, those disadvantaged in terms of education access, the elderly, the unemployed, and many indigenous peoples and ethnic groups like the Elmolo, Turkana, Samburu, and other marginalized populations. These groups are at a disadvantage in the new economy and must be supported to have requisite skills and computers, with Internet access. Beyond access, content must be relevant to Kenya's unique cultural settings. Former Permanent Secretary in the Ministry of Information Communications and Technology Bitange Ndemo suggested Africa should aggressively develop content in multiple local languages (2014, p. 9). President Uhuru Kenyatta reiterated that educators should ensure that Kenya's youth use ICT tools to acquire and share knowledge, bridge gaps between communities, and counter narratives of hatred with peace and tolerance and leverage technology to reinforce morality and responsibility (Kenyatta, 2015).

One component beyond online content, physical access, and ICT skills that must be addressed as well is that of attitudes toward ICTs. ICTs are mostly associated with younger "digital" generations, and the education system is best placed to change attitudinal constraints to reducing the digital divide. The assumption that computers are tools for certain groups like urbanites, educated, or middle-class folks is retrogressive. Attitudes that are culturally reinforced, such as bias against women gaining access to education, apply as well. In addition, to tackle the digital divide, several indigenous communities like the Maasai and Turkana and others need greater investments in education that supports both oral culture and the new digitalized data storage and retrieval platforms. And when these marginalized communities acquire relevant ICTs, continuous access must be ensured. Otherwise the digital use gap continues. This is about communities having active technology facilities, which are updated periodically to keep pace with changing information technology.

Examples of Initiatives from Developed Countries

Rowena Cullen stated that in Western nations, governments attempt to ensure that all citizens "have the opportunity to access and use effectively ICTs so that they can participate fully in the educational, social, and economic activities that depend on these technologies" (2006, p. 289). Cullen (2006) identifies at least four barriers to use of the Internet that include physical access to ICTs, ICT skills and support, attitudes, and content matters. These are barriers that also affect developing countries, albeit at more pronounced levels. In developed economies, among the strategies adopted for shrinking the digital divide was to provide funds to help prepare groups like Native Americans for careers in information technology (IT). We have to recognize that over the years, the United States has built a scientific infrastructure that established the United States as the premier science nation and leader in innovation in the areas of information technology (Goulden, Mason, & Frasch, 2011, p. 142). As a result, the United States serves as a model for nations aspiring to do well in development ICT infrastructures and also narrowing the digital development by providing access to most of its citizens.

All administrations to varying degrees allocate enormous resources and incentives to not only develop ICT infrastructures but also aspire to link scientific advances to the nation's social capital. Since the Internet mushroomed during Clinton's presidency, his actions deserve special scrutiny. American President Bill Clinton's administration provided tax incentives to encourage business corporations and other private donors to donate computers and sponsor community technology centers and training centers. Developed countries gave much emphasis to public-private sector partnerships and undertook firm steps that promoted innovative use of technology for communities that had traditionally been underserved. Again, in the case of Bill Clinton's administration, it provided funds to help train new teachers in the effective use of ICTs.

President Clinton's administration focused on narrowing the digital divide in the context of education reform. He also expanded the dialogue on providing Internet access through public library systems and after-school programs. In 1996, the administration authorized the implementation of the E-Rate program (Schools and Libraries Program of the Universal Service Fund). Beginning in 1997, the federal government directly addressed the technology gap between resource rich and poor communities by allocating funds from telecom taxes to the poor school districts. The E-Rate program was successful at increasing overall access of Internet resources within the nation.

At the local level, responses to the digital divide were equally successful. For example, in Arizona, the city of Phoenix introduced electronic access to government through programs such as "Phoenix At Your Fingertips" (phoenix.gov), a website that offered electronic access to city services. Citizens could explore public library digital media collections and also download audio books, eBooks, videos, and music. The digital media collection was accessible for free for those with a Phoenix Public Library card issued at public expense.

In the nearby city of Tucson, leaders including the mayor and council continuously talked about eliminating the digital divide in their city. In 2007, the city leadership impressed upon the digital signal providers such as Cox Television to address issues of the digital divide as the city moved to digital services. The city dropped some of its Public, Educational and Government (PEG) channels to give room for faster implementation of cable-based Internet connectivity. PEG channels delayed the shift from analog to digital until 2009 to enable a flawless transition. In some poor neighborhoods, Cox provided cable to public housing to facilitate easier Internet access.

Other cities like Scottsdale provided training programs and computer literacy facilities for their citizens. And in Texas, the city of Austin, considered a leader in the information-oriented economy, the leadership, through programs like the Austin FreeNet, worked hard to offer public access to the Internet for those who could not afford computers. The city teamed up with the Dell Foundation to equip several community centers and city libraries with the Internet and expanded broadband access. Other partners in providing support were the Bill Gates Foundation, Microsoft, and the America Online Foundation.

President George W. Bush's administration issued a rosy view of America's achievements with regard to shrinking the digital divide. In some ways, the Bush administration felt that much progress had been made to the extent that federal subsidies were no longer justified to continue supporting access to the Internet in less endowed regions (Garson, 2006, p. 99). Bush's 2003 budget proposed to eliminate some of the Clinton administration's information equity programs like the Community Technology Center (CTC) and Technology Opportunities Program (TOP) (Garson, 2006, p. 99). Yet, the reality on the ground proved otherwise. Several tribal communities in Indian country lacked broadband access.

For his part, President Obama focused on expanding high-speed (broadband) Internet services to school districts in economically deprived parts of the United States. In June 2013, he announced the launch of ConnectED Initiative, a program designed to enrich education in the K–12 levels. ConnectED was about empowering teachers and students by providing them the best technology and making the most of it. Under the program, by 2018, 99 percent of American students would have access to next-generation broadband. Obama's strategy included working jointly with ICT corporations to ensure that American students had the best technologies in the world. Among the corporations that collaborated to support ConnecED were Apple, Microsoft, Sprint, Verizon, Adobe, AT& T, Esri, Autodesk, and O'Reilly Media, among others.

President Obama continued to use his "bully pulpit" and in the State of the Union address to Congress in January 2014 he remarked:

> Last year, I also pledged to connect 99 percent of our students to high-speed broadband over the next four years. Tonight, I can announce that with the support of the FCC and companies like Apple, Microsoft, Sprint, and Verizon, we've got a down payment to start connecting more than 15,000 schools and twenty million students over the next two years, without adding a dime to the deficit. (Obama, 2014)

Furthermore, President Obama's concern for expanding Internet access was visible through his continued attention to bringing to the fore the issue of digitization of all schools. In January 2015, he challenged corporations to support educational technology connectivity in all the country's classrooms rather than acting to frustrate grassroots efforts by municipal entities that had demonstrated interest in expanding digital access in their jurisdictions. Cities like Cedar Falls in Iowa, Chattanooga in Tennessee, and Lafayette in Louisiana had made progress through supporting the development of high-speed Internet infrastructures one hundred times faster than the national average (Queally, 2015).

In his January 20, 2015, State of the Union address, President Obama continued to press for the expansion of high-speed Internet infrastructures. Obama's vision was for America to build twenty-first-century infrastructures for today's contemporary business needs. Having the fastest Internet was a key component of the overall development strategy for the country's infrastructure, which includes modern ports, stronger bridges, and faster trains.

In 2015, the Federal Communications Commission, (FCC) set a national benchmark for an upload speed of 3 megabits per second to replace the old standard of 1 megabit, established in 2010. The new measure for downloads was benchmarked to 25 megabits, an increase from the 2010 figure of 4 megabits. The new standards were aimed at keeping up with technology. President Obama's State of the Union Address highlighted his desire to "protect free and open Internet, extend its reach to every classroom, and every community, and help folks build the fastest networks so that the next generations of digital innovators and entrepreneurs have the platform to help reshape our world" (Obama, 2015).

A key component of the administration's vision is to encourage more private involvement in public infrastructure development. Obama's administration proposed an innovative financing plan known as the Qualified Public Infrastructure Bonds (QPIBs), which expanded existing bond facilities. These bonds allow local and state governments to issue tax-exempt bonds for infrastructure development. Private providers are then invited to manage the ICT projects. The financial proposal was similar to the Private Activity Bonds (PABs), introduced for raising funds in support of road construction projects. The major lesson from the United States is that ICT projects are accorded the same presidential support as other major infrastructures. In addition, these projects are implemented through public-private partnerships (PPP).

At the local level, in the United States, other innovative ways of increasing access to digital learning resources have been reported. At Salton City, Southern California, sixty-five miles from the border with Mexico, local communities access high-speed Internet through their school bus' Wi-Fi platforms (Dobo, 2014). The school bus mounted with a Wi-Fi router is driven up to the local high school each day for low-income students to access the Internet. At night, the bus is packed along a hot spot driveway and serves students until the battery fades away. There are also communities in the United States where communities have worked together to give every child tablet computers for use in the classroom and at home. Wi-Fi-fitted school buses are an important component of American innovation. This has allowed more and more schools in remote areas to access the Internet. It is noteworthy that there is still some work to be done, especially in tribal and rural communities where 39 percent of the people in those communities (about 23 million) lack access to 25mbps/3 3Mbps FCC established broadband speeds benchmark (FCC, 2016).

Notwithstanding broadband connectivity concerns and massive investments in digital education, online learning has helped American students enjoy advantages of twenty-first-century learning experiences. The proliferation of virtual schools has tremendously helped students to extend the learning hours beyond the typical school day. As a result, the quality of education in America is among the best among those reporting progress to the International Association for K–12 Online Learning (iNACOL).

Likewise, progress in other developed countries is remarkable. Schools were an important part of the expansion of ICTs in Canada, New Zealand, and other developed countries as well. For instance, in Canada, Community Access Programs (CAP) involved schools, libraries, churches, communities, and business agencies. In the case of New Zealand, a highly successful community training model was developed. Rowena Cullen (2006) observed that a loose network of local societies joined together to provide training for community members. Nonprofit societies that required members to pay a small fee were encouraged to train and have access to computer terminals in rural communities (Cullen, 2006, p. 309). All the various approaches to shrinking the digital divide require some measure of visionary leadership and skillful management.

The Digital Divide Context and Solution Effectiveness in Africa

Since Africa has among the poorest people on earth, the context of the digital divide transcends measurement of information equity and inclusion. Although progress has been made in terms of connectivity, African nations are still behind most regions (See Table 1). Internet usage is still concentrated in pockets of urban and semi-urban areas. Various ITU studies show that Africa ranks at the bottom of global Internet penetration and development of broadband infrastructures. High costs of providing broadband frustrated efforts such as the Nepad eSchool initiative developed to provide computers in schools (Ernst & Young, 2009). Africa's iGDP is at a low 1.1 percent. The iGDP measures the Internet's contribution to GDP and is a good measurement of investments in the ICT arena and also provides indications for connectivity and engagements in the digital platforms. According to McKinsey Consultants (2013), Kenya and Senegal were the best performers on Africa's iGDP index.

That said, Kenya is still among the best-placed African countries on the ICT Development Index (IDI), which ranks countries according to how well they have developed ICT infrastructures. Another index, the ICT Price Basket (IPB), compares the cost and affordability of nations implementing a host of ICT programs. On the IPB, it would appear that Africa is making strides in provision of ICTs but the continent is still not among the top performers globally (See, Table 4.1 below).

Affordability remains a huge problem in Kenya. According to Multimedia University of Kenya lecturer John Walubengo (2015), the costs of providing Internet services in Kenya are relatively high relative to national incomes. Walubengo argues that Kenyans spend 45 percent of their income to access broadband Internet services. And although Kenyans access most digital services through their mobile phones, the cost of these services remains high. For example, Kenyans spend 7.5 percent of their average incomes for 500 MB of data bundles per month (Walubengo,

Table 4.1. World Internet Usage and Population Statistics June 30, 2012

World Regions	Pop. 2012 Est.	Internet Users Dec. 31, 2000	Internet Users 2013	Penetration (% pop)	Growth 2000–2012 %	Users % of Table
Africa	1,037,380,925	4,514,400	167,335,676	15.6	3,606.7	7.0
Asia	3,922,066,987	114,304,000	1,076,681,059	27.5	841.9	44.8
Europe	816,372,817	105,095,093	518,512,109	63.5	393.4	21.5
Middle East	223,608,203	3,284,800	90,000,455	40.2	2,639.9	3.7
North America	348,280,154	108,096,800	273,785,413	78.6	153.3	11.4
Latin America/ Caribbean	592,994,842	18,068,919	254,915,884	43.0	1,310.8	10.6
Oceania/ Australia	35,815,913	7,620,480	24,279,579	67.8	218.6	1.0
World Total	7,012,519,841	360,985,492	2,405,510,175	34.4	566.4	100

Source: Spires, H. A. (2012, October 24). Pondering the digital divide across the globe. World View Global Education Symposium. Retrieved from http://www.slideshare.net/haspires/world-view-2012-digital-divide-final

2015). This is worse than Nigeria (5.6 percent) and South Africa (2.7 percent), which have much larger economies than Kenya.

Still, Kenya did not outperform its East African neighbors with lower GDPs. Countries like Rwanda, which initially relied on submarine fiber optics, were among the best performers in East Africa. Rwanda ranked seventh in Africa on the 2012 United Nations Broadband Commission for Digital Development's study of the most active broadband subscriptions per one hundred users. Rwanda, which distributed over 203,000 laptops to primary school pupils, ranks as one of the best performers in terms of government intervention in distribution of laptops to primary school students (Mungai, 2015). As was mentioned, Rwanda is only outperformed by Peru and Uruguay, which distributed laptops to primary schools as one way of providing affordable hardware to children from low-income communities.

Overall, Africa's change occurred when telecommunication platforms shifted toward greater usage of mobile telephony in contrast to desktop computers, which relied on cables and aerial grids. For example, Rwanda has also performed well in terms of expanding Mobile Government systems. Through its eNota Project, the country established a system where students access their national examination results through their mobile phones. Uganda has also experimented with PurcAI Mobile platforms that enable teachers to enter student grades via SMS. The proliferation of mobile platforms has increased Africa's utilization of ICTs. The move toward greater wireless broadband capabilities strengthened Africa's position as a consumer of ICT products. More importantly, Africa has made great strides in the mobile sector and has registered double-digit growth in mobile-cellular subscriptions.

Utilizing mobile telephones in government (M-government), has huge benefits for African governments. M-government cuts down communication costs and expands services in horizontal and lateral ways. Mobile phones enable government officials to reach persons in remote areas of the continent. And importantly, M-government is building new communities and networks that may organize to help exchange ideas on best education practices. This is certainly happening in Kenya, where communities are engaged in vigorous debates about solving the country's troubled education policy.

M-government also came into play after Kenya's security situation deteriorated following attacks by terrorist groups in schools and universities. Mobile phones are excellent tools for those in emergency situations. These tools have great advantage in personalization of services. In the case of emergencies, mobile phones will easily help law enforcement and peace officers to locate and reach individual persons.

Still, Kenya struggles with issues of continuous access through lack of power resources. Without securing electricity, schools will not be able to enjoy the full benefits of ICTs. At the moment, the majority of elementary schools are "day schools" as opposed to "boarding schools." Day schools need less electricity than the "boarding schools." In 2013, at least half of the schools lacked continuous access to electricity. 10,157 out of 21,222 schools were connected to the electric grid. Although the goal of national rural electrification is far from being attained, Kenya Rural Electrification Authority (KREA) accelerated the process of adding to the country's electricity consumers. By 2014, more than 80 percent of schools were closer to gaining connectivity to the national grid and therefore making it easier to access ICT platforms.

And even if connectivity was available, Africa's skills capacity is relatively low. Groups with poor education infrastructures lack skills required for utilizing Internet products. Computer literacy must be a part of the policy framework to make full use of the ICTs. Resources for skills development are as important as those for software, hardware, and connectivity.

The lack of resources is not only an impediment at the lower levels but stretches to the tertiary levels. In June 2014, the government admitted the country needs more than one thousand engineers in the telecommunications industry to support the ICT sector (Sunday 2014). The lack of quality high-end engineers was a hindrance to achieving growth in the telecommunications sector. More notable is that the lack of ICT skills worsened the digital divide between rural and urban areas. It is precisely for this reason that the government sought foreign assistance to help bridge the technical skills gap. For example, a Memorandum of Understanding

(MOU) between government and technology multinationals like Huawei Technologies of China was signed in 2014. The MOU focused on providing internships to Kenyans to further skills in Chinese high-tech industries. The Kenya Education Network supervised the selection process as one of the actors to implement the National ICT Master plan. The plan's key goal was to support skills development.

Building skills capacity must be done in a framework that includes groups that have historically been left behind. These would no doubt include women in rural Kenya, the elderly, and persons with disabilities. Households with poor disabled members present an even tougher challenge and must be a part of the strategy to increase Internet penetration. Increasing access to communities where poverty levels are high provide opportunities for narrowing the digital divide and mitigating social exclusion that may prevent some groups from realizing their economic and social potentials. African governments have made strides in increasing Internet penetration.

To illustrate the growth, one may note that in 1995, the total number of telephone landlines in the city of New York alone was by far greater than lines in sub-Saharan Africa. In 2014, the growth of mobile telephone lines in Africa exceed 635 million, thus depicting a steep rise in the continent's global connectivity. Because modern smartphones have multiple uses that include voice, cameras, music, and other forms of entertainment, Africa is no longer de-linked from the world's information system. And since the mobile phones provide avenues for data management and transactions, M-government applications are now possible.

Undersea Cable Infrastructures

The infrastructure for employing e-governance continues to grow. Since 2001, Africa has commissioned several undersea fiber optic cables. In the case of Kenya, private companies that include East African Submarine System (EASSY), The East African Marine Systems (TEAMS), Sea Submarine Communications (SEACOM), and Lower Indian Ocean Network (LION2) manage the submarine cables. The 2,700-kilometer-long LION2 cable is an extension of the initial LION cable, which connects Madagascar, Mayotte, and Reunion Island to Europe, Asia, and the rest of the world. The ownership of the fiber optic cables provided great redundancy for network stability, which boosted Kenya's bandwidth capacity. The cables are owned in private, public, and international partnerships. For instance, French Telecom-Orange had a key share in LION2. The government of Kenya owns a 20 percent share in TEAMS. Safaricom, Telkom Kenya, Kenya Data Networks, Wananchi Telecom, and Jamii Telecom are other investors with shares in TEAMS. Recognizing the need to serve its growing customer base, Safaricom acquired shares from its rival Essar.

The 2,700-kilometer-long LION submarine cable runs through the region to Madagascar. Because the cables run along the Coast, there is a cost advantage to cities along the East African Coast like Mombasa. In addition, satellite coverage in Africa has increased tremendously. Among the important providers is the Regional African Satellite Communications Organization (RASCOM), which launched its satellite RASCOM-QAF1R in 2010. Nigeria's NigComSat-1R added its satellites in 2011. Satellite firm iWayAfrica (Kenya) has a footprint in Kenya and has been a leader in encouraging backup services to supplement international fiber optic services. However, the satellite connections are quite expensive and have faced strong resistance from the terrestrial cable providers.

However, access to the Internet is not the complete story. Africa needs to grow its content capabilities because the continent has unique needs. African governments, through the Millennium Development Goals, recognize the role of the Internet in expanding Gross National Product. The Internet can lead to generation of jobs and new business opportunities and incomes. New applications in areas such as health and education will continue to be an integral part of the new economy.

The impact of new technologies in the area of education goes beyond information sharing. Applications in the education sector are catalytic and have implications for banking, security, public safety, disaster, and emergency management and other services.

Administrators at the Ministry of Education regarded ICTs as a partial solution to the teacher shortage in the country. In 2010, the country had a deficit of 61,000 teachers. This prompted then Director of Quality Assurance and Standards Enos Oyaya to argue that ICT platforms had the potential to fill in this void (Oduor, 2011). Online media had the potential to reach out to several learners because a single teacher could digitally broadcast lessons to students in geographically dispersed areas.

The government sought assistance from private providers to ensure that there was wide access to digital platforms across the country. The government saw ICT projects as a means to stimulate the economy and spur growth and visualized spreading technologies in rural constituencies. Through the Economic Stimulus Package, the government distributed refurbished computers to a select group of 1,050 schools (Oduor, 2011). Private companies like the Express Communications Ltd (ECL), an education programs website developer, Kenya Commercial Bank, and the Standard Group were among the key support for the pilot project geared toward narrowing the digital divide.

There were multiple facets to narrowing the digital divide. Under the country's Vision 2030 Development Blueprint, one way to expand ICT usage was to promote information technology in schools. Reports from the Teachers Service Commission indicated that a majority of 260,000 members of the TSC lacked basic computer knowledge. Efforts to create a self-help teaching platform received very little support from the teachers' body.

The Kenya Institute of Education (KIE) developed a KSh 24 million Elimika e-learning portal to boost use of ICTs. The project was meant to encourage teaching using ICTs. According to a Kenya ICT Board report, Kenya's digital divide was severe. It constituted lack of access, lack of skills, and issues with continuous access.

Of Kenya's 21 million Internet users, only 1 million had broadband speeds of 2mbs. Attempts by elites to faster 3G and 4G technologies would only exacerbate the divide by creating a huge difference in quality of ICT products across the different segments of Kenyan society. And according to data from the International Telecommunications Union (ITU), Kenya's broadband Internet costs were among the highest in the world. Neighboring countries like Uganda and Tanzania had cheaper broadband rates than Kenya. In rural schools, there was a need to establish computer infrastructure, including computers, laptops, electricity, and broadband Internet. In some areas, educators lacked interest in ICTs and exhibited "techno phobia" tendencies (Sunday Nation, 2011).

Perhaps Mohammed Mwamadzingo (2003) gave the most persuasive argument concerning the role of trade unions in narrowing the digital divide. Unions can encourage employers to provide incentives to encourage employees use ICTs. In his report to the International Labor Organization (ILO), Mwamadzingo suggests that trade unions ought to play a coordinative role in promoting an information technology agenda at the workplace. It is in the workplace where the newest technologies are applied.

Jubilee and the Laptops Project

Perhaps the most ubiquitous example of KNUT's attitudes toward implementation of IT policies was in rejection of the Jubilee Government's strategy of distributing laptops to all Standard One pupils in 2013. The idea of One Laptop per Child (OLPC) was as foreign as it can get. When first espoused in 2004, Nicholas Negroponte intended the laptops would cost no more than $100 and would be a means to facilitating digital inclusion and promoting development in less developed countries. The laptop projects were among the first initiatives to actualize the ICT4D agenda. By providing cheap laptops, countries would in essence be empowering children and preparing for future roles in social and economic development. In campaigns leading to the election of President Uhuru Kenyatta and William Ruto, their alliance platform included youth and women empowerment, through Uwezo Fund, and a digital revolution.

Kenyatta's Jubilee Alliance promised to provide laptops to 1.5 million elementary school children. The goal was to empower Kenya's primary school pupils to be competent in ICT operations, thereby helping reduce the digital divide. President Uhuru's vision was that early exposure to technology would be enabled through the laptop program.

In an April 2013 speech to a joint session of Parliament that brought together the Senate and the National Assembly, President Uhuru Kenyatta reiterated his resolve:

> My Government has committed itself to delivering on the promise of free laptops for our standard one children starting next year. Some have said this is too ambitious . . . I say that we cannot afford to leave any of our children without tools to compete in the digital age. Yes, our ambition is great but the scale of that ambition is the only one sufficient to meet the scale of our nation's challenge. As such, I call upon both Houses to work with me to ensure that in future, the laptops we provide are assembled locally. (Presidential Press Service, June 16, 2013)

The estimated cost of each laptop was KSh. 35,000 or roughly KSh. 50 billion for the project. Clearly, this was an ambitious project. The lead organization to implement the project was the Ministry of Education. The project was implemented without a systematic feasibility study. Not surprisingly, Christine Mungai (2015) compared Kenya's laptop project to similar failed projects in Nigeria and argued that corruption explained some of the implementation failures. Other observers argued the public may have been duped. In an opinion piece for the eLearning Africa Report, Leonard Mware speculated the project may have been a ruse. He wrote:

> Which leads us to the question, could this $300 million laptop project have just been a ruse for some businessmen or politicians to get paid back? Is this the reason why no one bothered to get a thorough feasibility study done before commencement? Could it be why we didn't bother to learn from the wealth of experience Kenya has? Was it really laptops for children or for greed? (Mware, 2014, p. 19)

Policy implementation frequently faces obstacles, if there are issues with problem definition and clarity of objectives. With regard to the laptop project, there is evidence to suggest that it was aspirational or meant to give credence to the Uhuru Kenyatta–William Ruto presidential campaign bid. The two never really provided concrete plans about the project's sustainability. As a result, the first obvious problem was that although the government had communicated its goals, its planning process was disjointed and excluded key stakeholders.

Second, the project was bound to face difficult challenges because of the lack of stable electricity in most rural schools. Without stability in the national power grid, laptops would not provide continuous services. This means that the digital divide would persist regardless of the presence of laptops in certain locations. And there was the additional cost associated with provision of stable electric power. Efforts to provide solar power panels ahead of the laptop rollout were unsuccessful due to managerial problems. The government announced it would supply solar panels to schools by end of 2013. It did not.

Next, the National Treasury did not provide funds to actualize the project citing concerns over the unsustainable Wage Bill. By 2013, Kenya's Wage Bill was over KSh 458 billion which was about half of the government's annual revenue collection. The Treasury and Office of the President wanted to balance the national budget through retrenchments and reductions in force and salary cuts. Relocating funds to the laptop project was seen as a politically less risky alternative.

Some of the funds previously earmarked for the laptop project went to finance the infamous Anglo Leasing debt. In 2014, KSh. 1.4 billion was paid to firms associated with one Anura Perera to avoid penalties and interests and meet contractual obligations. National Treasury Secretary Henry Rotich rationalized the payments on the grounds that paying off Anglo Leasing firms was "essential." Funds had to be reallocated from projects that had not yet been implemented, like the laptop project and others (Anyanzwa, 2014).

Although prior models of projects that support schoolchildren acquiring low-cost and low-power laptops around the world existed, Kenya's ICT policy faced managerial challenges. A well-known model was the One Laptop Per Child (OLPC) Foundation's project in which the supplied cheap computers led to increased use of new technologies in elementary schools. Kenya's policy implementers seemed to be muddling through. There was also considerable confusion concerning project design. Government officials differed on project specifics.

At one point, the government announced it was considering tablets over laptops for class one pupils in all public schools. The project proposals and feasibility study documents were not disclosed to the public. There was also considerable lack of specificity as evidenced in the government's official rhetoric. For instance, Cabinet Secretary Jacob Kaimenyi's reason for preference for tablets over laptops was not based on a documentable needs assessment plan but on hypothetical assumptions. Kaimenyi had observed that there were projections that in the next five years (i.e., by 2018), "laptops currently being used by majority of the people would be replaced by tablets thus the need to be ahead of time so that the gadgets are not declared obsolete. We have also established that young children prefer touch screen than devices that use a mouse" (Kimutai, 2013).

As a result, of insufficient funds and poor planning, the laptop for schools' tender was initially canceled. An initial offer had been made to an Indian company, Olive International, to supply computers to selected schools. The tender process followed through common stages such as technical and financial evaluations, best and final offer negotiations, and financial offering done through a diligent process. The initial evaluations were conducted at the Ministry of Education and the Ministry of ICT.

Later, there were allegations that the tender process was not above-board and had been subjected to manipulation. The Public Procurement Administrative Board (PPARB), the oversight body, and relevant Parliamentary committees expressed doubts about the veracity of the bidding process. In many circles, the selected provider had limited capacity to supply the required laptops. The PPARB doubted Olive's capacity because it was not an original equipment manufacturer. The Ethics and Anti-Corruption agency (EACC) vowed to investigate the flawed tender process. Close to KSh. 30 billion was at stake.

Jacob Kaimenyi, then cabinet secretary responsible for education, initially claimed that the process was without irregularities. However, other officials in the Ministry alleged there had been tender manipulation and that the same corrupt cabals had also participated in the theft of public funds allocated for free primary education in the previous Mwai Kibaki administration.

By March 2014, some members of the Parliamentary Education Committee with oversight of the Laptop Project ruled that the project was marred by corruption. The committee accused Kaimenyi of showing arrogance and "giving assurances that were proven misleading" (Okendo, 2014). Likewise, the Public Procurement Administrative Review Board cited irregularities in the tender (contracting out) process. The review board gave the government forty-five days to reevaluate bids by competing companies that included Hewlett-Packard Europe of the Netherlands and Haier Electricals Appliances Corporation of China, which had failed to win the tender. At a crisis meeting, Jacob Kaimenyi promised to take action on findings of the Public Procurement Administrative Review Board. The board has received petitions from two firms that lost the initial contract to Olive Telecommunications PVT Ltd, a company registered in India.

Sitting in Nairobi, in September 2014, the High Court nullified the tender for free KSh. 24.6 billion laptops project. Judges George Kimondo, George Odunga, and Mumbi Ngugi ruled that the tender process to supply 1.3 million laptops to Class One pupils in public schools lacked equity and cost effectiveness.

Because the "laptop for every standard one child" campaign promise was poorly managed, various stakeholders questioned its efficacy. Members of the opposition Coalition for Reforms and Democracy (CORD) opposed the project, citing corruption and seeing it as an ill-designed policy. Although the Kenya Publishers Association (KPA) was in support of the government's Vision 2030 plan for industrialization, there were reservations about the manner in which the laptop project was implemented. For the most part, KPA cautioned of the project because it threatened the print industry. KPA raised concerns about single sourcing of content and hardware. Simon Sossion, Vice Chairman of KPA, publicly complained that the procurement procedures were flawed and that the government should have involved all stakeholders in developing digital content for Kenyan schools (Wanga & Sigei, 2013). KPA accused the Kenya Institute of Curriculum Development (KICD) of not consulting with book publishers.

The government had stated previously that it would allocate KSh. 53.2 billion for the free laptop program as a means to transform the education system. In its vision, the government touted e-teaching and e-learning as policy strategies for not only improving access to information, communication, and technology but to replace textbooks and save money. The broad vision was branded as the ICT4E to signify the place of salience of education in national human development.

KPA officials also argued that the project design left out the input of key stakeholders. According to KPA Chairman Lawrence Njagi, KPA, as a key player in the production of educational materials that include teaching aids, textbooks and digital content, there was no desired partnership on the laptop project. KPA felt, for the one laptop per child program to be successful, there should be other accompanying projects.

Therefore, KPA recommended a requisite teacher-training program be established. The publishers also called for a discussion about the types of gadgets to be used by students. For instance, KPA provided a list of criteria for ICT tools to be adopted. Among the criteria is effectiveness for users, price affordability, and simplicity of software, Internet capability, and convenience of infrastructural factors like power. In addition, the technologies to be supplied should be "rugged enough" for students' needs. In other words, the laptops would be made of materials that do not break easily.

According to KPA, the laptop project would have been best served, initially through establishment of a pilot phase involving private and public sector partners. KPA's proposal called for government to participate less in areas that were best served through private vendors. KPA's statement also abhorred the "stalemate" between the Teachers Service Commission (TSC) and the trade union, KNUT. In 2014, KNUT had orchestrated a strike over unpaid pay increases.

KNUT chairman Wilson Sossion called for a strike ostensibly to pressure the government to honor a salary deal signed with the Mwai Kibaki administration, that is the Legal Notice 534 of 1997. KNUT protested that Labor Secretary Kazungu Kambi had dismissed as untenable the 1997 agreement. Teachers demanded various benefits including medical, commuter, hardship, and responsibility allowances. KNUT and expert educators opposed the laptop plan, arguing that any available funds be first used for other priority purposes. Moreover, the teachers' union opposed the laptop project because the funds would be best utilized for recruitment and promotion of teachers. KNUT called for the employment of an additional 40,000 teachers to meet the shortages countrywide. Union officials also sought for funds to hire 24,000 nursery school teachers. Most teachers' unions were concerned about the lopsided ratio of instructors to students.

At the same time, Kenya Union of Post Primary Education Teachers (KUPPET) demanded funds to be used "toward harmonization of allowances" (Oduor & Weru, 2013). KNUT also regarded the laptop project as an attempt to "undermine and destroy the teaching profession" (*Daily Nation,* June 13, 2013). KNUT's Secretary General Wilson Sossion expressed fear that the idea of laptops was "a highly suspicious project." And there was real fear that laptops would replace teachers (Oduor, 2013). Sossion's fears are not necessarily outrageous and have been expressed in the context of the proliferation of cyberschooling in the advanced countries (Moe & Chub, 2009).

Observers contend that labor unions have a tendency to oppose the cyberschool movement because it leads to hiring of fewer teachers. Promotion of e-learning, it is noted, reduces the number of teachers because courses are shifted online, thereby reaching a larger student population than in a restricted brick-and-mortar classroom setting. Another dimension to the union's opposition can be explained in terms of loss of union revenues. Fewer teachers hired are a direct threat to union membership and political power (Otenyo & Lind, 2011, p. 273).

Finance Cabinet Secretary Henry Rotich's budget speech for 2013 gave KSh. 119 billion for teachers' salaries and KSh. 53.2 billion for purchasing 1.35 million laptops, building capacity of teachers and rolling out computer laboratories for Standards Four to Eight in all public schools (*Daily Nation,* June 13, 2013). In his appending statement, Rotich argued that the laptop project would reduce costs of buying and replacing textbooks.

But the teachers' union did not provide a policy document with a cost/benefit analysis that outlined the long-term influences of the laptop school project. Still, others argued that the majority of teachers in Kenya were not computer literate and would not be able to guide children using laptops (Standard Digital Reporter, 2013). Others vowed to sabotage the laptop project if teachers were not well remunerated. By the end of 2014, the laptop project was clearly on the back burner of national policy implementation. Still, there were reports that the project was moving forward, albeit as a non-priority matter. Cabinet Secretary Rotich announced in 2015 that funds were reallocated to other projects. This followed shortfall in the budget following failure of donors to provide support for the country's development needs (Kubania, 2015).

The *Standard* newspaper (February 19, 2015) editorialized the withdrawal of funds as a "disappointment." The *Standard* noted that:

> [F]rom the outset, critics of the laptop project objected to it, insisting there were more pressing needs in the education sector and giving a laptop to a pupil studying under in succession. It would therefore follow the basic needs of pupils across the country (classrooms, teachers, water, food, electricity) before thinking about an expensive laptop rollout. (*Standard* editorial, 2015)

While the *Standard* editorial did not oppose laptops in principle and encouraged pupils to adopt new technologies, the paper had reservations about the political process and administration of the project. The editors further noted: "The benefits of exposing pupils to technology would have dovetailed with the plan to increase the human capacity in ICT in schools and training for teachers" (Standard, Editorial, 2015)

The country had trained at least three thousand master trainers to lead the capacity-building process. An addition of 161,000 teachers, drawn from public schools, was scheduled for training in 2015. The government of Kenya also implemented an electrification project that added more than 14,254 publicly funded primary schools onto the national power grid. In addition, government contributed KSh. 60,000 (less than US$700) to all primary schools to refurbish classrooms in readiness for the Integration of ICTs into Kenya's curriculum.

As prospects for reviving the laptop projects appeared to dwindle, President Uhuru Kenyatta announced that the administration would reconfigure the project to purchase portable tablets instead of laptops. Funds were subsequently allocated for the 2015/16 budget (Oduor, 2015). At least KSh. 17.58 billion was to be for the reconfigured project. The government announced it would shift the project's management and coordination to the Ministry of Information, Communication and Technology. The Ministry of Education was tasked with training teachers and through Kenya Institute of Curriculum Development develop relevant digital content to be used "across multiple technology platforms" (Mbatiah, 2015). Under the revised project, other ministries, like Industrialization, Energy and also Treasury would provide resources to cover at least 1.3 million pupils in 11,078 primary schools within two years. Cabinet Secretary Jacob Kaimenyi's political critics, especially MP Bernard Bett of Bomet East Constituency, argued that the project had been moved to the ICT ministry because of poor leadership in the ministry of education (Njagih & Kimutei, 2015).

An Example of a Squishy Project

The laptop project morphed into a multidimensional ICT enhancement one, referred to as the "digital learning" or "digital literacy" project. One would be tempted to call it a classic case of a squishy project. Uhuru's administration was simply yielding to pressure to showcase the administration's campaign promise. An Ipsos survey revealed that most Kenyans preferred school computer laboratories for lower primary school pupils to the laptop project as initially promised in Uhuru Kenyatta's campaign speeches (Wanzala, 2015). The Ipsos survey reported that close to 85 percent of those surveyed preferred computer laboratories for all students, while 14 percent preferred laptops for individual Standard One students (Wanzala, 2015). Twenty-seven percent of those surveyed believed that the project had stalled because of corruption in the procurement process. Nineteen percent regarded the Jubilee administration as dishonest and insincere in its intentions while 30 percent cited lack of funds as the problem. A small number attributed the project's problems to lack of planning (Wanzala, 2015).

In June 2015, the administration announced that it had given service ministries six months to deliver online content for the "digital learning project." The administration's focus was now on provision of online content, through the cloud, to 22,000 schools. The project's emphasis was now the promotion of digital literacy and not provision of hardware, which shifted to another institution. Moi University, Jomo Kenyatta University of Agriculture and Technology (JKUAT), Strathmore University (through its iLab Africa which would lead on cloud computing), and the University of Nairobi would now team up to provide locally assembled laptops. JKUAT had previously announced its ability to assemble laptops, with the help of foreign investors including JP Couto and Positivo BGH. Treasury would exempt the universities from paying Value Added Tax (VAT) on raw materials for the assembly of the laptops.

The Ministry of Information and Communication Technology was designated the lead agency. For accountability, oversight would be through consultative teams including officials from the attorney general's office, Treasury, Ministries of Education, Science and Technology, Industrialization and Enterprise Development, Energy and Petroleum, and Devolution and Planning (Ochieng, 2015). An ICT authority was established with members drawn from various agencies including Kenya Institute of Curriculum Development (KICD), the Teachers Service Commission (TSC), the Kenya National Union of Teachers (KNUT), and the Kenya Primary Schools Heads Association (KPSHA).

KNUT's Turnaround?

Because of the politicized nature of the project, the leadership at the Ministry of Information and Communication Technology continued to manage a publicity campaign in which the leaders continued to tout the virtues of the project. The ministry issued several statements touting the importance of the project and issuing warnings against corruption in procurement of the laptops. In September 2015, the ministry threatened that companies that engaged in procurement fraud would be banned from doing business in Kenya. A new date for launching the project was set for January 2016, which coincided with the election campaign season.

KNUT, which had previously objected to the initial laptop project, turned around and announced its support for the rebranded project. Through its chairman, Mudzo Nzili, the union pledged the members' support for the benefit of Kenya's schoolchildren. To further illustrate KNUT's turnaround, in September 2015, Secretary General Wilson Sossion, in a symbolic gesture, attended the occasion in which the ICT cabinet secretary, Fred Matiangi, unveiled the country's Digital Learning Program agenda. In November 2015, Matiangi's tenure at the ICT Ministry came to a close. President Uhuru Kenyatta appointed Joseph Mucheru, founder of Wananchi Online and former Google Kenya Country Manager, in his place. The principal secretary's position was also reassigned to an IT expert, engineer Victor Kyalo, a former CEO of the ICT Authority of Kenya. President Uhuru's cabinet reshuffle signaled a desire to fulfill his campaign promise to provide free laptops for primary school students. With a sense of urgency, the new team quickly pushed through some of Uhiuru's agenda.

Additional government efforts to revamp the laptop project were announced in February 2016 when a pilot phase involving 150 schools across the country, certified as an E-Ready component of the Digital Literacy Program (DLP), was inaugurated. Under DLP, a survey of 22,000 public primary schools was conducted to determine e-readiness. Three schools were selected from each of the forty-seven counties and an additional number of special needs schools were added to the list. These were the first recipients of free Internet services provided through partnerships with Safaricom. In addition, 11,000 schools would be supplied with 600,000 laptops by June 2016. The government also allocated funds for equipment security of the laptops in the selected schools. Further changes in the ICT sector emerged as the government announced the arrival of 5,000 tablets from China to be distributed to schools. The government also promised to begin local assembly of tablets by fall of 2016 (Wanzala, 2016).

The Digital Literacy program had five major components: (a) provision of content for digital learning (b), provision of digital devices for both learners and teachers, (c) capacity building for teachers and administrators (implementers), (d), establishment of local assembly for digital devices and related accessories and (f) broadband connectivity. The administration promoted the program by touting benefits such as: (1) development of skills for a knowledge economy (2) promotion of research and development, (3) promotion of local assembly of ICT devices and (4) job creation (Digischool Secretariat, ICT Authority, 2016).

Universities, Union Training, and Politics

Union leaders are first and foremost trained in Kenya's primary and tertiary education system. One cannot speak of union training in isolation from Kenya's entire education infrastructure. At the university level, Kenya's expansive public university system lacked a nationwide blueprint in terms of integrating ICTs to learning processes. Each university system adopted its own support systems and learning devices. In most cases, lecturer acquired their own tablets, laptops, and PC desk computers. Institutionalized support systems were lacking for the most part. Initially, units like computer science labs at the University of Nairobi offered computers but there were no systemic faculty training initiatives to incentivize wide use of programs like e-learning initiatives.

All the universities benefited from donor assistance in laying out ICT connectivity and establishing computer centers. The University of Nairobi, Jomo Kenyatta University of Agriculture and Technology (JKUAT), Kenyatta University, Moi University, Egerton University, and Maseno University all received donor support of varying levels to boost their Internet adoptions. As Maurice Amutabi and Moses Oketch (2003) demonstrated, the African Virtual University (AVU) added to the stock of ICT and computer skills training in the country. AVU teamed with local partners to offer several online courses.

Newer universities like the Multimedia University, the Open University of Kenya (launched in 2012) and a host of private universities, for example United States International University, Strathmore University, and others, also made significant contributions to the national pool of ICT human resources. These institutions not only expanded e-learning opportunities but also provided union members relevant experiences of navigating through various ICT platforms. Private universities that have affiliations with overseas universities adopted practices similar to those in developed countries and were early adopters of computer-mediated devices and the Internet (Munene, 2007, p. 78).

Of course, changes have taken place but at a slow pace. In most cases, initial campus-wide courses were supported through collaborations with donor agencies. Limited efforts through collaborations with consultancy firms financed through collaborations with the World Bank, and other bilateral donors, like the Great Britain's support for Moi University's library project, appeared to expand opportunities for skill development in the country. However, the expansion of university education has not translated into greater collaborations with unions, especially in training workers in computer skills and knowledge. And still the depth and scope of ICT education in the country has not resulted in the production of enough qualified ICT professionals with abilities to manage with competence the emerging e-government platforms. Keen observers point out that education preparation and training for these professionals was inadequate (Karshoda & Waema, 2007).

To say that labor unions need more training on ICTs is an understatement. In order to be involved in negotiations about curriculum and laptop projects, KNUT and other teachers' organizations must be informed about the transformations occasioned through the digital platforms. On their own accord, unions should have the capacity to utilize the emerging virtual offices and acquire new skills (Shostak, 1999, p. 165). Training in new technologies is necessary for union operations. Although COTU, KNUT, and the larger unions have research staff, the unions have not made much gain in developing digital literacy. A majority of union members do not have deeper understanding of ICTs and have not been exposed to programs that enhance their capabilities in new knowledge involving uses of technology at their workplaces.

Programs that emphasize use of devices for stimulating critical thinking and transformation of society are remarkably absent from training menus. For example, KNUT does not even participate in curriculum development that would advance learning processes that educate students about using smartphones for learning rather than texting and social networking, which is the main application in Kenyan society. Integration of mobile telephones in learning programs, especially in higher education, is necessary training. And because union members do not have the same level of digital literacy, professional development programs must be offered to them through union initiatives.

To implement successful staff development programs requires money and political will. Current research suggests that the two are rare ingredients in Kenya's landscape. Institutional instability at the National Industrial Training Authority was reported (Kubania, 2015). Moreover, the cabinet secretary for labor, Kazungu Kambi, dissolved the NITA, accusing its board members of corruption and embezzlement of funds (Kubania, 2015). The Central Organization of Trade Unions (COTU) filed an injunction at the Industrial Court to stop the minister's dissolution order. The back-and-forth disagreements between the national government and union leaders amplified the weaknesses in the nation's training infrastructure. Evident is the legal control structure that placed the cabinet secretary above the training system. As such, oversight and policy guidance with regard to ICT training was weak or haphazard. Through providing semi-autonomous and self-governing structures, with more consultative arrangements and without hierarchical rigidities would serve the different industries better.

Industrial training is bedrock for ICT development. Without training, workers and their leaders are unable to navigate the complexities involved in the increased use of digital platforms. The need for training in ICTs should be a movement, supported by key stakeholders like ICT corporations, labor unions, industry, universities, and the government departments. Workers with ICT skills are likely to earn better salaries than those without. And of course, companies and the government would reap greater productivity.

Training provided through the aegis of NITA should be based on philosophies that encourage competence and political neutrality. Those benefiting NITA should be able to perform at internationally recognized standards. And unions need to put in place mechanisms that emphasize training as goals, for the movement toward employee empowerment and upgrading of especially ICT skills. Union policies ought to place emphasis on training as necessary component of manpower planning. For this reason, COTU's role in engaging the cabinet secretary in NITA matters was expected, as a matter of technical rationale. Without union involvement in employee training, the importance of formal learning can be minimized in general public discussions about the quality of labor in society. COTU and other unions can help identify the challenges faced at the workplace and also be a part of the networks finding solutions to worker productivity. COTU and other unions have to be an integral part of the training infrastructures and contribute by providing ideas on reforms necessary for the country's workers to be digitally competent and reskilled in ICT applications.

Stakeholders, Data Management, and Policy Development

In tandem with building virtual platforms, there is need for all stakeholders to embrace technological changes and leverage ICTs in enhancing education. Technology changes quickly, and it is up to educators to stay on top of education. Stakeholders, including unions, have to retool and reskill the workforce and support innovation in the school system. All stakeholders now recognize that technology creates jobs and must be leveraged for the greater good. Among the areas where schools may use ICTs is in fund-raising (crowdfunding), data storage, conferencing, administrative transfer of funds, and other educational needs.

Mistakes have been made in the implementation of the Laptop Project. There are other lessons that arose from the attempts at advancing the digitalization of schools in Kenya. The first is to ensure adequate planning centered on students as end users. Policy makers should not focus only on the hardware—the computers, laptops, iPads and other tablets, or mobile phones. While much has to be done about the ICT infrastructures, stakeholders ought to advance the interests of the end users and be concerned with instruction techniques, data privacy, and professional development of teachers. Student data, especially grades, is vital for the integrity of the country's education system. Trade unions can do much more on that front by including in their collective bargaining portfolios measures that address learners and teacher initiatives.

Privacy of student data has become an important element in managing the increased digitization of schools. In America the Consortium for School Networking and the Data Quality Campaign produced a list of 10 Privacy Principles for Students Data (Roscoria, 2015). The ten principles are a groundbreaking template for developing countries as well and are listed below.

1. Student data should be used to further and support student learning and success.
2. Student data are most powerful when used for continuous improvement and personalizing student learning.
3. Student data should be used as a tool for informing, engaging, and empowering students, families, teachers, and school system leaders.
4. Students, families, and educators should have timely access to information collected about the student.
5. Student data should be used to inform and not replace the professional judgment of educators.
6. Students' personal information should only be shared, under terms or agreement, with service providers for legitimate educational purposes; otherwise the consent to share must be given by a parent, guardian or a student, if that student is over eighteen. School systems should have policies for overseeing this process, which include support and guidance for teachers.
7. Educational institutions, and their contracted service providers with access to student data, including researchers, should have clear, publicly available rules and guidelines for how they collect, use, safeguard, and destroy those data.
8. Educators and their contracted service providers should only have access to the minimum student data required to support student success.
9. Everyone who has access to students' personal information should be trained and know how to effectively and ethically use, protect, and secure it.
10. Any educational institution with the authority to collect and maintain student personal information should:

    - have a system of governance that designates rules, procedures, and the individual or group responsible for decision-making regarding data collection, use, access, sharing, and security, and use of online educational programs;
    - have a policy for notification of any misuse or breach of information and available remedies;
    - maintain a security process that follows widely accepted industry best practices; and

- provide a designated place or contact where students and families can go to learn of their rights and have their questions about student data collection, use, and security answered.

Several stakeholders endorsed the ten principles. Among these were the International Association for Online Learning (iNACOL), the International Society for Technology in Education (ISTE), the Association of School Business Officials (ASBO), the national Teachers Parent Association, and other important stakeholders in management of education policy. The point to be emphasized is the digital transformations come with responsibility that not only ensures 24/7 availability of student services and learning management systems but also protect data from abuse. Administrators and union members, as stakeholders, when using analytics of student data ought to privilege not only teachers' union business concerns and add on positive student outcomes, key of which is to transform the education sector.

Digital transformations do not occur in a vacuum. Administrators must be able to provide evidence-based policy solutions to problems of learning in the country. Arguably, policy formulation and implementation are pieces of the puzzle that Kenya and other African countries need to work on. The laptop project stalled partly because the policy was unclear. Implementations of any ICT projects in education will fail if policy guidelines are unclear and not based on solid data. Trucano (2009) challenges developing countries to embrace ICTs but at the same time formulate relevant policies to guide decision-making. He analyses the overall framework of policy platforms and argues that at least three models are discernable, in comparative terms. In other words, policies of ICT in education can be grouped along the following contours.

a. National ICT in education policy
b. National education policy that includes ICT
c. National ICT policy that includes education
d. Other variations.

One would argue that Kenya's current policy framework seems not to fall into a clearly identifiable scheme. Small wonder that funds for the Laptop Project were channeled to other uses, signifying low prioritization of the project. Granted that Kenya has a separate education policy, which has been changed incrementally, there seemed to be emphasis on expansion of primary and tertiary education. The mechanics of how to use technologies in curriculums were largely decentralized issues but not codified in any systematic fashion. As discussed in expert works (e.g., Kozma 2008; Tilya, 2008), coherent policy would provide rationale for use of ICTs in education. Besides, policy would set a clear vision and goals of how ICTs might advance the overall goals of education in the country. And, even if expansion is the stated goal, in most cases modern technologies are expensive and require a holistic and integrated development approach. Given that rural Kenya does not even have sufficient electric power to make much sense of basic technologies like telephones and interactive computer-mediated devices, it is conceivable that other infrastructural needs receive priority funding. With prices of devices becoming more and more affordable, tax regimes may support ICT hardware acquisition and eventually make equipment as cheap as household radios.

At independence radio programs were available but were mostly for nontraditional learners. Affordability will help but so will expansion of managerial capacity. The need for strategic planning cannot be overemphasized. Strategic thinking will no doubt involve networks of stakeholders including labor unions whose members implement ICT policy in education.

With the entry of the World Bank–supported African Virtual online (e-learning) ventures, strategic policy became necessary. Still, moderate computerization occurred but outside of a cohesive education framework. Vision 2013, the country's development blueprint, elevated the role of ICTs and suggested that education policy fit into the broad technology agenda. Recent expansions of ICTs in education, one would argue, are reactions to changes in the economy. Especially, an economy that is globalized and heavily dependent on ICTs as enablers of commerce and social life.

The ensuing policy framework neatly fits into the larger goals and rationalization of the country's key development partners, especially the World Bank and the United Nations. These multilateral development partners tend to support collaborative initiatives and frequently encourage partnerships with vendors of information technology systems. One notable example was the partnership between Microsoft and the government of Kenya. Signed in 2015, the goal was to include corporate global giant Microsoft in the National ICT Master Plan. In the plan, Microsoft agreed to support training for thousands of teachers to provide the skills necessary to sustain use of ICTs in the country.

In addition to working with global corporations and international development partners, the country's leadership retained strong relationships with African partners. In that regard, the country's prioritization of obligations to the African Union gave the national leaders the impetus to move forward with a robust push for ICTs in education and economic life. Both Presidents Mwai Kibaki and Uhuru Kenyatta prioritized African Union policies. In 2004, African heads of state committed their countries to expansion of ICTs, citing the merits of new information and communications technologies for better trade and cultural exchanges among member states. ICTs were also touted as instruments for improving health care, good governance, and expansion of education opportunities in Africa (African Union, 2004).

The broad ICT visions of the two multilateral institutions have concepts that reinforce each other and can be briefly articulated here. In the case of the World Bank (2003), ICTs may (a) offer potential benefits through improvements in efficient delivery of services, (b) bring markets within reach of most populations in rural communities, (c) improve government services, (d) transfer knowledge needed to meet the Millennium Development Goals, (e) increase access to education through distance (extended) learning, (f) enable and facilitate a knowledge network for students and train teachers, and (g) broaden availability of quality education resources.

Similarly, the United Nations vision (2005) includes goals such as (a) expanding access to quality education in developing countries, (b) boosting literacy levels, and (c) providing universal primary education in developing counties.

Moving toward digitalization entails encouraging cultural shifts. There is no way that Kenya and other developing countries can successfully embrace digitization of the education sector without changing cultural attitudes toward ICTs. ICTs are beyond mobile phones and social networking tools that are popular. Mobile devices can also assist students in their learning efforts. The efforts to expand digital skills should begin at early stages, with the goal of arming students with critical ICT skills before they enter the job markets.

Again, trade unions should be well positioned to help achieve coordination of ICTs and teacher training geared toward attainment of cultural change. Digital inequality is also about creating an environment that advances knowledge sharing and fosters innovative approaches to solving societal problems. Stakeholders have a duty to ensure that cultural attitudes foster innovation and that national and local policy development promotes improved understanding of the full capabilities of ICTs. Such an approach reinforces well-known digital effectiveness frameworks that go beyond simple access and draw attention to opportunities brought about through acquisition of ICTs.

Finally, since the UK-based Overseas Development Institute (ODI) reported that Kenya was among the leading African countries in matters of collecting and managing data, the government's support for the ICT sector had begun to receive international recognition (Kariuki, 2015). Having a culture of using data provides an obvious advantage for policy makers to leverage ICTs for development. Therefore, it was important that school administrators and the Ministry of Education provide adequate resources and funding to ensure that digitization processes are sustainable and not short-term endeavors. This requires use of data so that the link between investments in ICTs is compared to the benefits accrued. In other words, the relevant ministry and stakeholders should tap into databases for purposes of strategic planning. Data can also be used to measure the scope of the digital divide for purposes of extending access to use of ICTs.

The ODI report said it well when it noted that investments in better quality data means that Kenya can borrow at cheaper rates from the International Monetary Fund (IMF) and other financial markets, which prefer to work with "accurate country-level profiles of schools" (Kariuki, 2015). The implication of increased use of data-driven administration is that education officials, school principals, and teachers must now acquire new skills. There is no way that a digital society can emerge without incorporation of learning analytics and monitoring software to help administrators intervene in areas that require attention and therefore rectification. Such areas may include knowing about student access to digital devices and their familiarity with web-based resources.

A new era of data-based decision making is now at hand. The reality is that contemporary reporting of workflows requires staff to be able to assemble information for timely decision making. Fortunately, new ICTs have the ability to accelerate these processes and offer new insights that add to organizational effectiveness and efficiency. ICTs have the unique advantage of being able to store and distribute actionable data in more transparent ways than previously possible.

Although increased data analytics is the way forward, governments should continue to narrow the conditions, that create information resources inequalities. Ultimately, the digital divide is not just about installation of infrastructure and distribution of computers and other mobile devices to school students. The divide is very much about continuous access to programs on the Internet. Continuous access is in turn, a function of software updates, investments in reliable Wi-Fi resources, deployment of suitable access points, and replacement of devices that frequently break down. The job of administrators is to provide, through budgeting, sustainable funding strategies. Administrators are also required to be aware of industry standards in the field of new wireless networking technological systems. In modern schools, wireless networks must be installed to the satisfaction of end users. This means that administrators must consult with teachers and students who are the cornerstone of digital classrooms and the effectiveness of new ICTs in the education sector.

CONCLUSIONS

In conclusion, there is evidence that the digitization of Kenya's economy is still a work in progress, and much work remains to be done in the area of shrinking the digital divide, especially in rural centers. Education policy, particularly provision of computers and tablets, is currently being pursued, albeit in a haphazard manner. A globalized education, facilitated through computers and other ICT devices, is well understood among the various stakeholders, including trade union members. The next steps will require realization that ICTs have changed the way work is done and it is up to stakeholders to realize that the future means fewer textbooks and increased use of digital formats for enhanced learning. Primary and secondary schools will be expected to use tablets and e-readers for assignments and general learning. Digital texts are considered more efficient and better equipped for modern teaching and learning experiences. Teachers and other union members are expected to be savvy about using online and open-source databases of information. The era of the traditional workplace is gone and the education systems must move along for the benefit of society. To guarantee a future workforce that can help society move forward through training for ICT skills, a national education and digitization strategy supported by unions must be implemented.

FIVE

Trade Union Members' Attitudes toward ICTs

Implications for Participation in Governance

INTRODUCTION

The involvement of unions in an ICT-driven economy depends, in part, upon members' ability to understand the benefits of new technologies and, especially, uses in personal terms. Union members also regard ICTs as instrumental devices, especially for mobilization in group matters. ICTs help in enhancing power available to stakeholders in governance processes. Good communication strategies enabled through social media and other platforms assure union members of access to collaborative governance systems. If satisfied with ICT tools, members can and are always willing consumers of ICT products, thereby giving discursive legitimacy to government policy on new technologies. At the same time, union members dissatisfied with aspects of ICT-driven economies will show their disapproval through various means, which includes political action and refusal to support certain products.

Scholarly attention to attitudes of union members toward ICTs and various applications of computer-mediated devices in African society and at work situations are rare, if not inadequate. There are implications for not paying attention to attitudes of union members toward changes emerging from the increased consumption of ICT products. Most important, attitudes determine the level of participation in policy activism and governance associated with ICTs. Further, knowing union member attitudes is an important window into the behaviors of concerned groups, especially as relates to supporting policy prescriptions and embracing

ICT-driven changes in the workplace. In social sciences, behaviors are closely associated with beliefs. When union members believe certain technologies add to their positive experiences, this may translate into support for greater absorption and use of those technologies. From a theoretical perspective, psychologists regard such behavior as reasoned action, which illustrates the complex relationships between attitudes and behaviors (Fishbein & Ajzen, 1975). Scholars focusing on information systems have developed a model for predicting individual attitudes and behaviors of users of technologies that perhaps, captures the emerging trends in absorption of ICTs in Kenya.

The technology acceptance model (TAM), as articulated in several research works, for example, Davis (1989), Davis, Bagozzi, and Warshaw (1989), Mathieson (1991) and Adams, Nelson, and Todd (1992), among others, offers plausible explanations and useful insights on the unfolding interaction between union members and ICT artifacts in Kenya and other countries.

At the core of the TAM as applied to the electronics industry is the idea that users have to have a certain degree of trust before embracing e-commerce and online shopping experiences (Gefen, Karahanna, & Straub, 2003). In addition, for the more technology-savvy users, especially at the workplace, perceptions about existing software and administrative decision support and maintenance influences operational uses and by implication absorption (Lederer, Maupin, Sena, & Zhuang, 2000; Morris & Dillon, 1997). Still, great work exists that points to attitudes and acceptance being functions of intrinsic and extrinsic motivational variables (Teo, Lim, & Lai, 1999). The intrinsic incentives are associated with psychological and emotional rewards that flow from using the various ICT applications, such as the ability to interact with friends and family on social media or even to support family through uses of mobile money. Using ICTs for such purposes offers a sense of solidarity and feelings of belonging and possibly happiness for end users. At the other end of the continuum are the extrinsic rewards, which one may suggest are tied to the needs of union members as workers. In which case, the use of ICTs aligns neatly with rewards at the workplace. Using computers, for example, enhances productivity, which translates into promotions and salary raises. Therefore, how union members behave toward organizations using a particular ICT device or application (app) is a function of their attitudes or more appropriately the level at which they accept and use the respective new technologies. These attitudes may also be derived from union members' interactions with family, friends, and colleagues already making use of particular ICTs or apps.

Regardless of the specific strength of interactions with other users of ICTs, union members are also affected by variables such as income, gender, age, and types of jobs they perform. One may argue that union members in rural communities, especially teachers, are affected by issues such as connectivity and may not be expected to be aware of the full potential of the gamut of Internet resources available to their counterparts in urban settings such as in Nairobi.

Attitudes toward technologies are also shaped by organizational culture, especially the goals that are established by employers. One would easily note, for example, that shifting from typewriters to word processors was definitely advantageous to office workers, who could now save time by taking advantage of the added tools like spell-checking software. In a sense, such machines gave workers greater satisfaction and conjured positive attitudes toward the changes in workplace technologies. In today's world, software and online resources such as Google Tasks are handy in organizing work. Further, note-taking apps such as Google Keep, Evernote, and OneNote allow important information to be stored in the cloud for easy access. Besides, several time-tracking programs are widely available for use in various work settings. These technologies aid employee productivity and also influence behaviors associated with changes in the workplace, if and when those technologies are present. Thus, ICTs can and have been known to shape attitudes toward job enrichment and improvement of productivity.

Aside from productivity consciousness, attitudes toward ICTs have much to do with safety and health outcomes for the workers. In any case, it is reasonable to observe that some new technologies provide better safety and protect employees from harmful hazards associated with previous technologies. Union members will almost always approve of use of such technologies at the workplace or in society. On the other hand, as members of society, union members will be less supportive of technologies that produce contrary safety and health outcomes for workers.

One may observe that the increase in information technologies in the workplace is, in part, a managerial function. This means union leadership has to be aware of the needs of members, and the first step toward that awareness is to take stock of attitudes toward technologies among members. Doing so means the union leadership is making an effort to meet the expectations of its members' needs. As was previously described, awareness of computers has become an integral and expected component of workers in the twenty-first century. Access and computing proficiency have the effect of motivation for some employees. However, an interesting observation is that in many instances, attitudes toward technology are a moving target. This is because the extent to which motivation is conditional impacts on job security. Employees who are union members considered some forms of computer technologies to be irrelevant to their aspirations and in some cases intimidating. Historically, Kenya's labor force exhibited similar reactions to proliferation of other forms of technological change. Comparative analyses of goals and attitudes toward technology applications in different developing countries or against practices in the developed world are few. In Great Britain, "Opposition to technological progress has never been confined to a single class, monarchs, governments, religious authorities, merchants, farmers, workers, and learned professions have all attempted, at one time or another to impede or prevent various innovations" (Aaron, 1965, p. 12).

Archival records indicate that technological innovations were rejected or accepted based on whether or not they were introduced at a time when the economy was static, shrinking, or contracting (Stern, 1937). For a moment, consider the example of the sewing machine. There was widespread resentment at its invention during the 1830s. The fear then, and now, was that machines, as aspects of technological change, would render jobless the thousands employed in that industry. It was therefore, not a surprise that, Frenchman Barthelemy Thimonnier (1793–1857), the inventor of the sewing machine, was the target of hateful assassins who wanted him dead rather than alive. Although jobs are a major explanatory variable in resentment against new technologies, there are also psychological and cultural reasons that explain attitudes toward new inventions. In modern African society, the arrival of revolutionary ICTs like mobile telephones and computers is no exception.

Since the age of ICTs is here with us, the various applications constitute a major shift in the way work is done, and have the potential to displace jobs. There are several ICT applications that could be examined and discussed in relation to the impact on employee attitudes and overall role in society. Already the ICT sector represents over 5.3 percent of Kenya's economy. According to the 2015 Economic Survey, the ICT sector expanded in areas such as mobile money, Internet usage, and mobile telephones (Republic of Kenya, 2015). According to Vision 2030, the growth in the ICT sector, as a fraction of the GDP, is expected to hit the 10 percent mark by 2017.

In this chapter, the focus is on the most widely applied forms of new technologies, beginning with mobile money. In subsequent sections, we consider general attitudes toward computers, mobile phones, and e-government in a general sense. The chapter is an overview and appraisal of Kenya's union members' attitudes toward ICTs in general. An important point to make is that the discussion reflects on individual behaviors and attitudes derived from a limited sample of union members.

Trade Union Members as Consumers of ICTs and Applications

Trade union members in Kenya are major consumers of the country's mobile banking market. An overwhelming majority of union members (92 percent) have exchanged money through Safaricom's M-PESA (mobile money) and other money transfer protocols. There is increased evidence that mobile money transfer systems, lending platforms like M-Kopa, and remittance companies such as Dahabshill have fueled a new economic infrastructure in the East African region, especially the rural areas. According to informed World Bank estimates, 80 percent of those with cell phones also used mobile money (Vaughn, Fengler, & Joseph, 2012). In 2012, there were about 60 million mobile money users in the world. One in three of these were based in Kenya, making Kenya the largest player in mobile money transfers in the world. Omwansa and Sullivan (2012) argue that M-PESA, after its inception in 2003, crystallized into a viable problem-solving ICT innovation transforming the lives of millions of Kenyans.

Kenya achieved this success thanks to its liberal regulatory environment. The Central Bank of Kenya (CBK) eased entry into money markets by reducing requirements for operation. Safaricom was also an aggressive market leader, having developed an infrastructure that covered the whole country. Safaricom was able to create a brand that customers trusted and reached out to its customers, focusing mainly on establishing loyalty through agent networks. By 2007, the service had attained a level of sophistication in which both banks and customers were no longer skeptical of its veracity. Safaricom made mobile money the "go-to" financial service for low-wage workers in Kenya. Customers could pay for goods and services and send money to relatives in rural areas through virtual money. M-PESA was also available for payments to a host of government services, including settlement of court bonds and fines. According to data from the Central Bank of Kenya, by the end of 2011, Kenya's electronic payment sector was dominated by mobile money transfers and transacting over KSh 1.2 trillion (Mumo, 2012). In 2013, Safaricom reported revenues from M-PESA totaling KSh 21. 8 billion, up from KSh 16.8 billion generated in 2012. According to the *2015 Economic Survey*, in 2013, total mobile money transactions were worth about KSh. 1,902 billion, which increased to KSh. 2,372 billion in 2014 (Ochieng, 2015).

At this time, simple money transfer options had expanded to enable customers-subscribers (*wateja*) to access payment services, which included emergent Lipa Na M-PESA platforms targeted at SMEs. By December 2014, Safaricom had approximately 19.5 million customers and 250,000 agents and, following an agreement with MTN, was hoping to expand its customer base across other markets in Africa.

In 2014, the Central Bank of Kenya (CBK) reported that mobile phone transactions amounted to KSh. 2.37 trillion, compared with KSh. 1.9 trillion in 2013 (Masinde, 2015). At that time, daily transactions were at around KSh. 7.3 billion. Safaricom reported that it enabled transactions of KSh 101.3 billion per month through the same platform and attained revenues of KSh 26.6 billion. According to the *Economist*, Kenya led the world in Mobile Money transactions because "it had several factors in its favor, including the exceptionally high cost of sending money by other methods, the dominant market position of Safaricom, and the regulator's initial decision to allow the scheme to proceed on an experimental basis, without formal approval" (*Economist*, 2013). Mobile money transactions are expected to increase because of increased competition from new players, namely Orange, Airtel, MobiKash, Tangaza Pesa, and Equity Bank (Masinde, 2015). Equity Bank is Kenya's largest bank by customer base, and its entry in the mobile money services generated much interest in the financial business sector. Equity Bank, through its Finserve subsidiary, launched its own Virtual Money Network Operator (VMNO), which by mid-2015 had registered over 394,606 users (Sunday, 2015).

The Lipa na M-PESA platform was embraced by a section of *matatu* and small transport companies. By 2013, 1,300 PSV *matatus,* buses, *boda bodas* (motorcycles), three-wheeler *tuk tuks,* and taxicabs had adopted Lipa na M-PESA services, thereby requiring customers to discard cash payments for plastic cards redeemable at Equity Bank and Google Beba Pay prepaid cards. Google's entry into Kenya's electronic payment systems was in its pilot stages (Mumo, 2012). The Beba Card allowed users on Citi Hoppa buses in the Nairobi area to load money and make fare payments by swiping cards on handheld devices installed in buses and enabled through near field communication (NFC) technologies. Beba Cards are based on Google's Android systems and have been applied in banking systems in the developed countries.

In the meantime, the Kenya Bus Service (KBS) and Kenya Commercial Bank (KCB) operated the Abiria Card, and the Matatu Owners Association was licensed to make use of their My1963 Jinice card in conjunction with Safaricom. The Beba Pay facility uses Near Field Communication (NFC) technology that allows card holders to make payments by tapping on an NFC-enabled phone. The plastic payment cards were integrated as payment components of the existing virtual money platforms.

Through the National Transport and Safety Authority (NTSA), the government had initially gazetted September 2013 regulations to ban the use of cash money for payment of bus fares. Cabinet Secretary for Transportation Michael Kamau's order outlawed use of cash in matatu vehicles and imposed a fine of KSh 100,000 or imprisonment not exceeding one year for noncompliance. Some transport operators resisted the move and workers demanded more time to absorb the changes. The Matatu Welfare Association (MWA) called for more time to educate members of the public. According to MWA Chairman Dickson Mbugua, most members of the public did not even know where to buy the cards (Wanzala, 2014). Several low-paid workers saw the move toward a cashless fare as rushed and insensitive to their conditions. Additional concerns regarding systems interoperability emerged as the different devices failed to communicate to each other. For example, the Abiria card (Mastercard brand) could only be read by terminals associated with the servicing banks.

On the other hand, Safaricom's M-PESA terminals used Near Field communication systems that could not accept rival companies and only supported the My 1963 card. As a consequence, Matatus, using devices from Kenya Commercial Bank and Equity Bank issued cards refused to take the My 1963 cards, "citing security reasons" (Achuka, 2015). The National Bank of Kenya (NBK) also registered the Na3card cashless fare that empowered Matatu operators to accept payments via different platforms that ranged from cash to electronic cards (Mwakio, 2015).

This disorder in terms of systems inoperability prompted Matatu Owners Association (MOA) to suggest a single Pamoja Card associated with the Diamond Trust Bank (DTB) to issue a card that would operable across the sector. Not all stakeholders were against cashless devices. A section of matatu owners led by the MOA officials argued the cards would reduce losses incurred through theft from matatu crews and *manamba* conductors. A good number supported the program but worried that the cost of gadgets was high, ranging from KSh 14,000 to KSh 30,000. Matatu owners wanted support, in loan form, to acquire the digital devices.

Some journalists saw the drive toward a cashless Matatu industry as a "battle to control billions of shillings in commissions," involving banks and politicians with vested interests in the policy. Vincent Achuka, writing for the *Daily Nation*, posited that:

> A fierce battle to control of billions of shillings in commissions from cashless payments in public service vehicles is one of the main reasons for the slow uptake of the system, three months after it was launched. On one side are the commercial banks that maintain their system that uses EMV (Europay, MasterCard and Visa) based cards is secure and the most appropriate. On the other is mobile telephony giant Safaricom, which insists that its Near Field Communication card is the standard approved by the government for the purpose. (Achuka, 2015)

Equally notable, the government, through the Kenya Revenue Authority (KRA), saw the move toward plastic money as an efficient strategy toward reducing tax fraud. According to the KRA, the transport sector generated over KSh. 205 billion that was frequently not properly collected due to fraudulent practices. Anticorruption crusaders also supported the move, arguing it would act as a disincentive for paying bribes to corrupt elements in the traffic police department.

The immediate impact of the money transfer service was to empower low-paid workers by providing access to banking and financial services from which they were previously excluded. With a subscription of over 18.2 million, M-PESA changed the banking landscape in the country and the African trade union movement at large. For instance, in 2014, the Tanzanian Informal Sector Worker Union (ISWU) unveiled plans to establish a mobile money transfer service. Dubbed Dau-Pesa, the money transfer platform would enable subscribers to pay for various services in Tanzania, Kenya, and Rwanda. Dau-Pesa's transactions were designed to move through mobile carriers such as Vodacom, Airtel, Zantel, and Tigo (Linington, 2014).

Following the success of M-PESA, Safaricom launched M-Shwari in November 2012. M-Shwari was introduced in partnership with Commercial Bank of Africa (CBA) to become one of the largest mobile banking services. M-Shwari is designed as a savings and loan product. In only two years, M-Shwari grew to disburse loans amounting to KSh 29 billion (over US$278 million in 2014). Reports show that the service processes an average of 50,000 loans per day (Standard Reporter, 2015). CBA does not demand security for loans extended and depends on a credit scoring system. Research shows that 59 percent of M-Shwari customers were male and the highest usage was among the twenty-four to thirty-five age cohort (Standard Reporter, 2015).

According to InterMedia surveys, 15 percent of all registered mobile money holders used M-Shwari savings accounts (Kaffenberger, 2014). Although the service was popular, rates of savings for purposes of buying a future product or payment (goal-driven saving) were still low, but the deposit rates were high (72 percent) among those sampled in the survey (Kaffenberger, 2014). Most of the savings reported were for short-term purposes.

Following the example of Commercial Bank of Africa (CBA), the Cooperative Bank of Kenya (CBK) joined the mobile banking fray. The Cooperative Bank formed the M-Co-Op cash, a strategy to decongest banks through issuance of micro-loans and deposits. M-Co-op Cash customers use mobile phone account numbers to apply for loans, pay utility bills, and make deposits. The strategy was premised on the notion that Kenya was already a leader in the cooperative movement and there was an adequate customer base.

The surge in mobile money businesses also attracted Kenya Commercial Bank (KCB), which launched M-benki, a platform that relied on Safaricom's system to allow bulk payments through the digital platforms. Likewise, Family Bank initiated micro lending through its digital avenues. Family Bank linked its services with Safaricom's M-PESA electronic platforms. These services demonstrated the popularity of the convergence between telecommunications and financial sectors. More important, Kenyan society was experiencing a transformation from paper money to cashless currencies.

INDICATIVE SURVEYS AND DATA COLLECTION

The discussion is based on analysis of data from surveys of union members in Eldoret, Kakamega, Kisumu, Nairobi, and Nakuru counties. Teachers and other union members were randomly selected in urban and semi-urban centers. In each county, sets of questionnaires were distributed to union and nonunion members who worked in mostly public organizations. For the surveys, private schools were excluded, but there was no separation of teachers to demarcate whether they were in secondary or primary education. The survey instrument determined whether one was a union member before proceeding on with the rest of the questions. In total, 300 surveys were sent out but only 140 responses were received. All the respondents were youthful, with ages ranging from twenty to forty-seven. No one above age forty-seven was in the limited cohort assessed. All the respondents had greater than high school education, with just fewer than 40 percent having earned a college degree. In addition, informal meetings took place with stakeholders in the union movement. These surveys were conducted on various dates covering 2012 and 2013. Admittedly, the sample size was small but helpful in establishing the underlying union experiences with the ICT-driven economy. The sample size limitations are complicated by another unpleasant reality about conducting surveys on trade unions in Kenya. As researchers Jane Master and Mohammed Mwamadzingo (2012) reported, COTU and its affiliates have a poor record in matters of maintaining a credible database. The two scholars add that some of the unions affiliated with COTU do not have reliable information about their members, whether these are found in rural or urban workplaces. COTU is not alone; KNUT also did not have a reliable register of members to work from. So, the research occurred under difficult logistical circumstances in terms of organization and administration of the prepared questionnaire instruments.

In terms of structure and organization, the questions were organized along three major themes. First were sets of questions aimed at determining comfort levels with ICTs in general, to include computers and mobile services. The second set was designed to tease out perceptions on the impact of technology and need for technologies. The questions also shed light on the importance of ICTs in the economy. The third set of question covered issues concerning usage of ICTs.

The questionnaire included demographic data and information about education and whether or not the respondents were union members. Additional data was obtained from narratives on union attitudes toward information and communication technology policy in society. In this study, the goal was to have a sense of perceptions of a small representative sample of the union population depending on the issue at hand. Further work beyond surveys was included to understand attitudinal trends within key union sectors. Data was also compared to existing databases on general attitudes toward ICTs and technology in general. While the analysis may not be perfect, because of the logistics of carrying out the surveys, the results seem to coincide with general outlooks within the larger society. In this regard, it may well be that union member attitudes are not far from the larger society's attitudes toward ICTs.

The questions applied in the study were meant to address comfort levels with payment through computerized or mobile services and systems. Many of the responders felt that some employers were not ready for change and unwilling to move toward online payment platforms. There was a general concern over lingering traditionalism and a fear of the unknown. Nevertheless, union members felt that new mobile money platforms were an easy and safe way to make transactions. Most felt that mobile money is more efficient and can be accessed anywhere in the country. Most felt that mobile money was the quickest way to get money in cases of family emergencies. Moreover, it made banking easier, which was a much better outcome than previous systems that were prone to delayed payments. Although the merits of mobile money were advanced, there was a vast majority of those who felt that M-PESA was not suitable for proper accounting and record keeping in government accounting.

The survey revealed that many government accountants were frequently corrupt and lazy and insincere in how they performed business. There was wide acknowledgment that ATMs have made it easier for people to access money anytime and anywhere.

The questions were also meant to address issues about perceptions of the effects of information and communication technology on people's lives and the relative need for investments in such technologies. The perceptions were varied and, for the most part, responders acknowledged that ICTs had transformed individual lives. Most agreed that ICTs made it a lot easier for people to communicate and also send and receive

Table 5.1. Comfort Levels with Payment Through Computerized and Mobile Services and System (%)

	Yes %	No %	%No response
1(a). Have you ever received your pay through M-PESA or any other electronic mobile money transfer?	50	50	0
(b) Would you accept to receive your pay through mobile money transfer like M-PESA?	50	30	20
2. Would you be willing to receive your pay through M-PESA/Mobile Money Transfer?	70	20	10
3. Would your personnel manager be willing to pay you your dues by mobile transfer?	20	60	20
4. Would you be comfortable to pay your employee by M-PESA, ZAP Airtel or any other mobile money transfer service?	50	50	0

Source: Author

Table 5.2. Perceptions about the Impact of Technology on People's Lives and the Need for Technology (%)

	Yes	No	Somehow	Don't know
4.(a) Have computers transformed the place of work for you and the people you work with?	80	0	20	0
Should everyone learn computer skills?	90	10	0	0
Do you know people who think that computers take away jobs from people who would be secretaries or even clerks?	70	30	0	0
In your opinion, do workers need computers in their offices?	80	20	0	0
Should government buy all workers computers?	70	30	0	0
Should everyone have a computer and mobile phone?	60	40	0	0
Will a techno city change your life? (Malili Technopolis)	20	80	0	0
Do computers make your living standards better?	40	60	0	0
Do computers increase efficiency and output at work?	98	2	0	0
Do you as a teacher or government worker think that computers and the Internet make learning better?	80	20	0	0
Does Tom Mboya Labor College (In Kisumu) train workers how to use computers?	10	0	0	90
Should students in primary schools learn how to use computers and other mobile devices?	70	30	0	0
Do you worry that computers are not private and that anything that you write on it is recorded?	60	40	0	0
Do you worry that text messages (SMS) are never really erased?	60	40	0	
Do trade unions have rules and policies on using computers and mobile phones at work?	20	20	0	60
Does your trade union have a policy on online programs that are dangerous to children?	20	40	0	40
Can trade unions play a role in technological innovation?	40	40	0	20

Source: Author

money. A majority of those interviewed revealed that ICTs made it much easier for families to live in different towns and yet feel connected to each other. In addition, ICTs enhanced business transactions and helped add value to business enterprises.

The proliferation of ICTs in the workplace was also seen to be a positive change. Those interviewed felt that computers and, especially emails made work much easier. In addition, paper cabinets were seen as taking away too much space. Therefore, a majority felt that saving data and documents on electronic devices and in the cloud saved paper and money and was more accurate and efficient. In comparative terms, computers reduced much of what would be done by labor and meant that employees would suffer from less fatigue. Computers had also made it much easier for workers to find information (through Google) and read e-books that were previously hard to find. The downside of the new ICTs was the reported overuse of social media. Social media was criticized for wasting time and cutting into family time. The majority, 90 percent, had Facebook accounts and a smaller group had Twitter handles. These two social media sites, together with WhatsApp, were considered as possible disruptors at the workplace.

Responders also criticized online shopping during work hours. Also criticized was access to online pornography, especially during work hours. Responders felt also that the level of computer literacy in the Kenyan workforce was improving but still relatively low. Many of those interviewed expressed support for teaching children computer skills but there was skepticism that the government would provide computers for all schoolchildren. Union members were not critical of children playing video games because these exposed them to learning about modern technologies. Union members felt that ICTs were the way of the future and "everything" will be about computers and mobile phones.

These questions also probed the importance of ICTs and technology in general. Kenyan union members interviewed, by an overwhelming majority (80 percent), acknowledged that workers needed computers in their offices. Sixty percent preferred that the employer (mostly government) provide computers and mobile phones at the workplace. A vast majority reported using computers for social media and also official record keeping purposes. Still, there was concern that computers were known to infringe on privacy and that union members were concerned that government would monitor their communications (60 percent). Union members also reported that they did not know much about policies toward ICTs.

For teachers sampled the vast majority (80 percent) agreed that the Internet made learning better and easier. Members of KNUT regarded the proliferation of ICTs in education sector as a good thing. A majority touted the virtues of e-books, and search engines, especially for students wishing to learn more about a topic. The availability of the Internet was seen as an important step in enhancing education standards in the country. Seventy percent felt that primary school students should learn to use computers and other mobile devices. This support can be interpreted to mean that union members had, in principle, agreed with the overall goal of President Uhuru Kenyatta's Laptop project. But the survey did not specifically ask about the implementation process and other politics surrounding the project, which is the subject of chapter 4 in this volume.

Although official government policy documents like Vision 2030 had articulated the importance of ICTs in the country's development, there was not much information about the flagship ICT projects. For example, when asked if they had heard about the Malili Technopolis (Konza City) project, only 20 percent affirmed. This was a shocking result, considering that information about the proposed city was frequently in the news. Perhaps, this is a reflection of the mistrust of government and perceptions of corruption in numerous projects that have been promised to Kenyans. An alternative interpretation is that respondents probably saw the Malili Project as less of a priority and more of a white elephant.

The set of questions addressed whether or not respondents were using the available technologies. Fifty percent reported having received payments through M-PESA. The majority preferred to receive salaries through mobile money transfers (70 percent). The most revealing information was that a majority of union members had never taken any online class.

Table 5.3. Are Union Members Using Available ICTs? (%)

Questions	Yes	No	Don't understand
Have you ever checked your pay through computers? (Whether your salary has been deposited on your account or not)	20	70	10
Have you ever received an Imprest through M-PESA or other Mobile money?	10	60	
Have you ever taken a class online?	0	100	
Have you ever received a government service online? (Example, permit, license, tax return, or other certificate)	30	10	60
Have you ever made a work-related decision through the text message? (Example: called your colleagues on work matters)	90	10	
Do you read news items about KNUT or COTU through the Internet?	50	30	20
Have you ever checked KNUT's website?	10	70	20
Do you have a functional computer in your office?	60	40	

Source: Author

Still, e-government applications like paying taxes online and receiving government online services through the Internet were not reported. Overall, the levels of e-government services were quite low. This was in spite of the majority reporting that they had computers installed in their places of work (60 percent). Consistent with other surveys, the majority reported that they use the Internet for social media purposes and not for e-governance. Although social media took much time, responders used computers for data storage and simple packages like Word, MS Office Publisher, Excel, and other statistical packages for financial management.

Explaining the Results and the Question of Gender

In previous studies, (e.g., Liaw, 2002; Wong & Hanafi, 2007), it was found that male students had more positive perceptions of computers and ICTs than females in general. There is also the widely held belief that men users have more positive attitudes toward computers (Durndell & Thomson, 1997). However, learning opportunities for women around the world have changed the narrative. Still on a global stage, differences in ease of use, scope of usage, and access are still an issue, in part because there are discrepancies in IT courses offered to different gender (Broos, 2005). Davis (1989) argued convincingly that the perceived ease of use of computers had some influence on relative frequency in usage. In many instances, amounts of training on computer applications shaped perceptions of ease of use. It can be argued that female users had less exposure and, therefore, much higher levels of anxiety in making use of new ICTs, especially computers (Jackson et al., 2001; Kay, 2006; Whitley, 1997; Woodfield, 2000).

Not surprisingly, in many countries, corrective measures are part of the development agendas. For instance, in Malaysia, Vision 2020 privileges Smart School Policy with a heavy infusion of information technology education in educations for all. In Malaysia, all secondary schools have a well-equipped computer laboratory and students are taught IT applications. The results in Malaysia have changed the access and usage of IT products in that country, illustrating that policy matters.

Gender policies have an impact on attitudes of female or male teachers toward IT when other variables are accounted for (Lee, 2003). Like elsewhere, attitudes of those who have taken computer and IT-related courses change their perspectives about ICTs in general and are more accepting of technology (Bhattacherjee & Premkumar, 2004). In Africa, much like in the developed world, acceptability of ICTs in education is a function of the training and competence of teachers and officials in the education sector (Derbyshire, 2003; Mudasiru & Modupe, 2011). Empowering teachers and learners is therefore an important piece of the puzzle that explains the acceptance of ICTs in education and society in general. The point is that simply supplying schools with laptops and other ICT products is not sufficient; their effective use is a function of a competent education system. Teachers must have not only the competence but the right attitudes toward ICTs (Kadel, 2005). Positive attitudes by those in the learning communities are strongly associated with the interest on the part of teachers and officials in the education sector.

The larger number of women in the sample shows remarkable expansion of girls' education in the country. Reports also indicate that Kenya's women score above global average in adoption and use of mobile telephone systems (Mutegi, 2015). According to a Groupe Speciale Mobile Association (GSMA) report, *Bridging the Gender Gap: Mobile Access and Usage in Low and Middle Income Countries*, globally, over 1.7 billion females in developing countries do not own mobile phones. Women were also, on the average, 14 percent less likely to own mobile phones than men, which created a huge gap in the usage of different applications and exacerbated the digital divide. Although the gender gaps exist, women were making progress and were using phones for basic services.

Kenyan women had overcome many barriers and were now among the best-placed African nations in terms of gender equality, ranking at 37 out of 142 countries surveyed (GSMA, 2015). However, 23 percent of poor women in Kenya were reported to have never sent any SMS, signifying that the overall penetration of ICTs in the country was still a work-in-progress (GSMA 2015, p. 28). Forty-two percent of women used Facebook via mobile phones. At the same time, fewer women than men used Twitter (20 percent) through mobile phones in Kenya (GSMA, 2015, p. 28). A study by the World Wide Web Foundation (2015) reported that few women who use the Internet leveraged the online platforms for economic empowerment.

Globally, women owned fewer mobile phones than men, making it much harder for them to participate in ICT-driven economic activities. For Kenya, the gender gap was relatively small, at 7 percent, which meant that women were a key player in the country's use of M-PESA applications. Mutegi (2015) reported that "half of the women in Kenya who owned or borrowed a mobile phone declared they had received money and topped up credit through mobile" facilities. Women in Kenya were frequent users of M-PESA, but they are more receivers than senders (Mutagi, 2015). Women also used mobile phones for Internet access and SMS communications at rates similar to Kenyan men (89 percent women versus 91 percent men) (Mutegi, 2015).

Consistent with the survey of union members, women utilized mobile phones to communicate with relatives and friends. This discovery is not unusual but follows patterns found in most countries (Teo, 2001). And consistent with similar surveys on mobile technology penetration, women experienced frustration because of the high costs of mobile telephones and limited access to electricity. Moreover, issues of technical literacy, and network quality, discussed in the survey above, were also reported in the GSMA study.

General Attitudes toward E-Government

Attitudes toward e-government, telemedicine, virtual currencies like M-PESA and mobile phone applications are probably associated with individual union members' perceptions of ICTs. A union member perceives a particular technological application to be helpful depending on proximity issues. If they have had a good experience with any of the applications, the member generally appreciates the use of that particular technological device. One the other hand, a union member will view a particular application in abstract terms, if they have never had the opportunity to make effective use of the technology. These arguments are probably similar to theoretical frameworks developed by those who study social psychology and apply it to market research.

Proximity is, in part, a function of affordability. Although at least 60 percent of Kenyans have access to the Internet, it is well recognized that services are out of reach for most teachers and low-wage workers. According to the International Telecommunication Union (ITU) figures, Kenya ranked 146 out of 165 in affordability of broadband Internet services (ITU, 2014). ITU statistics report that Kenyans use up to 45 percent of their average monthly disposable income in order to use broadband connectivity. The idea of data bundles promoted by companies like Safaricom appears attractive but the average charges, ranging from KSh. 3,000 to KSh 5,000 per month, are way out of the reach of ordinary Kenyans. Just as a case in point, consider that a day watchman's (security guard's) monthly salary in Nairobi, Mombasa, and Kisumu is just around KSh. 9,000. Data bundle allows users of mobile phones to access the Internet through lower rates. By comparison, Ugandans pay up to 32 percent of their average incomes on broadband Internet, which places it at number 139 on the ITU rankings for 2014. Kenyans spend about 7.5 percent of their average incomes for data bundles per month, placing Kenya at number 111 out of 150 surveyed economies (ITU, 2014). According to the United Nations (UN) Broadband Commission standards, countries should spend far less on broadband availability; roughly 5 percent of incomes should go to broadband costs. Thus, high costs and poor content development are major hindrances to the country's match to a mature information society. The survey confirmed that affordability is an issue for union members.

As mentioned, affordability is not the sole factor limiting ICT usage. Both e-government and e-commerce depend on speed of the Internet and content of materials presented. And whether an individual purchases a product is frequently associated with how well it is presented through a host of communication devices. The television, newspapers, and radios can frame a particular technological device in a manner that persuades consumers to purchase it. Individuals in the labor unions are much like other consumers of ICT products and services. They choose tablets over laptops depending on how these devices are presented in popular media discourses. One with experience using tablets will tout the advantages of similar devices and one who has had a lousy experience will most likely view the devices in less glowing terms. The same mindset applies to ICT applications in different job settings.

The time it takes for workers to learn particular programs and applications was found to be a key determinant of the favorability of making use of the particular technology. Therefore, knowledge about ICTs is crucial in leveraging new technologies to work situations. Another driver of attitudes toward ICTs is the risk perception, frequently associated with overuse of applications such as mobile phones or even the Internet. The debate as to whether mobile phone emit some form of radiation or whether using computers has hazards are subjects for the medically inclined scholars of workplace health and safety concerns. But there is the risk factor that often attracts public commentary and endless debates.

At a much wider scale, the Internet is seen as an instrument of good and evil. If a union member perceives it to be more of the latter, then increased use of online resources is considered as less desirable than if the experience with technology yields positive outcomes. The Internet is home to millions of websites considered to promote cultural decadence and immorality. In that case, the more a member has access to some of the adult links, the greater the persuasion of its disruptive contents. But the conclusions are entirely subjective and not uniformly embraced by union members. The larger point is that ICTs that are considered risky for workplace tranquility and a safe environment, the less likely that those particular applications are welcome within the larger body of the trade unions. A most important variable shaping union member attitudes toward ICTs is the cultural space they occupy. By cultural space, one might refer to the cultural worldviews toward ICTs. ICTs lend themselves to scrutiny, especially because globalization through ICTs has weakened, rather than strengthened, the position of low-wage workers in African countries.

Unions respond to applications of ICTs and other technologies by adopting featherbedding practices. Featherbedding can be defined as "a labor working rule which causes the firm to hire more labor units of a particular type than it would at the existing wage, assuming technology and social norms to be given" (Weinstein, 1965, p. 45). Unions impose the working rules as a result of potential unemployment (Weinstein, 1965, p. 54). These are practices meant to ensure a level of stability and equilibrium in the labor markets. Another motivation is minimization of the insecurity of incomes. More important, unions desire to maintain and increase members' wage incomes and employment opportunities by imposing a variety of make-work rules and policies on employer units (Simler, 1965, p. 55).

The assumptions of featherbedding will vary according to the industry. In most of sub-Saharan Africa, where government jobs are frequently the main or major monopolies, the practices are based on assumptions of guaranteed wages. Where competition is emerging, the shape and form of featherbedding can be reconfigured. Likewise, the low level of capitalization of state-owned enterprises and other key firms complicates the shape and form of featherbedding. Many employers hire a good number of unskilled workers to serve as "messengers," receptionists, tearoom cleaners, and clerks. The foregoing assumption is, therefore, closer to the alternative view that featherbedding "is the practice of requiring the employment of person whose labor is not needed . . . resulting from the feeling that a worker has vested interest in his/her job" (Berg & Kuhn, 1962).

One interpretation is that Kenya and other African countries have high levels of unemployment and unions are not a disinterested component of the political patronage and spoils systems that come with the seizure of political power through ethnic alliances. Therefore, in the case of Kenya, unions will be involved in featherbedding practices as a part of the complex nature of securing jobs for factions that union leaders are part of. Workers will then act to expand patronage-based employment. This method is wasteful but politically expedient, since in Kenya, the public sector is the default source of formal employment.

Where technological change is seen as threatening, employees adopt a self-interested attitude and work to frustrate efforts to introduce new technologies. When computers were introduced in the workplace, civil servants and especially those with secretarial jobs regarded computers are threatening, mostly because they had to learn new skills to keep their jobs. Later, there was much consensus that introduction of computers eliminated some jobs but created more. Much like software, the Internet initially caused anxiety but quickly became the norm. Evidently, history is replete with examples of displacement of workers occasioned by introduction of new information technologies. In the 1970s, when spreadsheets were introduced, some firms reduced employees in occupations like account clerks and bookkeepers (Goldstein, 2015). At the same time, firms reported increased demand for accountants, meaning that the introduction of spreadsheets required employees to be retrained and acquire new skills. Therefore, members of unions should be educated to continuously upgrade their skills and not wait to be displaced by new technologies.

CONCLUSIONS

Much of the discourse on union members' attitudes toward ICTs has been devoted to an examination and validation of uses of various applications in daily life activities. To identify the circumstances and commitment of union members to increased uses of ICTs, similar studies on attitudes are needed for other African countries. African countries need to have a sense of the implications of the proliferation of ICTs on workplace behaviors and, especially the instrumentality of new devices for worker participation in shared governance and quality-of-life enhancements. Knowing union attitudes provides a window for management to improve on relations with workers, especially in the context of promoting national development. The scope of the study was limited by the small sample size and should be regarded as a first look at the attitudes of a selected group of unionists. Perhaps case studies that target, for example, COTU (K) affiliates may shed further light on the big questions of potential for ICTs to substitute much of the labor in some of the old industries. Important COTU affiliates that would be of interest include the Banking, Insurance and Finance Union, Tailors and Textile Workers Union, Kenya Union of Domestic, Hotels, Educational Institutions, Hospitals, and Allied Workers, Communications Workers Union, Kenya Local Government Workers' Union, and the Dock Workers Union, among others. Notably, leaders in these COTU affiliates have focused more on collective bargaining agreements (CBAs), job security, leveraging unions to provide welfare services such as legal assistance, financial aid, and housing for members, and training for members. Evidently, there has been a marked lack of robust ICT training, even where human resource development initiatives are a strong element in union benefits. Investments in training on the role of ICTs in the new economy is a necessary component of increasing awareness of the potential of ICTs in society and must be supported by COTU and KNUT as the leaders in the trade union movement.

Granted, union members from the data sources considered were asked limited attitude questions; their observations offer consistency of results but data adjustments can be made in future studies. From the emerging and preliminary evidence, the biggest influence on day-to-day activities for the average member of society and union members is the mobile telephone. Mobile phones, computers, and tablets are now a common feature in Kenyan society. The advantage of the mobile phone is that people have them all the time. And at work, smartphones bring benefits such as reference databases and are an important tool for ease of communication, especially for purposes of e-governance and national development. However, evidence also confirms the existence of digital exclusion in organizations stemming from inadequate broadband desktop capabilities. Yet, in most instances, everyday experiences with ICTs influence overall computer attitude statements.

Union member expectations are shaped by their experiences with various banking systems. Interactions, content, and features of digital devices also help them make decisions about which products to use. Also, interactions with trusted friends and relatives and peers are important influencers regarding which ICT devices to trust and adopt for both work and social purposes. Union members are also citizens and must engage government, especially in matters of participation in ICT policy development. This is important because government regulation does provide structure that determines which ICTs are imported into the country and the nature of business evolution. Business responds to customer needs and therefore business also has a role in shaping attitudes toward the ICTs adopted.

The missing link in this discourse is the relative failure of the e-government and e-governance models among unions and affiliated organizations. It is well known that in developed countries, email is the most utilized channel for communications within organizations. One would think the expansion of Internet infrastructures would have resulted in greater embrace of digitalized government in Kenya. That is not the case. As the research indicates, the shift to a mature e-government system takes time, and governments have to set aside funds to maintain the system even as new forms of data storage and retrieval emerge. In particular, cloud computing, which may be a valuable instrument for centralization of work management and storage of data for shared governance, is remarkably underutilized. And it is not an idea that is appealing to elements of the civil service prone to massive corruption. However, the main reason why cloud computing is weak in local and county governments is the lack of awareness and competence within the leadership cadre.

Competence will entail increasing resources for data analytics and expanding awareness, eradicating silo mentality among different ministries. Information has to be shared interdepartmentally and among different programs with similar interests. For example, traffic congestion in Nairobi may benefit from data from ministries such as Lands and Physical Planning, Transportation, Housing, and Urban Development and various police departments. Siloing in ministries, such as Lands, contributes to loss of information and risks for corruption. Integrating new technologies requires a change in the mind-set of the administrative class. Eradication of the silo mentality will go a long way in inculcating the culture of data analytics and promote good governance in general. This can be possible with increased attention and changes in attitudes toward ICTs. Union members, like other workers, will need twenty-first-century skills, which are largely associated with ICTs. The goal for unions is to encourage training in ICTs, widely defined. And with the speed at which technologies are changing society, training programs must be rolled out with a sense of urgency. As studies on power indicate, the ability to acquire intangibles such as knowledge and technology and information devices that hold crucial data is an important asset for any organization seeking to extend its influence beyond mandated authority. Still, union members have to be allowed to learn new applications at their own pace. Unions must encourage members to share experiences about interactions with new technologies and also be able to provide feedback to the leadership when ICTs cause difficulties in productivity and workplace management.

In sum, this analysis shows that characteristics of union members and structural variables influence how best they absorb and use ICTs, communicate with each other, and conduct daily transactions. There is evidence that structural issues, especially weak computer Internet systems (lack of continuous access), appear to consistently disadvantage union members from exploiting the full potential of ICTs. Increased availability of mobile phones has however changed the nation's communication landscape. Although computing literacy has improved, the rise of digital citizens required for greater union activism is a work in progress. As theory suggests, ICTs do not necessarily change power structures at both organizational and national levels. It is therefore reasonable to assume greater absorption of ICTs at personal and organizational levels will lead to new visions of digital democracy. ICTs offer additional space for union participation in the new economy, beginning with relevant attitudinal changes.

SIX

Productivity Discourses, Information Technology, and Unions

INTRODUCTION

Organizations are established to achieve specific missions and goals, which may be services and/or products within a time frame. Human resources are a key element in the production of goods and services. To achieve declared goals, people in organizations must be productive. Unions traditionally engage employers in discussions about productivity. Trade unions and their supporters have continued to demand better pay for working people. In many ways, union leaders in Kenya have been pragmatic and understood they cannot, on their own, overturn the capitalist system and transfer ownership of the means of production to workers.

Still, union leaders do not see themselves as outsiders in the often supercharged identity politics that characterizes Kenya's history. As such, ideological arguments revolving around class are minimized. One common feature of national politics is that union leaders celebrate when political elites raise minimum wages and secure legislation and administrative directives that increase employee benefits such as medical care, housing, and commuter allowances. By working through existing structures, union leaders in Kenya have opted to, for the most part, enter into collective bargaining agreements with their adversaries, namely government leaders and industry bosses or employers with whom they have to maintain communication channels. To ensure successful labor-management relationships, unions have to keep abreast of technological advances that support efforts to improve productivity, which in many instances is the primary area of focus for employers. Chapter 5 presents an elaborate discussion and description of productivity discourses in Kenyan public management systems highlighting the special role of ICTs.

Common sense tells us that productivity discourses have been around for a long time. The reality is that organizations often put in place systems to encourage greater productivity without making a big deal about it. In other words, organizational leaders assumed that simple gestures such as participatory management approaches, improving worker's conditions of work, and offering various rewards passed as commonsense strategies for organizational sustenance. And because productivity was even difficult to define and measure, scholars of emerging labor-rich African societies paid very little attention to the nitty-gritty elements of the interaction of labor and new technologies.

The evolution of public productivity in African countries can be traced to the movements for clean government, especially the anti-corruption strategies that sought to end political patronage and incompetence. For most of sub-Saharan Africa, the emergence of the civil service was associated with the discourse and implementation of Africanization, which was meant to provide jobs to Africans (representativeness) and to replace departing colonial administrators.

Colonial administrators did little to encourage an inclusive merit-based civil service for African natives. In colonial times, the British administrative class developed recruitment and selection criteria for themselves. This tradition was not incorporated in its "indirect rule" administrative strategies in colonial Africa (Otenyo, 1998, p. 8). In the mid-1960s, the African ruling elite hurriedly pursued Africanization for political reasons. The ensuing search for professionalism was conducted in the spirit of nationalism. Namely, the early careerists wanted to demonstrate that Africans were ready to manage their own affairs.

Amishadai L. Adu, a pioneer in studies of African civil service, commented that the colonial civil service valued efficiency of services and devotion to duty (Adu, 1965, p. 13). The early careerists took pride in civil service traditions, but soon patronage and corruption of the 1970s turned the situation worse. The philosophy of modern management changed to privilege politics at the expense of competence and performance. There is general consensus that after independence, the civil service in African countries deemphasized efficiency as a core value to be attained (Hailey, 1942 p. 252–6; Olowu 1987).

Arguably, the most criticized underperformers were the strategically important State Owned Enterprises (SOE) or parastatals. Solomon Kagwe (1986) wrote:

> The performance of public enterprises, however, did not correspond to expectations and the anticipated growth in most cases did not occur. Further, despite the fact that development plans that were prepared were highly sophisticated in terms of economic model building and

> statistical database, they were not implemented. The failure to implement these plans was blamed not on plans themselves but on administrative inadequacies and this diagnosis led to greater emphasis being given to questions of implementation and administration of development plans. (p. 22)

Performance Measurements

The failure of SOEs to implement performance measures and contracts cause much strife in African administration. As a result, the World Bank and other donor agencies began demanding changes in governance of these institutions, including the parent government ministries. Reformers also called for the introduction of Western-style management practices like Management by Objectives (MBO) and Performance Evaluation and Review Techniques (PERT). In Kenya, the Ndegwa Commission called for the introduction of MBO techniques, thereby requiring that government ministries set clear and precise objectives for each manager (Ndegwa, 1971, p. 89). The manager would also meet goals set in an agreed-upon time frame. In addition, MBO techniques required establishment of standards of performance and job improvement plans. The World Bank Report of 1984 was an important statement on energizing the productivity and governance debates. Its objective was to promote good governance, meaning efficiency, less corruption, and an end to cronyism.

Later on, as the neoliberal agenda took root, the emphasis shifted to the idea of privatization of public services, as a means to raise funds to pay debts and also promote efficiency, strongly associated with the private sectors. After 1990, the privatization and cost-sharing ideology permeated the administrative centers. Some authors saw the emerging order as a component of liberation management, which emphasized higher and results-oriented performance.

At the global level, expert observers note that the search for greater productivity is a major facet in the global public management agenda (Kettl, 2005). Thus, for example, in the United States, the Government Performance and Results Act of 1993 was a manifestation of this movement toward accountability and increased productivity. Perhaps, associated with the emergent New Public Management (NPM) approach, the goal was to enhance service delivery through downsizing and increased use of technologies.

NPM was widely embraced in Great Britain and the Commonwealth. Permutations of performance measurements were encouraged in the United States, as well. President Bill Clinton promoted a National Performance Review Agenda that gave emphasis to productivity. His successor, President George W. Bush, instituted the President's Management Agenda (PMA) through which the government would promote e-government and uses of ICTs and launch outsourcing initiatives. One would argue that the search for performance measurements and the pivot toward higher productivity is not unrelated to the greater advances in new communication and information technologies (ICTs). Later in 2004, President George W. Bush put forward the Program Assessment Rating Tool (PART) that was intended to continuously evaluate the performance of federal programs. PART was a scorecard in which failing programs would be pruned and successful ones rewarded.

Recognition of the importance of productivity in the modern workforce was described in Peter Drucker's (1994) work on postcapitalist society. Drucker saw productivity as a challenge that faced the post-capitalist society as it moved toward a knowledge society (Drucker, 1994, p. 83). For most societies, with the rise in the knowledge-based services, the productivity of knowledge workers was an important component of the productivity of society as a whole. Drucker argued that the lowest levels of productivity were in government employment (p. 84). For Drucker (1994), the low productivity in government was a huge issue because government employees were also the largest component of workers in the service industry.

In developing countries, especially in Africa, where the bulk of formal employment is in the government sector, raising productivity must be a key component of increasing development. Unless African societies learned how to increase productivity in the public sector, the countries would continue to face stagnation and there should be no expectation that real incomes would be increased. In many instances, in both Africa and the developed world, the use of technologies was touted as a modernization strategy. As Drucker put it, the new information technology underlies the strenuous efforts of corporations to "reengineer." Organizations that want to be more productive are also expected to be those that are willing to learn. This is the lesson for African bureaucracies. Reforms that introduce new ways of doing business are not just for modernization purposes. Productivity in the workplace demands that employees seek self-improvement, while managers reengineer work structures to eliminate areas that lead to less productivity.

Ruling elites have to minimize the organizational politics and power components of new technologies. As is speculated, in Kenya, new technologies also fulfilled the control function for the political elite, who sought greater control of day-to-day administration especially of strategic agencies like the Ports Authority, strategic parastatals, and vital departments of the Office of the President. In implementing changes, the Office of the President, for example, sought tools for shifting power to those allied to its core interests. Officers with affiliation to the ruling party were most likely to receive the most support for their new technologies, including the supply of mobile telephones.

Public service reformers, especially those associated with the World Bank and IMF, have long advocated for accountability in Kenya's public service. Governments were urged to institute measures that increase productivity and to encourage performance contracts. In many instances, the process has been more symbolic than meaningful because suitable metrics have not been designed or made useful. Injecting performance and productivity measures was also associated with convincing donors, civil society, and interested journalists that African bureaucrats were doing their jobs as prescribed in law and public policy. These organizations are crucial partners in the problem-solving networks for advancing the cause of greater productivity in society.

Although, as Itika (2011) points out, "productivity is an indicator of how best resources are utilized in organizations," managers must know what they are measuring (p. 32). Although as Peters (2001, p. 125) suggests, performance is linked to service quality, even assessing management capabilities and organizational achievements can be challenging if budgets don't allow it. Managers in civil service positions often complain of poor budgetary allocations and late disbursement of allocated funds, which weakens their ability to measure contract performances. Productivity bargaining is not a strong forte of the trade union managers either. One reason is that perfect measuring devices are absent for the most part (Kirsh, 1964 p. 127). Collective bargaining aims to attain industrial peace, but the challenge of linking wages to productivity weighted upon accurate scales and statistical perfection is not easy to realize. Not surprising, productivity measures are rare in economies with high unemployment.

Thus, for instance, negotiations, especially between KNUT and the Teachers Service Commission (TSC) and Ministry of Education, are mostly about salaries and benefits (allowances). The government as an employer has not shown any skillful negotiations in matters of work measurement, which include efforts of individual teachers who face different hardships (fatigue and contingencies) at work. As a result, many a union, including Universities Academic Staff Unions (UASU) has failed to show why university teachers should be paid a uniform salary across the different public university systems in the country. Productivity agreements must describe work measurements to make sense of the tasks associated with work and employment. It is foolish to assume that work measurements are applicable in all job situations and categories.

Evidence suggests that in most cases where work measurement is possible, managers in national civil service seemed to have no clue as to what to measure. Most did not even have a record of ministry assets and resources. The problem was also present in local governments, which rarely used performance data for management. Governments across the board (municipalities, parastatals, schools, hospitals) did not even keep records on solid waste, absenteeism, ghost workers, and so on. Evidence of this gross managerial failure can be seen in unending efforts to count numbers of ghost workers. In the case of Kenya, more than 12,500 fictitious names were discovered after President Uhuru Kenyatta ordered biometric registration of civil servants in September 2014. The 12,500 "ghost workers" were subsequently struck from the payroll (BBC, 2014). For decades, Kenya's administrative state failed to utilize information systems that could gather and produce data crucial for human resources and productivity decisions. Furthermore, as was initiated in advanced economies, simple electronic performance monitoring devices could have, with newer artificial intelligence devices, been put to use. As Angel (1989) and Edwards (1990) demonstrated, computer-mediated technology in support of performance measurement has been around for a long while.

Perhaps, human resource information systems (HRIS) are not well-developed or understood in Kenya. HRIS are used for the acquisition, storage, manipulation, analysis, retrieval, and distribution of information about human resources (Tannenbaum, 1990). Data can be used to support administrative decisions and to store employee records electronically. The systems are good tools for forecasting, analyzing, and supporting decisions such as merit pay, benefits, productivity, and retirement issues. In developed regions like the UK, client server architecture, intranets, workflow, and integrated GroupWare are terms that are well known in human resource circles (Ball, 2001, p. 677).

Today, the market for affordable HRIS software has grown. To use HRIS, IT skills must be present in organizations. It also means that mangers have to develop strategic thinking to match organizational needs. Evidence suggests that that is where authorities in developing countries go wrong. Systemic weaknesses are not only evident in personnel and budgetary processes. Decision making is poorly managed and lacking in sophistication in all areas of service delivery.

Small wonder, then that productivity improvement decisions for delivery of public services was lacking, most likely due to lack of enthusiasm on the part of the managers. For instance, Geographic Information System (GIS) mapping technologies were unheard of in most regional districts and local governments. The issue of nonexistent ghost workers became a contentious issue only after the Wage Bill grew out of proportion and the Office of the President ordered a head count in 2014. Salaries, it would appear, were the major metric that political leaders understood and talked about. Productivity-based metrics were decidedly a back-burner issue.

Kenya and other African countries rarely used performance measures to know which service providers outperformed their peers. So, for example, in Kenya, it is not known whether Nakuru Municipality garbage collection and sanitation management outperformed that in the cities of Kisumu or Eldoret.

At the highest level of government, President Kibaki appeared to want to connect productivity to performance metrics and rewards. In April 2010, when officiating at a function in which results of previous performance contracts were announced at the Kenyatta International Conference Center, he remarked:

> I wish to clearly indicate that implementation of performance contracts is not a selective requirement. This goes for all public institutions without exception. We must therefore place punitive punishment for those who fail to implement the program. (Kibaki, 2010)

On the same occasion, Kibaki called for performance-merit based pay structures in the national public service bureaucracy. "I would, therefore, like to see institutions, particularly the Public Service Commission of Kenya, introducing flexibility in recruitment and promotions based on demonstrated merit not just the years served" (Kibaki, 2010). But his words were not matched with actions. Even after his successor, Uhuru Kenyatta, became president performance contracts remained "unactionable" instruments of symbolic political leadership and not management.

To a large degree, the performance contracts signed between ministry and parastatal chiefs can only make sense if these result in greater accountability. In the information age, there is the expectation that ministries keep track and act on the existing web-use measures. Most websites track numbers of people visiting the sites. Higher-order measures for information systems should go beyond that and include measures on security breaches, production ratios, and calls-for-help indicators.

Kenya's experience may be epitomized in the security field. Statistics and reporting can show the percentage of fires extinguished, losses, response times, incidents per on-duty and emergency staff, response times, and effectiveness in tracking down terrorists, and safety education and training within the law enforcement academy.

Since 2013, the country's security situation deteriorated following terrorist mass shootings. Even though government heads had signed performance contracts, the high rates of unresolved murders and successful terrorist attacks provided ample evidence of poor performance. But it took political pressure to force the national police chief's resignation. Opposition politicians used metrics to agitate for change in security management. The government also responded by changing the laws of the land, thereby shifting the blame to the legislative branch rather than the failed implementation strategies of the executive. The executive has not been known to compile data upon which actions are pegged. Kenya's performance measurements of "mini movement" (evidenced in rudimentary performance contracts) is virtually absent in the local and county administrations. For the most part, the devolved units have observably been riddled with politics and incompetence.

Lack of Productivity Collective Bargaining

Worldwide, the prevailing economic conditions have worked to weaken labor and probably done much to influence resurgence in concession bargaining and productivity bargaining practices (Berman, Bowman, West, & Van Wart, 2016, p. 470). Productivity bargaining is associated with collective bargaining agreements (CBA) in which there are stipulations concerning work rules and practices with goals of achieving increased productivity (Horton, 1976, p. 409). This implies that union demands for worker gains are reciprocated through had work and attainment of increased outputs. Judging from a May 1, 2015, speech by President Uhuru Kenyatta, there seems to be indication that the government wanted labor unions to embrace productivity bargaining more enthusiastically. President Kenyatta raised the minimum wage by 12 percent but justified it in terms of productivity. Kenyatta remarked, "Last year we did not increase the minimum wage because we should work first. Today, we have increased the minimum wage because we have earned it" (PSCU, 2015).

Productivity bargaining was also in the news after KUPPET and KNUT argued for increased salaries at the Employment and Labor Relation's Court based on the need to match pay to inflation. Teachers' unions disputed productivity bargaining agreements, terming them as a tactic "to delay settlement of their rewards" (Wanzala, 2015a). On the other hand, the Ministry of Education and Teachers' Service Commission (TSC) announced the intention to peg teachers' pay to performance. Under the New National Education Sector Plan (NESP) proposals, teachers were required to teach a specific number of classes and lessons. The plan also sensitizes the idea of quality education for all students. The move toward productivity bargaining has been touted in the Education for All Movement, which recognized the need for reducing absenteeism and incompetence within the teaching fraternity, globally. Kenya has bought into this plan and sought to make it a part of collective bargaining, especially as concerns basic education (Wanzala, 2015a). In some instances, it is referred to as the Teacher Performance Appraisal and Development (TPAD) strategy. Under TPAD, appraisal of teachers would be based not only on time management, teacher safety and conduct, and mastery of professional knowledge but on innovative practices. These would entail applications of ICTs in teaching and student activities.

In 2015, the TSC began to sensitize its employees toward utilizing performance appraisal systems that would form the basis for promotions and demotion. The TSC warned "lazy" teachers they would not be promoted and that performance appraisals would measure knowledge, content, engagement, and professionalism. With funding from the British Council, TSC launched a pilot Teacher Performance and Integrity Program (TPIP) in which absentee teachers would also be subjected to sanctions. The programs were initially rolled out in Kitui, Kwale, Kisumu, Samburu, Uasin Gishu, and Nyeri counties (Oduor, 2015a). School head teachers supported the idea of job evaluations and performance-based promotions, thereby going against both KNUT and KUPPET (Nyassy & Gicobi, 2015).

The vigorous introduction of performance-based promotions is in direct contrast to COTU's prevailing belief that wage increases should be pegged to cost-of-living indexes and the poor working conditions that most union members are subjected to. To illustrate, during Labor Day 2016 festivities, COTU Secretary General Francis Atwoli dramatized his position by challenging the leadership of the Federation of Kenya Employers (FKE) to substantiate their own productivity at work. He argued that there was no formula in place to measure productivity and "the government has no way of measuring productivity so FKE cannot pretend to know how to do it" (Mutambo, 2016). Atwoli added; "This language of productivity in Kenya cannot work. In Africa, it is only in South Africa where they have some semblance of productivity" (quoted in Mutambo, 2016). The differences in perspectives can be attributed to the lack of agreed-upon performance measurement systems in Kenya and other African countries where patronage systems are still strong. In addition, most public organizations in Kenya have no strategic plans to invest in performance management technologies. Even though multinational corporations like IBM have some presence in Kenya, absorption of software such as IBM performance management solutions, which may address some of the productivity measurement concerns, are not officially embraced in most organizations at national and county levels. Remarkably also, trade unions have not themselves been keen to transform their structures and performance measurement practices to be economically successful as sustainable organizations.

Regardless of the challenges of measurement as outlined in Horton's (1976) work, political executives and managers from development partners now expect unions to give back to society more value by way of greater efficiency and productivity. As a result, discourses of performance contracting have proliferated. Importantly, observations reveal that Kenyan trade unions have not been at the forefront of the drive for performance measurements in the vocal local governments and teaching professions that have huge membership bases. Instead, the primary concern is to agitate for allowances and pay raises. As an example of the probable discomfort with performance contracts, secondary school head teachers, many of whom were unionized, demanded a pay increase of "more than 100 percent as a condition for their signing performance contracts" (Ngare, 2008). However, there are no studies or reviews to show the differences across county services to demonstrate that performance contracts and reporting led to higher efficiencies and effectiveness in service delivery. As a result, the payoff in service measurements that underscores the contract processes remains to be seen.

Another example of weakness in Kenya's collective bargaining system is the underdevelopment of the productivity bargaining approach. In the productivity approach, management would offer salary increases conditionally. For example, management would request unions to change work rules and practices and adopt those that increase productivity and quality of products and services. In the case of teachers' unions, it would be expected that the Teachers' Service Commission (TSC) would demand from KNUT to use practices that result in good teaching and improved outcomes from the school systems. When it became apparent that Kenya's education system was producing graduates with questionable skills and competencies, the unions should have taken the initiative to work jointly with the Ministry of Education, TSC, and other stakeholders to establish action teams and plans that would find ways of increasing productivity and quality of services offered. As far as records show, this was not the case.

Guidelines on productivity bargaining set up by KNUT typically refer to inflationary trends. While the increase in cost of living is important, it is essential that workers are aware of the need to be more productive. KNUT, KUPPET, and other unions in the teaching profession have stayed away from productivity bargaining that demands teachers account for the performance of schools not only in national standardized examinations but also by the impact of their teaching and community service.

Although education scholar Ishmael Munene (2014) observed that collective bargaining agreements in the country's university system were helpful in helping "cushion union members from the deleterious effects of inflation," he disclosed members considered merit-based systems as an "anathema" (p. 21). A one-size-fits-all approach to managing pay levels seems to be the prevailing norm for most trade occupations.

One may argue that trade unions have not necessarily refused to be a part of productivity bargaining that hold members accountable. The issue of pay and compensation in Kenya's public service is too politicized to the extent that the principles of pay equity are riddled with corruption. Yet, for example, teachers recognize that organizations like the Teachers Service Commission (TSC) and the Salaries and Remuneration Commission (SRC) must first be accountable themselves before fronting their cost-saving allowance withdrawal, salary delays and slashing, and biased promotion agendas. Unions, for example, opposed the SRC bid to harmonize salaries of teachers with those of the members of the civil service placed in government ministries.

Therefore, the focus of performance measurement still remains at the rhetorical level, whereby politicians and head of administrative units continue to exhort officials to effectively deliver services to the people. As far as one can observe, Kenya's administrative process has failed to match the "efficiency rhetoric" to use measurable "outcome measures." While the country's GDP grew, the ranks of the dispossessed and poor rose. Revised GDP per capita statistics indicated a rise from $994 to $1,256, meaning that Kenya had joined the lower Middle Income Countries bracket (Munda, 2014; World Bank, 2014). The rise in GDP denotes output of goods and services grew to make the country the ninth "richest" country in Africa. The country ranks fourth after Nigeria, South Africa, and Angola as the fourth largest economy in sub-Saharan Africa (BBC, 2014). The World Bank considers Sudan a sub-Saharan country, which would place Kenya at number five (World Bank, 2014).

A Kenya Institute for Public Policy and Research Analysis (KIPPRA) study showed that more than 21.5 million Kenyans lived in poverty (*Daily Nation*, 2014). The figures for rural poverty necessitate a national conversation, especially in view of failure to achieve the Anti-Poverty Millennium Development (MDGs) goals. Anti-poverty strategies included participation and strengthening of all stakeholders in the country's production of goods and services. In addition, the state's role in setting minimum wages and price controls, subsidizing education, and guaranteeing public sector employment were efforts that unions supported.

Not all of the prescribed policies are likely to be helpful in the long run. Economic critics regard low-wage and low-labor economies to be less likely competitive. Low-wage countries are mostly associated with less industrialization and lower productivity. In other words, to compete as a low-wage, low-labor-cost economy causes a productivity gap. Brown and Walsh (1991) made that observation with reference to Britain. Most likely, the same principle applies to Kenya and other low-wage African economies. Argued differently, low-wage economies are unlikely to advance in overall productivity.

In addition to the low-wage predicament, the expansion of the gap between rich and poor working classes, government's policy-monitoring capacity required serious human capital development. Capacity building in data-driven service-monitoring are likely to support existing efforts aimed at achieving growth with development. Information systems, which generate data about productivity in all sectors, provide crucial support for managerial and executive decision making. The implication of the growth in GDP is that productivity in certain sectors may have improved, but at the expense of quality of life and human development. And since a nation's output is a function of its productive enterprises, workers and their unions are a part of this growth.

Scientific Management, Productivity, and Motivation

The principal idea in productivity discourses is that managers and workers should work together to increase productivity. Perhaps in some ways this stems from scientific management and Frederick W. Taylor's search for the "best practices" that would lead to a win-win situation between employers and employees. Taylorism was about maximization of efficiency, especially among the low-level blue-collar workers. Taylor thought that management lacked information about how much work was generated by each worker and therefore did not understand each worker's limits. Therefore, he called for research to determine the productive capacity of each worker, which led to the standardization of operations, tools, and equipment. Overall, scientific management, as one of the key twentieth-century philosophies, aimed at maximizing employee productivity (Thite & Kavanagh, 2009, p. 7). Today, we see standardization in tools such as keyboards on computers.

One of the flaws of Taylorism was that work was rewarded through increased pay and sanctioned by threats of dismissal. He saw workers as appendages to machines and favored individualist solutions rather than group and therefore union pressures. Although Taylor's philosophy is still visible in different work settings, other perspectives on best ways to improve productivity became the focus of organizational humanists. For instance, Abraham Maslow, a pioneer in psychological humanism, advanced a theory of motivation that assumed workers had a hierarchy of needs that gave them the push to work hard in their workplaces. In his words, "self-actualization" or "self-realization fulfillment" would lead to satisfaction and serve as a key motivating factor for the worker.

Maslow and other organizational humanist scholars and practitioners illustrated the deep connections between productivity and motivation. In a country with high unemployment, the traditional assumption is that workers should "be grateful that they have a job that pays the bills." Therefore, as Chester Barnard had stated, pay alone should not be a key motivator. It has never been.

Maybe, social motivation may be presumed to exist in most employment situations. Social motivation is attributed to John Calvin and the Christian Protestant ethic that posits the idea that having work confers human dignity. It follows that one without work is deprived of a key element of selfhood and social solidarity. Associated with sociologist Emile Durkheim, social solidarity implies that everyone's well-being is a function of each one's contribution. From an African point of view, "members of society exist because others have made it possible." In Luo language, the popular reflection of this ethic can be found in the idiom *cham gi wadu* (eat or share with your brother). For the AbaLuhya, it is akin to *eshinyu ni eshinyu* or *yours is ours*. Underneath this form of communal *Ubuntuism* lies the logic of work as good for society. Therefore, without work, society cannot be sustained and, therefore, work has an enriching intrinsic value.

In organization theory, intrinsic rewards are known to be motivators. Leading organization theory researchers Mclleland, Atkinson, Clark and Lowell (1953), Herzberg, Mauser, and Snyderman (1959), Gellerman

(1968), and Ducker (1991) remind us of the importance of establishing a motivating work environment for attainment of higher productivity at efficient costs. Following Porter and Lawler (1968), employee satisfaction and performance are related in interesting ways. Satisfied employees most likely perform at a higher productive level than the unsatisfied lot (Durst & De Santis, 1997). Could it be that workers are satisfied because they feel they have done their job to the best of their abilities? That would be the case when there is a feeling that one's contributions are recognized and that people are dependent on that employee's efforts.

In many instances, productivity conjures the image of work measurement—hence the emphasis on performance contracts by Kenya's government leaders. For managers, productivity is about efficiency and effectiveness of programs, individuals, units, and organizations. Measurements can also consider impacts of programs and services offered. Public organizations like police and immigration often have multiple and sometimes intangible outputs. For example, in evaluating the police force, do managers factor in those servicemen that deter crime by simply being present at events or place? On the surface, a policeman sitting at the fence, watching over a graduation ceremony, may appear to be "unproductive"—just hanging around. But is that really so?

As Adam Smith suggested in his *Wealth of Nations,* "The labor of some of the most respectable orders in the society is, like that of menial servants, unproductive of any value, and does not fix or realize itself in any permanent subject or vendible commodity, which endures after that labor is past" (quoted in Shafritz, Russell, & Borick, 2013, p. 301). The point is, not all labor can be measured accurately, in part because productivity does not lead to a direct measurable product.

The question then becomes, just what do these measurements of productivity look like? The answer is not straightforward. Each organization has to put in place its own unique performance measures. The press is often misleading when it issues a blank pass and makes awards to officials, claiming they outperformed others. A good instance has been the report cards highlighting that some county managers were more productive than others. Such measures may not be accurate because of the context. A veterinary official in Wajir should not be compared to one in Kakamega. The ecological conditions are dissimilar. Standards for measuring productivity must always be contextualized.

Productivity cannot be measured outside of a consideration of government rules and regulation. We must factor into consideration political patronage and poor supervision. Certainly lack of accountability is a huge hindrance to increased productivity and must be a big part of the discussion on productivity. In some instances, it is nonsensical to ascribe grades to work done. Nonetheless, we have to start from somewhere. Benchmarks and best practices indicators can help in some organizational settings.

Before we delve further into productivity discourses, we must consider civil service reforms in Kenya. Although reforms that came with structural adjustment programs were intended to prepare the state for corporate investments, underneath the deregulations and market-driven policies was the desire that a lean government would be more efficient and productive. Most likely, the unintended result of the Golden Handshake and other retrenchment policies known as the Civil Service Reform Programs (CSRP) was to further lower further the morale of already underpaid public officials. The attrition exacerbated the frustrations of Kenya's tribal and patronage-driven civil service. Those not directly affected by the retrenchment programs of the 1990s were scarred.

The reductions in force contributed to more absenteeism, lack of enthusiasm, and in some cases lowered loyalty. Some civil servants argued that they would not respect accounting officers known to have been appointed based on tribal loyalty and not competence. Compounding the problem is that the public sector policy failures are riddled with blame avoidance. A case in point is the failure of the police departments to arrest and prosecute criminal gangs and politicians known to fuel corruption and ethnic schisms. Evidence suggests that high-level civil servants blame one group or the other over failed contracts like Anglo Leasing, Malili ranch purchase (for Konza Technopolis), poor workmanship on Thika Road, and other major projects. Negativity and blame avoidance (indecision) are symptoms of multiple forces, key among which is maladministration.

After the 2007 elections, a poisonous atmosphere proliferated in the public organizations. Many middle-level managers commented that tribalism affected their productivity. Measuring productivity became a farce as tribal biases covered performance appraisal lenses through which public officials were evaluated. In accordance with Kenya's political culture, performance is not tied to financial rewards or sanctions.

Proponents of performance measurement and reporting practices argue that administrators should be able to track results, compare outputs, and assess the efficacy of strategies for processes and practices adopted. If the correct measurements are in place, it is assumed performing civil servants will be rewarded in a manner that is congruent with their efforts. Conversely, nonperformers would be subjected to a variety of sanctions, trained, or offered opportunities for improvement.

However, missing from the debate on productivity in African countries is the incompetence of the managers themselves. Most managers in public service rely on unclear indicators and are poor at writing usable reports. The net result of unclear indicators is mistrust and declining levels of data collection. In classical organization theory, failure to report accurately was considered antithetical to sound management. Indeed, in the traditional functions identified in Luther Gulick's seminal work, reporting is as important as is planning, organizing, staffing, directing, coordinating, and budgeting. The import of the failure to put in place sound measurements and reporting regimes is a steady decline in quality of public administration.

One may trace the low productivity regime to the political, social, and technological environment in which public service is located. As the literature suggests, performance and productivity is a function of organizational environment. Where politics creates a lack of trust, no meaningful productivity measures can be expected. Moreover, Kenya's policy choices are done in a less-than-transparent manner. There is a lack of freedom of information laws that support scrutiny of how decisions are made in the country's top executive bureaucracy. And with tight budgets, low use of productivity software, and a heavily ethnicized civil service, the public sector has generally received a failing grade in its ability to deliver any quality public services.

We know from research that morale is not always associated or linked with productivity. But when we examine the effect of tribalism on morale, we find a fairly direct relationship. In instances where members of one or two ethnic groups dominated some of Kenya's strategic departments, there were accusations of deteriorated levels of productivity. Efforts to control civil servants by the dominant groups created an uneasy relationship in the workplace, which resulted in the belief that hard work would never be rewarded so long as ethnic patronage was the dominant human resource management value.

Professionalism was shunned, resulting in the "hanging coat" phenomenon, a pervasive tardiness and absenteeism habit common among some civil servants. It is widely believed that a good number of public officials were not "technically" at work but instead hung coats or jackets in their offices to symbolize their "presence or availability." Others were said to be making "technical appearances" and simply read newspapers in offices, in quiet protest of the lack of professionalism in the politically charged civil service.

And there was the little-discussed phenomenon of internal brain drain. In Kenya it referred to misallocation of human resources. For instance, internal brain drain may mean not allocating duties to a qualified individual for fear that they would expose the bosses' incompetence. Another variant of internal brain drain common in Kenya's public service is the creation of meaningless positions in which office occupants have no clue about how to proceed. The net result is to lower morale and productivity among the better-qualified professionals. In many instances, patronage encouraged nonproductivity. In other words, even when employees were there, they made no contributions, perhaps they did not care, and the supervisors and political executives lacked skills or resources to motivate employees.

In tandem with reducing patronage and inculcating professionalism, controlling corruption is a challenge for the public sector. Kenya does not rank well on Transparency International's Perception of Corruption Index (PCI). Corruption, as most scholars know, has a direct effect on productivity. Corruption can have a direct effect on productivity in instances where public officials embezzle public money and purchase products and services that contribute to inefficiencies. Corruption through falsification of records and lack of integrity may also affect an organization's effectiveness and efficiency.

In the case of Kenya, civil service reforms have not been tailored to combat mega corruption. Without crushing corruption, through political will, increased productivity through improved efficiencies and effectiveness is unattainable.

Unions must do their part to inculcate values that promote productivity. Unions must work with employers to develop productivity indictors.

For their part, managers should find remedial measures to help workers achieve the agreed-upon productivity targets. Mangers are obligated to monitor and report performance and take action to fix weaknesses found in the production chain.

An often-cited goal in most economies is that workers should improve in their service delivery as a patriotic endeavor. For members of the political and their allies in the business classes, greater productivity is a path to a larger national cake. Deployment of information and communication technologies is just a part of the strategy by management to increase productivity. Deployment of ICTs cannot be alone. It has to be supplemented with ethical executive leadership, human resources management, and prudent financial skills.

Given the grim assessment of Kenya's workplace ethos, the point must be emphasized that using ICTs in many instances enhances productivity. An alternative argument is that lack of ICTs is a barrier to achieving certain efficiencies and lowers productivity. The arguments here discount Robert Solow's (1987) contention that the impact of IT investments did not generate convincing benefits in productivity statistics. From the point of view of Kenyan society, the "productivity paradox" is methodologically flawed. Observable data show the benefits of ICTs, especially because societies with labor surpluses and undercapitalized information resources were missed in his initial thesis. At any rate, for example, mobile phones save much time and money and support decision-making in developing countries that had dysfunctional and nonexistent telephone landlines. The evidence of increased productivity is, in such instances, indisputable. Yet, we must, following the research findings of Kraemer & Dedrick, (1994; 1997), Roach (1988), Lee (1999), and Lucas (1999) and others give credence to the importance of substantive methodological problems associated with productivity measurements and recognize that productivity is a function of other variables beyond ICTs (Kellough, 2012; Perry & Rainey, 1988). Undergirding the productivity discourse is the question of how to determine the barriers to productivity. The discussion below outlines a few that have been widely debated in national forums. The list is not exhaustive or mutually exclusive but serves to highlight the major challenges that must be understood by both employers and union members.

BARRIERS TO PRODUCTIVITY IN KENYA

Understanding productivity starts with observations of the human resources systems. Productivity is more than increasing numbers of output. Research also shows that productivity is not about enhancing employee satisfaction. Satisfaction can be up and not necessarily raise levels of productivity (Swanson & Holton, III, 2009, p. 99). Yet, like satisfaction, productivity is about the people in organizations. Although employees have most responsibility for ensuring productivity, there is more. Other variables exist. Organizational performance has a lot to do with structural problems like poor leadership and lack of resources. Organization theory teaches us that to increase productivity, employees and employers must do certain things. Starting from the employee side of the equation, one can identify existing human and structural barriers. Cumbersome and rigid civil service rules—for example, wasting time to get clearance for travel to Tanzania or other neighboring countries—frustrates productivity.

Time-wasting practices like taking too long at teatime and coffee breaks also undermine productivity. A vast number of public bureaucrats are unproductive because of what Peacock (1983) referred to as "on-the-job leisure," habits that are associated with an indolent employee. Time wasting is also evident through employee accessing social networking websites like Facebook, WhatsApp, Twitter, and Clickbait 24/7. Multimedia University of Kenya lecturer John Walubengo (2014) observed that close to 40 percent of an eight-hour working day in local corporations is probably spent on social media and websites like LinkedIn and Youtube.

And at the middle-management and lower cadre levels, it is not uncommon to witness public servants spend increasing amounts of time surfing the Internet. Some spend most of their working lives online, which has implications for productivity. Any productivity losses from use of ICTs at the workplace should be a workplace policy issue. Evidence is emerging that much time can be wasted through ICT interruptions, especially social media and text messaging during official hours. According to Assa Munene and Ycliffe Nyaribo (2013), workers in Kenya spend well over an hour a day on social media. Poor work habits, as reflected in visiting social media websites and apps during work time, are largely associated with younger workers. Yaacov Cohen has illustrated that this phenomenon is pervasive even in developed countries and has morphed into what psychologists regard as "online compulsive disorder" (in Ogeto, 2016).

Walubengo (2014) opined that the debate over the pros and cons of social media and the relationships to productivity also appraise the importance of providing "breaks," in which case connecting to social networks during work times benefits, especially the younger workers. The point is, organizations that do not have appropriate policies that confine and structure social media use are likely to grapple with productivity issues, especially if employees spend too much time on the ever increasing social media outlets.

And since, according to IDC Mobil phone tracker reports, smartphones are outselling PCs 3:1, they may be disruptive if individuals spend much time using search engines (including Bing, Google, Yahoo!) and for e-commerce, informational queries, online games, and other applications in work settings. These search platforms are rich in data and have innovative voice, gesture, mixed-modal dialogs, and touch-activated capabilities.

Productivity is lowered through lack of "a work ethic and culture," which in the end is a drawback to the country's economic recovery (Devani, 2003). Among the poor work habits are poor time management skills while using emails. Tate Carson (2015) advises that emails should be used correctly and that much efficiency can be gained through automating responses to unclear messages. When one receives vague emails, it is best to send automated responses. Software apps exist to this end. For example, a free text expander software app like FastFox for PCs and Text Expander for Mac allow users to insert commonly used texts that cut short time spent on sloppy emails that clutter inboxes. Carson (2015) also advises that much efficiency is derived when email messages are effective and easily understood. In response to web-surfing activities that reduce productivity, some digital media groups like AccessKenya Group introduced a web filtering tool that enabled companies and the government ministries to manage their time schedules in a cost-effective and productive manner (Kinyanjui & Okuttah, 2011). The product, Zscaler Web Security Cloud Solution, was the first such intervention in the East African region. Similar cloud-based web filtering tools are in place in Nigeria and South Africa.

Other time-wasting processes must also be considered in relation to featherbedding and other tendencies to shun effective technologies. One example is the delayed and halfhearted implementation of digital data storage facilities. Ministries in Kenya have been slow at adopting electronic archival and retrieval systems. As evidenced through poor record keeping in ministries like Lands and Physical Planning, the matter must be considered with outmost urgency. As a result, President Kibaki's administration talked about reforms to promote efficiency and effectiveness in service delivery. Furthermore, in 2012, then Minister of Public Service

Dalmas Otieno announced a five-year plan to move the country toward a paperless correspondence system.

The project would entail scanning and electronically archiving all files and data in government ministries. The plan also envisioned that all correspondence, including government circulars, memoranda, and vouchers would be electronically transmitted. The government saw this strategy as not only a means to promote transparency and accountability but to increase productivity. Virtualization ensures that fraud detection is simplified. Electronic records are likely to save time and with excellent cloud enabled backup, the well-known phenomenon of "lost files" would be a thing of the past. In the pre-digital old days, citizen complaints of missing application forms and documents hiding in someone's desk or cabinet made government and other bureaucratic work unbearable.

Paper-based registries are known to be less efficient and considered obsolete in advanced countries. Experts agree that digitalized platforms are more productive and also provide better services to citizens. Digital or electronic document management systems have the advantage of being able to identify and capture data with greater accuracy than paper formats. When correctly designed, the digital systems also check all the information entered and only forward or reroute forms that are completed. This gives administrators more time to deal with other pressing work-related issues.

Improved document management plans provide advantages beyond saving money. Constituents, especially in the devolved counties, are likely to accrue benefits by saving time. It is much easier to cross-check documents in Ministry headquarters through online and cloud-based archives and other automated document management technologies. Because of enterprise software that can capture and route information automatically to field offices, one does not need to travel from the county office but with a click or touch access vital data. Document management solutions improve service delivery in areas like immigration, pensions, land registration, birth certificate registration, and so on.

Another approach to enhance productivity in the civil service was through seeking support of the International Business Machines (IBM) Research Lab. Also in 2012, IBM signed a Memorandum of Understanding (MOU) with the Kibaki administration to contribute toward including data solutions and advanced analytics and cloud technologies for managing government operations. The IBM technologies were designed to deter fraud and enhance efficiency and productivity in government ministries. IBM's investments introduced advanced technologies that provide smarter solutions for transforming both government and business in the country. Included in IBM's support analytics is the area of management of traffic jams, which are one of the main contributors of low productivity in Nairobi and other large African cities.

In addition to building paperless bureaucracies and introduction of data solutions, the procedures of conducting government business must be scrutinized. Some procedures and rules waste time—the idea that certain procedures are in place for control purposes comes in mind. Wallace Sayre put it nicely when he suggested that administrators might go wrong if they give more emphasis to procedures and structural rules in organizations instead of the purpose for which the techniques and rules and processes were designed.

Poor Organization of Schedules and Lack of Clarity in Goals

Several observers of workplace dynamics note the correlation between work-related stress and poor productivity. Stress has been reported in Kenya's civil service, particularly associated with incivility and tribalism. Tribalism can be a negative factor as it creates the perception that certain employees are favored in personnel decisions like posting, promotion, or even task assignments to plum positions.

Psychologists report that people respond to pressures in a variety of ways, including being underproductive. When employees feel unsupported, because of their gender, religion, or ethnicity, they are unlikely to perform at their best. Moreover, if the workplace is poorly designed or lacks appropriate facilities such as clean restrooms or has poor lighting and unventilated and unsafe rooms, employees will not be enthusiastic about their workplace (Smith, 1979, p. 40). The same lack of enthusiasm exists when the work systems are not conducive to high-level productivity, and stress may occur. Schedules of duties that are insensitive to needs of employees are frequently cited as impediments to productive life. Employees who feel they do not have much control over work processes or are assigned tasks that are not commensurate with their training and experience are not likely to be productive.

Unsatisfactory work conditions exist in many rural and urban schools. Images of leaking roofs, students studying under trees, and lack of basic infrastructures like textbooks and washroom facilities are stress factors that not only lead to health concerns but also contribute to low productivity. An Education International (EI) conference held in Nairobi in early 2015 reported a survey on the working conditions of teachers across the globe, showed that nearly half of the teachers in Kenyan schools were ready to "quit their profession because of unfavorable working conditions" (Oduor, 2015b).

Organizations that lack clear goals are unlikely to experience higher productivity. A good example was the establishment of political ministries that lacked focus. For example, President Daniel arap Moi created a Ministry of Political Guidance. President Kibaki also created several ministries and units of government including one for National Cohesion that had vague goals. When organizational goals are vague, difficult to define, and contentious, productivity suffers. Workers find it difficult to be motivated if the organizational goals are ill defined and workers may hardly be committed to unclear goals.

Corruption as Barrier

Corruption comes in different forms that include bribes, embezzlement and fraud, extortion, abuse of power including misusing privileged information, conflict of interest, and favoritism based on different motivations. Jreisat (2012, p. 163) lists corruption as one of the features or traits of administrative systems of developing countries. Transparency International (TI) ranks Kenya as one of the most corrupt countries in the world. In the 2013 Corruption Perceptions Index, Kenya ranked at 136 out of 177 countries (Transparency International, 2014). TI reported that in 2015, Kenya was ranked at number 139 out of 168 countries. In 2015, the country retained the same scores and was seen as one of the countries which lacked public access to information. A study by the institute of Certified Public Accounts of Kenya (ICPAK) reported that the country lost Sh 69 billion per year due to corruption (Kithi, 2014). According to the institute, corruption in Kenya raised the cost of living by at least 15 percent. The World Bank also warned that due to rampant corruption, Kenya fell behind its neighbors, Tanzania and Uganda, in attracting foreign direct investment (FDI) (Omondi, 2016). Corruption in administrative areas like procurement and inefficiencies resulting from corruption made it difficult for the economy to realize its full potential. Translated in economic terms, corruption is uneconomical and leads to inefficiencies.

The literature on corruption supports the thesis that corruption undermines economic growth due to its negative effects on long-run economic and political stability (Aidt, 2009; Mo, 2000). Corruption also tends to favor certain groups in the economy, leading to inequalities. For the most part, combating corruption has been one of the popular slogans in Kenya's electioneering. From the economic standpoint, corruption is seen as negative behavior because it hinders innovation and is a disincentive to private investments. According to Mo (2000) and de Vaal and Ebben (2011), the effects of corruption are generally detrimental to developing countries like Kenya, which are desperate to accumulate human capital for faster economic growth (Aidt, 2009; Mo, 2000; de Vaal & Ebben, 2011). The International Monetary Fund (IMF) considers corruption as a hindrance to foreign aid inflows because funds are diverted from their intended projects (IMF, 1995). Munro (1995) and Assane and Grammy (2003), also provided empirical evidence that corruption lowers economic growth, especially in developing countries. With growth hampered, economic distortions can result in a vicious cycle of underperformance and uninspiring productivity.

Corruption hinders productivity because it rewards employees whose ethical behaviors are questionable. Ethical employees may lose morale and be discouraged from producing at their optimal levels if the system rewards the corrupt and inept. Unethical behavior is considered unprofessional and there is a positive relationship between being ethical and being more productive. In other words, for the most part, the most productive officials are likely to be those that are also ethical.

Unethical practices were reported in the procurement of ICT products, especially as concerns the Laptop Project. Prior to that, the country had been treated to a scandal known as the Anglo Leasing Project, in which security gadgets and passport printing systems were imported from France and Britain by less-than-transparent means. In addition, Anglo Leasing involved payments to ghost firms that did not deliver Very Small Aperture Terminal (VSAT) equipment including modems, satellite Internet access dishes, the purchase of police surveillance systems, and other ICT devices for an E-Cops Security Law and Order Systems Project. Anglo Leasing resulted in loss of millions of public funds through kickbacks to dubious companies.

Although the British government eventually charged some of the individuals involved in the scandal, the response in Kenya was muted. Former Permanent Secretary for Governance and Ethics and anti-corruption crusader John Githongo released tapes implicating senior members of the Kibaki administration in the scandals (Mugonyi, 2008; Wrong, 2009). Among those adversely named were ministers and the postmaster general of all accused abuse of authority through granting special deals to "M/S Spacenet, Universal Satspace and First Mercantile Securities Corporation for purposes of establishing data networks" (Ogemba, 2015). These business deals were allegedly executed without competitive bidding and without regard to transparency.

Authorities in Kenya are cognizant of utilizing ICTs to advance the cause of transparency in government operations. In 2014, President Uhuru Kenyatta directed that all state-owned enterprises and public universities utilize automated procurement systems. The president went on to launch the Integrated Financial Management Information System (IFMIS) e-procurement system, touting its promise for curbing the incidence of corruption. The e-procurement system entails enterprise resource planning, maintenance and repair, sourcing, ordering, tendering and e-market sites, and e-reverse auctioning, which involves invitation of groups to compete against each other and supply a specified good or service. The online procurement initiative was managed through the National Treasury and was started as a pilot project covering nineteen parastatals. IFMIS was considered a much better tool than the manual procurement systems that were in place in the majority of Kenya's ministries and parastatals.

At the launch of IFMIS, only 30 percent of the parastatals had partial automated procurement systems. An even smaller number (14 percent) had fully automated e-procurement systems (Wanzala, 2015). Like other business-to-business (B2B) innovations, electronic procurement can work only if there is trust. E-managers establish websites that provide room for qualified and registered buyers and users of goods and services, including the government. Conducting business through web portals muse be based on laws, policies, and procedures that are fair to all participants. E-procurements do save money and offer increased access to markets without additional supplier market efforts. E-quotes, for example make it easy to find the best offers fast.

Although Kenya has launched e-procurement platforms, the country's leadership must be aware of the need to develop capacity to manage the systems. E-procurement systems are not that simple. The software includes complex supply management and auctions calculations. In addition, several applications involve Enterprise Resource Planning (ERP), which involves the use of software to coordinate resource planning. Most authorities report that e-procurement must ensure that goods and services ordered are reliable, with warranty provisions and cost-efficient invoicing and cost tracking (Baily, 2008; Neef, 2001). This implies putting in place robust repair and maintenance systems.

Combating corruption can be helpful in recovery of assets corruptly acquired, thereby providing resources needed for productive endeavors. The United Nations Convention Against Corruption (UNCAC) has given charge to nations to help prevent corruption through training and implementation of codes or standards of conduct so that public officials can perform effectively and honestly. Ultimately, it is up to leaders to have political commitment and institute effective strategies and anti-corruption measures (Smith, 1999, p. 193). Commitment on the part of political leaders can ensure that resources are allocated efficiently, thereby enhancing possibilities of increasing productivity. For their part, citizens must put to use the full range of social media platforms that educate society on the dangers of corruption, while promoting transparency in government operations. Social media has unmatched advantages of disseminating information about corrupt individuals to a wide range of key stakeholders. Shaming corrupt businesses and individuals associated with government is a small way of raising the costs of corrupt behavior. At the same time, government entities are more accountable when they conduct public affairs in transparent and accessible ways.

Corruption within unions has traditionally received little attention. But infighting among the country's various trade unions has been widely reported in the media. Some of the fragmentation within the union movement was attributed to corruption. Remarkably, in response to the formation of the Federation of Public Service Trade Unions of Kenya (PUSETU), COTU's leader Francis Atwoli described the founders of PUSETU as "politically motivated to protect corrupt senior members of society" (Nyassy, 2014). In making those remarks, Atwoli positioned COTU as the voice of public morality and protector of interests of workers.

Unions, as part of society, are not oblivious to the need for greater transparency and accountability. Unions have traditionally raised concerns about corruption in government. For instance, in 2013, the acting COTU Secretary General George Muchai denounced "corrupt government officials who evade strict and stringent labor inspections" (Jamah, 2013). Francis Atwoli, the substantive COTU Secretary General, has strongly opposed corruption in government, especially in relation to misappropriation of social security funds collected from workers (Sum, 2014).

In March 2015, Atwoli described President Uhuru M. Kenyatta's actions against corruption as "bold" and encouraged the Ethics and Anti-Corruption Commission (EACC) to continue fighting corruption. This was after Kenyatta called upon members of his cabinet and other public service officials to resign for being mentioned in an EACC report on corruption. Atwoli was reported to have said that, "It is a bold step by President Uhuru Kenyatta and the Jubilee Administration of commitment to fighting corruption and he has the backing of workers who have been victims of graft suffering low pay and lack of morale" (*Standard* Reporter, 2015).

Inflexible Systems of Position Classifications, Poor Job Descriptions

Most government ministries lack well-drawn-up classification and job description systems. Several senior civil servants spend most of their time performing odd "duties assigned from time-to-time." In many instances, these assignments are political in nature, in the service of political masters. Most government ministries do not schedule periodic job analysis and evaluations. Without periodic job analysis, managers do not have a good grasp of actual tasks performed and may not put in place appropriate job contents.

Without suitable job analysis, the contents of government jobs might be confusing and further hamper motivation within the body of workers. Designing jobs may be a challenge in a highly politicized environment. Job content, if done professionally, leads to satisfaction and motivation. If the incumbent finds aspects of a job "beneath" their skill level, the loss of productivity is a no-brainer. For example, a deputy secretary assigned duties of supervising clerical staff is unchallenged and likely to be unproductive. The point is, employees may be motivated to perform at higher levels of production if the job content is suitable and appropriate to skills, knowledge, and competencies of incumbent holders.

And even when policy and executive managers face stressful assignments, it is important the organizations adapt practices that are effective at ensuring productivity levels are high. Beverly Potters's (1985) ideas capture key attributes of preventing burnout in many organizational settings. For example, she recommends "stress inoculation" as an alternative way of sustaining productivity in the workplace. Stress inoculation works like a vaccination (Potter, 1985, p. 133). Kenyan managers need stress inoculation from tribally centered managerial practices. More energy is focused on sustaining patronage systems than on creating organizations that truly value merit and productivity. Professionals stressed out by organizational factors that devalue their efforts to professionalize the civil service, and techniques for preventing toxic political invasions in the workplace are a way to enhance productivity in all sectors of Kenya.

Poor work habits include perennial absenteeism and tardiness. Keen observations of Kenya's civil service reveals low productivity on the part of many an employee. Both central and county governments report uncomfortable levels of tardiness. For instance, in Garissa County, employees have been observed to miss work and warned "days of hanging coats on the office chair and disappearing unnecessarily from public office are long gone" (Jubat, 2014).

In a public dispute with the Kenya National Union of Teachers (KNUT), Education Cabinet Secretary Kaimenyi publicly disclosed the poor work ethic among some of the nation's teachers. Kaimenyi disclosed that close to half of the teachers in schools "are never in class when they are supposed to be, while another 20 percent abscond work altogether" (Wanzala, 2015c). The Global Monitoring Education for All 2000–2015 Report released in April 2015 confirmed that 20 percent of teachers in public primary schools did not teach at the time they were required at the workplace. Roughly 40,000 primary school teachers out of 200,000 absconded from duty and continued to earn salaries. The National Adolescent and Youth Survey Report of 2015 attributed the high rates of absenteeism among teachers to low pay, poor economic status, and heavy drinking (Kajilwa, 2016). Absenteeism was therefore a huge problem for education sector in the country and required attention.

External and Internal Brain Drain and Work Conditions

A common conceptualization of the bureaucratic anomaly is the brain drain problem. Some call it human capital flight to signify the loss of an important resource for productivity. Going by numbers, Kenya is considered one of the "most heavily brain drained" nations. The estimated number of Kenyans working abroad is between 500,000 and 1.8 million (Ojanji 2006). Of these, at least 50,000 skilled workers work in the United States alone. Critics argue that the brain drain phenomenon is one of the reasons for delayed development in Africa. Okwaro Plato (2015), a commentator with Gravio Africa Consulting, considers the loss of intellectual capital in Africa as a product of the brain drain. According to Plato

(2015), the inability of Africans to use information for their own uplift will linger on, if nothing is done to curtail the brain drain to Europe and the United States, which use the skilled capital for their own growth. Plato's commentary in the *African Executive Magazine* asserts:

> When African men and women of ideas, who will give birth to new ideas, have fled to Europe and the United States, then the so-called African Renaissance cannot occur in Africa. It can only occur in Paris, London and New York. There are more Soukous musicians in Paris, than in Kinshasa; more African professional soccer players in Europe, than in Africa. (Plato, 2015)

World Confederation of Labor Information Officer Andre Linard, quoting data from the International Organization for Migration (IOM), disclosed that one third of Africa's intellectual resources lived outside the continent (2002, p. 47). According to Linard, many graduates from Africa did not return home immediately or put off returning home for "as long as possible" because the conditions in Africa were not attractive (2002, p. 47). He recommended that African governments institute policies that encouraged "brain gain." There have been voices for imposing a brain-drain tax to lure back talents lost to developed countries. Among those voices are consultants from the McKinsey Institute in Washington, DC, which advocated for the return of IT experts from developing countries (Linard, 2002, p. 49).

Observers contend that one of the key factors fueling external brain drain is that a good number of Kenyans with specialized training return to Kenya only to be "offered job designations that do not match their qualifications" (Ojanji, 2006). Researchers in the scientific fields are frequently underpaid or lack essential facilities like well-managed and equipped laboratories. Still, funding for research hinders productivity among top scientists, thereby feeding the external brain-drain pipe. In the end, these highly skilled human resources leave the country.

Ironically, in the medical field, a good number of members of the profession leave Africa in general for lack of modern equipment that would greatly aid and enhance the quality of medical service delivery. Such devices include Computed Axial Tomography (CAT), or Computed Tomography (CT) scans that supplement X-ray machines for imaging any or all parts of the human body. Indeed, Magnetic Resonance Imaging (MRI) machines are recent additions to Kenyan hospital infrastructures. For instance, even in vast areas like Kirinyaga, the installation of MRI machines in Catholic Church-run hospitals took place for the first time in 2015 after Karira Mission Hospital in Mwea installed one (Kamau, 2015). Local leaders noted that without imaging and diagnostic devices, patients had previously "either died while on the way to Nairobi" or had their conditions worsen, and installing MRI was a game changer.

The situation in Kenya is similar to that in other parts of sub-Saharan Africa because health care budgets are relatively low and do not show commitment to the Millennium Development Goals (MDG). The governments of Kenya, Uganda, and other sub-Saharan African countries have failed to meet millennial goal targets in increasing budgetary allocations for health care services and underfunded supply of vital lifesaving technological equipment and investments in manpower acquisition, training, and development.

In Uganda, the high rate of medical brain drain created a huge shortage of medical workers, resulting in a lawsuit against the government of Uganda. In 2015, a think tank, the Institute of Public Policy and Research (IPPR), sued the Uganda government for neglecting its medical professions, which in turn resulted in brain drain (Mwesiga, 2015). The consequence of this has been an overstretched health system that has resulted in the untimely deaths of many Ugandans.

The records of the Kenya National Union of Nurses (KNUN) show that nurses working in Kenya were among the most "frustrated in the world" (Gathura, 2015). Thousands wanted to leave the country because both the national and county governments had neglected health workers. And at Kenyatta National Hospital (KNH), the country's major referral treatment center, the levels of burnout were also among the highest in the world. The net result of continued burnout was increased turnover of the experienced nurses and other health workers. Kenyatta National Hospital was also in the news after the only two radiotherapy machines used for cancer treatment broke down in March 2015, adding to the frustration of both patients and health workers (Mathiu, 2015).

Still, after the government purchased additional machines, there was evidence that the country lacked medical engineers to operate new equipment for scanning cancer patients at Kenyatta National Hospital (PSCU, 2015). President Uhuru Kenyatta acknowledged the scarcity of skilled medical engineers in a speech to university chancellors and called for universities to offer market-oriented courses.

Research shows that the major cause for frustration and exit from Kenyan health facilities was "poor working environment characterized by too many patients, inadequate facilities, and patients' relatives" (Gathura, 2015). In an interview with the *Standard* newspaper, Esther Seka Odanga, a senior nurse, opined, "It is frustrating to work in conditions where everything from drugs to requisite instruments are in short supply or absent altogether. It is painful to see patients whose lives could be saved die while you watch helplessly" (Ombuor, 2008). It does not surprise that several reported cases of strikes by health workers are about salary and working conditions. For instance, in the March 2015 strike by members of the Kenya National Union of Nurses, Vihiga Chapter, officials complained that the county hospital workers were exposed to health hazards through issues such as "unpaid water and electricity bills" (Iungai, 2015). Lack of continuous supply of water and electricity in county hospitals was reported in other parts of the country.

Also reported as problematic was the lack of drugs (pharmaceuticals), long working hours, and inadequate or missing facilities. In partial response to the lack of medical equipment, the government, in 2015, launched an innovative project whereby medical corporations would install and manage the equipment, including digital X-ray machines, ICU facilities, kidney dialysis, and machines for use in the theaters. The government teamed up with international corporations including Belico SRL (one of Italy's manufactures of renal dialysis equipment). Others were China's Mindray Biomedical Co, a theater equipment supply company, Esteem Corporation, a theater central sterile services unit originating in India, and General Electric for the supply of radiology equipment. Through contracting out, hospitals in the country would modernize the health sector and perhaps motivate and improve the productivity of health workers.

From the examples of members of the health care community in Uganda and Kenya, we recognize that brain drain is a multifaceted issue. In developed countries, the large-scale retirement of elderly baby boomers from government has reduced the talent pool in certain areas (Hays & Lavigna, 2009, p. 161). Although significant numbers of baby boomers are involved in the ICT industries, younger generations probably dominate the talent pool of ICT experts.

Regardless, in the advanced nations, brain drain is claimed because younger workers are also known to shun employment in the public service. The same sets of conditions are not widely found in African countries, where most of the population is younger. Instead, the brain drain can be attributed to a whole different set of variables. Most important are factors that misallocate human capital and other resources.

Brain drain can be as detrimental to productivity as the lack of commitment and poor motivation due to poor pay and systemic organizational mismanagement. Any aspect of management that causes an otherwise good worker to leave public service may cause the phenomenon termed brain drain. The misdirection of labor resources is more damaging if the few bright stars leave government jobs for lucrative professional jobs in other sectors. If the star employee stays on the job but is underutilized or frustrated by work conditions, one may also consider the misallocation of resources as *internal brain drain*. Arguably, mismanagement through overstaffing, wrong assignments, tasks, and roles constitutes internal brain drain. This is because human capital is misallocated.

In many instances, internal brain drain is about waste of talents. Able workers, especially in the scientific fields like IT, are "wasted" if the government agency does not provide them with commensurate assignments and equipment. Realistically, overdependence on "expert" IT professionals displaces equally qualified nationals, thereby producing a variation of brain drain. Evidence of brain drain can be discerned from the "steady stream of really good people leaving government agencies for jobs with the UN and international NGOs" (Shaikh, 2010). As international development consultant Alanna Shaihk (2010) elaborates, the major reason for the move away from government agencies in developing countries is that public sector pay is poor and "not always regular." She adds,

> The problem is not that sexy UN jobs are pulling people out of government. The problem is that people are pushed out of government jobs by poor working conditions. It's not a demand problem—it's a supply problem. People who want to leave their government jobs will find a way to do it. If it wasn't NGOs and the development sector pulling them out, it would be the private sector or international emigration. (Shaihk, 2010)

Furthermore, the lack of incentives is acute in areas such as IT and other ambitious skilled professionals. Kenyan IT workers create the brain drain effect because work conditions are unsuitable for optimal productivity. Internal brain drain is also associated with economic hardships caused by politics and corruption. Poor leadership leads to professionals moonlighting in all manner of jobs including serving as Matatu drivers, subsistence farmers, and *Mitumba* (secondhand clothing) retailers. An excellent account of this misplacement of labor was evidenced during the vetting of candidates for top positions in Kenya's police force. One commandant of Kenya's Police Air Wing reported that his unit had only two out of twelve operational planes (Ombati, 2014). In addition, pilots at Kenya Wildlife Service earned KSh 4500,000 compared to KSh 125,000 paid to Kenya Police pilots (Ombati, 2014). According to commandant Rogers Mbithi, the Air Wing department suffered from loss of pilots moving to other sectors. The vetting exercises also revealed that several senior police engaged in other jobs, including sale of vehicles.

Working conditions affect productivity in more than one way. Physical and psychological environments were found to be powerful motivators and boosters of productivity. The Hawthorne experiments provided a clue into the importance of working conditions. Just for the sake of illustration, an employee working in Lamu, Garissa, or Mandera in the desert heat most likely will want air-conditioning. At the psychological level, one has to examine employee relationships. Job frustrations will increase in environments where tribalism and sexual harassment are rampant.

Frustrations will also appear in workplaces without sufficient Employee Wellness and Employee Assistance Programs (EAPs). Several of Kenya's public organizations have welfare associations that support employees during bereavements and other calamities. EAPs cater to worker's psychological needs like counseling and support services. When an employer invests in Employee Wellness Programs (EWPs) that promote health education and quality-of-life issues, important benefits in terms of higher productivity may accrue.

Already Kenya has reported an increase in obesity among its middle-class workers. According to data from the Global Disease Burden, from a study by the University of Washington's Institute of Health Metric and Evaluation (IHME), six million Kenyans are overweight and 1.8 million are classified as obese (Kariuki, 2014). High levels of obesity are associated with several diseases, including diabetes and heart conditions, that have a negative impact on productivity. Employee Wellness Programs (EWPs) that target workers with obesity concerns are becoming popular in Western societies and can be replicated in Africa. Research shows investing in employee health and emotional stability through welfare interventions lowers voluntary attrition and absenteeism, which leads to higher productivity (Berry, Mirabit, & Baun, 2010).

With the rise of the idea of the Internet of Things (IoT), there is potential for governments and businesses to provide wearable fitness trackers. Verizon (2015) reports that wearables make it easy for patients to monitor their conditions from the comfort of their home or even at the workplace. According to Verizon (2015, p. 9), "IoT-enabled wearable devices can also play an important role in preventive medicine. By encouraging the population to lead a *healthier* lifestyle, the incidence of obesity and other conditions that can be a factor in many serious conditions can be reduced."

Lack of Sufficient Training Opportunities

Economies that are heavy on producing goods and natural resources are likely to experience slower growth in their GDP (Andersson & Karlsson, 2007; Powell & Snellmann, 2004). Such economies rely on low-skilled, poorly paid manpower. In the current "knowledge society," successful economies will be those that are driven by new technologies and high levels of human capital (Obradovic, 2009). Countries with great education systems are better positioned to produce knowledge economies. It follows that access to higher education and training opportunities enhance development in human capital. Training, especially in the ICTs, is an essential ingredient of improving the quality of human capital.

Kenya has a deep history in development of manpower in the service of low-level manufacturing industries. Closely supervised by the Directorate of Industrial Training (DIT), the most beneficiaries were personnel in craft and technical arenas. Implementation was frequently assigned to Village Polytechnics, Kenya Polytechnic, and other technical schools all geared toward production of skills for an import-substitution and export-manufacturing base.

Following ILO's philosophy of institutional training, Kenya adopted training regimes for the emergent manufacturing sector. Emphasis was on modules of employment skills (MES) approaches. It was a system that claimed to have global applicability through its supposedly high degree of national adjustability. Proponents touted the connections between labor skills and production requirements. Its emphasis on on-the-job training techniques was based on Taylorist principles. However, on close examination, the approach did not lead to production of highly skilled and sophisticated experts.

Traditionally Kenya's university system failed to integrate sufficiently with the country's thin industrial and technical base. Kenya's technological capacity in all areas of technology and applied science has never really grown beyond its 1975 levels. Then, the percentage of qualified technical personnel was rather low (Mikkelsen, 1987).

Skills structure did not reflect changes in industrial processing. Even with the proliferation of universities, progress in developing high-end skills in the IT sector remains a challenge. Former ICT Cabinet Secretary Fred Matiangi, speaking at the launch of @iLabAfrica and @iBizAfrica at Strathmore University Auditorium in September 2014, disclosed that the lack of adequate specialized skills in the ICT sector threatened the successful implementation of government programs (Sunday, 2014). Lack of ICT personnel weakened the government's efforts to digitize databases and automate processes in both county and national governments. Providing training opportunities for workers in the ICT sector was therefore a huge challenge.

The devastating result of shortages of Information Technology (IT) workers, scientists, and development engineers means that African countries were likely to be confined to consumption of IT products. Most research and development work would therefore remain in the industrial countries, in parent MNCs, and research institutions thereby weakening the ability of developing countries to acquire the necessary skills for sustainable growth in IT sectors. Bennell (1981, pp. 17–18) found that to be the case in traditional manufacturing enterprises. Similar trends exist in industries that are heavy on IT systems. Without sustaining production and nurturing of IT skills, control of the process is lost, with devastating results in the area of productivity. The situation is made worse when African organizations shun prudent management practices like conducting comprehensive manpower surveys to assess skill levels.

Culture, Political Will, and Political Strife

Related to training and development is the concern over organizational cultures in most national institutions. Then chair of the Kenya Association of Manufacturers (KAM), Arun Devani (2003), offered a most serious indictment of Kenya's inability to secure high productivity levels in all sectors and also attract greater manufacturing capabilities. Devani (2003) argued that Kenya's political system neglected investments in basic service such as sewerage, crime control, roads, and water, which affected productivity within the manufacturing sector. In addition, Kenya's education system created incompetent graduates and technical personnel, unable to produce efficiently. Devani (2003) also criticized the lack of "acceptable work culture" in the country as a factor that contributed to low growth. This perspective from a noted manufacturer, which places blame on work ethic, is not a new observation. There are certain cultural norms and practices that hinder organizational productivity. Among these are nepotism and poor time-management skills. Many Kenyan cultures have yet to embrace the art of efficiency in use of time.

From the management (employer) perspective, perhaps the most obvious barrier to increased use of productivity techniques has been the lack of political will and appeal. Performance measures and contracts go against the dominant value of political spoils and patronage. Arguably, the coalition government of 2008 was one that reinforced the tradition of spoils. The government was formed after a disputed election. The two largest coalitions partners, one led by then Prime Minister Raila Odinga (Orange Democratic Movement, ODM) and the other by President Mwai Kibaki (Party of National Unity, PNU) shared ministry slots on a partisan basis. The two leaders built not a civil service but a patronage human resource administration in which their allies were appointed to high offices. Even though performance contracts were in place, some senior members of either party owed their allegiances to their party leaders and not the general public. Ministries were divided into ODM and PNU departments, making it difficult to hold anyone accountable and exacerbating accountability battles at the national level.

As was mentioned in previous chapters, attainment of full employment through economic growth is a key area of interest to trade unions. Although trade unions have for the most part demanded better remunerations, employers have continued to call for greater attention to productivity issues. Discourse on productivity is associated with union interest in raising standards of living for workers. It is argued that real wages in Kenya have been on the decline since the election of President Uhuru M. Kenyatta, 2013. This has resulted in increased labor militancy through strikes and other legitimate means of protest and agitation.

Ironically, the increase in real wages after 2003 may have been associated with the emergence of new technologies and ways of doing business. For example, money transfers through electronic remittances from Kenyans in the diaspora led to increased foreign exchange earnings and benefits to millions of families in the country. In addition, emergence of M-PESA-increased availability of instant cash for the rural and urban poor. ICTs, especially mobile telephones, are also responsible for improved efficiencies in communications. Without doubt, there is a positive relationship between productivity and improvement in living standards.

Perhaps the question of political will can be further explained through examination of differences in labor productivity within various departments. Arguably, departments and units that have the most political patronage are most likely to suffer from low productivity. A reasonable explanation is that employees who feel "protected" will be less accountable for the general use of time. The same applies to workers who are entitled and feel that they can spend government time doing their own private business without much to fear.

Observation techniques lead us to compare production in various units. Crude measures such as time spent at the workplace, output of work, and efficiency in delivery of services point toward a widely held belief that Kenyans produced at lower levels and added value at much lower levels than is expected of a country that seeks to gain in terms of human development.

The effects of lower wages in the civil service can be one factor leading to low productivity in ministries. The theory holds when comparison is made between public sector producers and their counterparts in private industry. Theory would suggest that higher rates of output for services like education would be realized if teachers were paid highly. In fact, the numerous strikes called by KNUT would suggest so. Yet, we know, that salaries alone are not a predictor of better productivity. Strikes in themselves are a political act that lowers productivity. Frequent strikes among public officials, teachers, nurses, and in the private sector reduce output.

Likewise, political rallies held on workdays are a loss and waste of public funds. Dealing with strikes takes up management time that could be used for other organizational development purposes. Strikes in education institutions are notorious and are known to directly affect worker productivity. When the University of Nairobi students go on strike, or take to the streets, the losses in productivity are enormous. Compared to developed countries, developing countries like Kenya lose more from unrest and labor or trade union militancy. Thus, if workers of educational institutions are on strike, the net effect is to lower productivity within a whole range of public service-delivery systems.

Even if we held salaries constant, the productivity of teachers and other public servants in Kenya is not at the level one would find in for example, Washington, DC, or London. Measured in terms of the volume of output per man-hour, it is clear that a police officer in Kakamega is less productive compared to his or her counterparts in cities located in the developed world. In advanced countries, the level of professionalism is much higher and officers account for their time at work. A simple explanatory variable is the obvious use of technology including vehicles in advanced society. Police departments in advanced societies normally report to accident scenes in a matter of minutes in part because of superior communication and transportation equipment.

Not to stress the resource scarcity issues, it is not unheard of for members of the public to be told that police will not arrive at an accident scene because their vehicles lack petrol (gas) or spare tires and that citizens affected should provide their own petrol (gas). In addition, staffing levels, especially in registries, are much higher in Kenya than one would find in developed society. Labor unions in Kenya do not necessarily oppose overstaffing of office machines. For example, "lift" (elevator) operators are hired to push a button for the senior civil servants, even though the machines are automated and do not need someone to simply push a button. The point is, relatively little skill is required for operation of "lifts." The same idea applies to photocopy machinery. Differences in salary levels do not cause differences in technologies applied. The two are very different variables but must be considered in this discourse.

Perhaps we can add to this list the challenges associated with poor commuting systems in most of urban Kenya. The Nairobi metropolitan area suffers from intractable traffic congestions that impact on the nation's productivity. Traffic congestion results in loss of manpower hours and adds to the high cost of doing business in Nairobi. Although the Ministry of Transport and Infrastructure and the county government have developed strategies to ease congestion, long-term strategies will cost money.

Beyond money, improvements in productivity have much to do with human organization, economics of scale, and attitudes toward work. In the private sector, it is easy for multinational corporations to require higher levels of productivity and embrace practices adopted in parent companies in the overseas subsidiaries. That logic is missing in Kenya's public sector. Indeed, a visit to Kenyan embassies abroad shows that labor practices associated with Kenyan civil service are much in place in the overseas units. With the exception of few technological infusions, embassies tend to continue practices, borrowed from home departments. In other words, there is very little organizational learning going on.

In many instances, Kenyan embassy staff is not completely insulated from patronage hires and are subjected to similar organizational "codes of regulations." In many instances, the civil service codes of regulations are dated and unenforced. This discussion leads us to conclude that comparisons of labor productivity can be done. In recognizing the sources of advantages of government departments in developed society, one may begin to find solutions to low productivity in developing countries. Arguably, in a globalized world, productivity should be compared internationally as a means to encourage competitiveness.

CONCLUSIONS

In conclusion, critics are quick to identify several factors that work against increased productivity in developing countries such as Kenya. Data shows that the United States, the most productive country in the world, happens to be the most advanced in terms of increased consumption of ICT products. While the role of digital innovations in increasing productivity is still a subject of debate, evidence suggests investments in digital technologies such as in the service sectors has enormous benefits. A study by the American Enterprise Institute shows that in 2015, for example, the Gross Domestic Product (GDP) in California, with a workforce of about 19 million people was higher than that in France, a country with over 25 million workers. (Perry, 2016). California also happens to be a state in which labor unions are strong. Workers in America embrace values such as efficiency and effectiveness, which are also given full backing by the political elites. There is something to learn from countries that have higher productivity values and organizational cultures. There is a direct correlation between increased productivity and the removal of barriers to productivity that have been addressed in this chapter. Cultural adjustments and incentives are needed to make ICTs work for the general growth in African economies, including Kenya's emerging digital economy. Stakeholders, who include trade union members, have to be a part of the adjustment to the digital technology for increased national productivity to be realized.

SEVEN

Trade Unions and Internationalism

Emerging Governance Networks

INTRODUCTION

The global economy has been variously described as "neoliberal" and driven by "globalized consciousness," a force that seems to challenge the power of nation-states. Manfred Steger (2003) observes that globalization is a contested concept that refers to different and competing realities. He underscores the fact that globalization is transformative and refers to processes which shift human contact. For Stager, globalization is happening in dynamic ways involving creation of "new and the multiplication of existing social networks and activities that increasingly overcome traditional political, economic, cultural, and geographical boundaries" (Steger, 2003, p. 9). Much of the connectedness is fueled by technological innovations and especially information and communication technologies, which include satellite televisions and Internet connections. He offers the following definition: "Globalization refers to a multidimensional set of processes that create, multiply, stretch, and intensify worldwide social interdependence and exchanges while at the same time fostering in people a growing awareness of deepening connections between the local and the distant" (Steger, 2003, p. 13).

Stated differently, globalization, defined in terms of connectedness and economic integration of human populations across the world, has produced goods and services that are widely available anywhere on the planet. And at the heart of globalization is the information revolution, driven in large part by achievements in the information and communication technologies (ICTs). From a lay perspective, globalization engenders internationalism and its attendant social, economic, political, and technological consequences. Moreover, there is widespread agreement that, in current phase of globalization, nations that control technologies are likely to be leaders in global commerce and development. Therefore, policy makers in African societies are well advised to understand the ramifications of ICTs for national economies.

Globalization, propelled through ICTs, has had tremendous impact on national economies, especially job creation and associated distribution of wealth and prosperity. Of particular importance is the reported shift in the global economy that has resulted in an altered balance of economic power and lowered the world's gross national product in some cases. Another unintended consequence is that some nations are forced to return to trade restrictions and other efforts to protect domestic industries and jobs (Milakovich, 2012, p. 216). The loss of jobs is the worst-case scenario for all trade unions, especially in countries with high rates of unemployment. And if institutionalized replacement of jobs through ICT-enabled automation leads to a weakened labor movement, there is bound to be a reaction on the part of union members. This chapter discusses the linkages between trade union activism, ICTs, and emerging governance networks, especially the possibilities for increased internationalization of labor movements in Africa. And there is sufficient reason for this exploration.

IS THERE AN INCENTIVE TO ENGAGE EMPLOYERS IN A GLOBALIZED WORLD?

Perhaps, we should first wonder why unionized workers should engage their employers in a world that seemingly favors the owners of capital. In the private sector, corporations can reject government policy prescriptions to raise minimum wages and even fail to implement safety regulations, based on the argument that such policies are anti-business. By threatening to move where lax regulations are welcome, the incentives for workers to organize are reduced. This implies, to some extent, that solidarity among labor groups must be international, as it has been for most of the past century.

As was described earlier, Kenya lost thousands of factory jobs due to movements in industries such as those in the clothing and apparel sector. This was, in part, because Kenya, like other African countries, had diminished capacity to isolate itself from an economy driven by global economic forces, including the World Trade Organization (WTO). Moreover, national trade union organizations were particularly vulnerable and weakened in negotiating wage increases in the wake of global trends toward labor market deregulation. Developing countries found their ability to implement welfare policies incompatible with the desires of those driving globalization, especially, the attendant platforms that relocate capital to regions with lower wages. These were, in general, places where nations provided legal incentives, in order to compete for capital and other investments. Among the legal regime frameworks is weakened union bargaining capacity.

Globalization, one may argue, has certainly restricted the policy options available to countries such as Kenya that had previously streamlined incentives for capital inflows but lacked capacity to prevent job losses. It is, therefore, not hard to see how forces of globalization are partly responsible for generation of pressures on unemployment and national labor markets. The resulting deindustrialization is therefore, in large measure, explicable by the actions of global companies, which account for a huge section of the world's productive capacity and economy and had stronger leverage than union fraternities.

Not surprisingly, the era of globalization has forced countries to adjust their governance structures in order to draw more benefits from the new economic order. Accordingly, unions in developing countries have to build capacities to apply skills, which enable workers to draw maximum benefits from the changed global economic structures. Fairbrother, O'Brien, Junor, O'Donnell, and Williams (2012) correctly point out the trade unions have to change with the times and to retool their management and negotiation practices in response to forces of globalization. More important, they call for greater collective action rather than individualizing efforts to advance labor's cause.

Unions must understand that the nature of work and structure of organizations have changed, and the new knowledge-based economy, which is pegged to distribution and use of information, requires new approaches to conducting labor affairs. Within this reality is that unions have to encounter governments that invest substantial funds into ICTs, which, in countries like Kenya, are now recognized as the drivers of productivity and economic growth. The African state has traditionally been weak when negotiating with global ICT corporations. This in itself is a fact that disadvantages union leaders in the wider scheme of things.

Failure of the state, especially in Africa, to negotiate better terms of investments in sectors run by international corporations means institutions serving employees and workers have to be equipped to play a greater role in humanizing all negotiations. Evans (2014) argues that the strong international connections forged through global interactions and trade should foster new internationalism and bring together unions to solidify their causes. ICTs can be, and are being used by unions to mitigate the effects of trade imbalances and distortions of national economies brought about through globalization. Most important, ICTs make it possible for different members to coordinate their governance structures and provide a platform for union activism. ICTs alone are insufficient, and it takes leadership to help move the union agenda forward.

Unions have witnessed the forces of international trade and transnationalism affect the plight of workers, on a global scale. For example, the North American Free Trade Area (NAFTA) opened doors on union transnationalism in unprecedented ways. This implies unions can build solidarity across borders rather than be complacent with restrictions imposed by national governments. Kay (2005) suggests NAFTA allowed unions to forge international cooperation to bolster their causes even in the midst of restrictions imposed through state legislation. A similar argument may be presented for unions in East Africa, where regional governments frequently stifle activism. Trade unions in Kenya can, therefore, increase their bargaining power through collaborations with other regional unions as a reaction to the expanding economic regional linkages. With cultural and language barriers breaking down, communication among workers should expand rather than be limited through national attempts at fragmenting trade unions.

A similar argument in favor of unions expanding membership supports the contention that globalization may, after all, offer opportunities for unions to flourish in unfavorable political climates (Trubek, Mosher, & Rothstein, 2000). This argumentation articulates the contention that global connectivity allows unions to form rules that give many different national labor unions direction about possible causes of action concerning their missions. Similarly, Lindell (2010) concurs with the argument that transnationalism has positive effects when it comes to building informal coalitions of workers.

Transnationalism can also be seen as boosting union memberships among the rank and file, meaning expanded political clout, even if unions are inactive in their local governments (Anner, 2009; Martin & Brady, 2007). Langevin (2010) adds that the fear of globalization is reason enough for unions to come together and solve their problems. In other words, Langevin finds merit in strengthening union power through internationalism, much like global multinational corporations have established common agendas to leverage their power and thin out labor unions in global and transnational enclaves (Geer & Hauptmeier, 2008). This concluding chapter offers a snapshot of unions as members of global, transnational, and virtual organizations. We explore the various ways in which the new economy requires unions to engage ICTs. There is a strong element of internationalism and solidarity that is enabled through ICTs. These connections empower workers and are a huge part of the modern labor movement, hence, a fitting way to appreciate the role of ICTs in contemporary collective bargaining and labor activism.

Union Members as Consumers of ICT Applications and Digital Workers' Unions

Although unions have responded to emerging ICTs, there are differences among nations. Richer countries fall within networked societies and are high consumers of modern ICTs. And industrialized nations also enjoy better services, in terms of equipment and software packages. Work settings in industrial societies are likely to be better programmed and, hence, adherents of Neo-Taylorism than the emerging market.

Internally, unions employ a host of new ICTs and are getting attuned to various applications. Members are savvy about uses of M-PESA and other popular apps. In addition, internal memos and decision making in the areas of collective bargaining are frequently conducted in new media. Besides, the existence of the Internet of Everything (IoE) makes ICTs an essential component of daily living.

Unions all over the world are taking advantage of ICTs to network and fight for the rights of workers. Unions have several mechanisms for engaging with policy makers and their members. Union members traditionally contact political figures, administrators, and other unions to advocate for change in employment policies and workers' rights. Unions are also actors in collective action issues of international concern. This means that union leaders have to make an effort to be data literate and help organizations understand possible biases inherent in manipulations of data against worker interests. Unions also want to be a part of the new economic frameworks and to utilize ICTs in their workplaces and as a means to safeguard membership employments.

In tandem with emerging economic trends, the growth in numbers of ICT workers calls for a reset in matters dealing with new growth areas in membership. In other words, interests of Africa-based workers in IT sector will somewhat have to be reconfigured into various trade unions. This has already happened in India and Europe, where IT workers are joining unions. In India, for example, the Union for Information Technology and Enabled Services (UNITES) tapped into the more than 2.3 million IT workers and positioned itself as the voice of workers in this large sector. Although unionization of IT workers is growing and encouraged by the International Labor Organization (ILO), rates differ by subsector and region. Most likely, employees in the assembly lines unionize at higher rates than those in the software development industries and services. This is likely to be the case in Kenya as well, where telecommunication sectors are unionized. And there is additional reason for protecting the rights of IT workers. Article 41 of the Constitution (2010) offers the legal framework for workers to participate in union activities in order to attain reasonable working conditions and be subjected to fair labor practices by management. The Bill of Rights in chapter 6 (section 35, 37) of the Constitution is about equality of all people and reinforces the principle of freedom from discrimination in section 36. The constitution also guarantees freedom of association (Section 52) and in section 59, reiterates the principle of rights of workers and trade unions to collective bargain.

Although the ICT sector is not the leading employer in Europe, numbers of employees have grown steadily since the 1970s. ICT jobs in Kenya are increasing and becoming a part of the new economy. It is possible that the ICT sector, as a fraction of GDP, will continue to grow. In Western Europe, ICT accounted for at least 6.3 percent of GDP. This shift signifies changes in the role of manufacturing as a player in economic growth. Even though the shift to more service-oriented economies has taken place, the rates of unionization among IT workers vary with subsector and from one country to another. Evidently, unionization in telecommunication is strong globally. After all, most countries had telephone utilities like postal and telephone services managed through parastatals. The telecommunications sector was previously a strong province of the public sector and was a huge employer in many European and African countries. It is the area of hardware production, dominated by subsidies of multinational corporations, that has experienced zero or low unionization rates. Employers tend to have much bigger leverage in labor-management decisions. American-based ICT software and hardware corporations like IBM and Google are known to take cues from their parent organizations, which are largely anti-union in their practices. Many favor outsourcing ICT workers to places where labor is cheapest. Core ICT workers in Africa's so-called Silicon Valley are not generally unionized. The situation is complicated by gender and age dynamics.

An attendant concern is gender equity in information technology (IT) professions. In many parts of the developing world, there are still age- and gender-related disparities among IT workers. Empirically, ICT work in Kenya is strongly correlated with age, which means that applications for workers in older age brackets are unlikely to be the focus of policy makers. Yet, one must recognize that the population of Kenya, like that of other African nations, is largely youthful. Thus, careers in ICTs are again associated with the youth. Additionally, there are still major issues concerning involvement of women in IT-related industries.

Regardless of the disparities, the main challenge is in the area of highly skilled IT workers, where Africa lags behind other economies. Yet, there is evidence that unions are impacted by ICTs regardless of the proportion of their contribution to GNP. Key areas emerging in the twenty-first century include the changing nature of the global economy and the increased introduction of virtual reality (VR) applications and substitution of labor by automated devices stemming from advances in artificial intelligence (AI).

Artificial Intelligence and Robotics

It is now common knowledge that advances in artificial intelligence (AI) and robotics are changing the nature of work. Automation and robotization have already changed the industrial sector in America, resulting in stagnating wages and a crushed middle class. Autonomous and semiautonomous systems are increasing rather than being reduced. The fear of automation is not new. Benjamin Kirsch, a former member of the the Wage Adjustment Board in the United States and other observers of the American labor movement once predicted automation will weaken labor unions (Kirsh, 1964, p. 172). Although he was concerned about technology in general, the versatility of the ICTs makes them a more potent force in displacement of humans by machines. ICTs are evolving so fast that they are a huge driver of the uncertainty that comes with automation.

Recently, an important paper published by Oxford University scholars Carl Frey and Michael Osborne (2013) suggests that the cost of producing robots has declined and will lead to further substitution of labor by machines. In their estimation, 47 percent of jobs in the United Kingdom (UK) are at risk and will be automated. The net result of this is to deskill future employees and also change the meaning of work. Examples of the unfolding changes are evident in new technologies such as Google's driverless cars that easily replace taxis and bus drivers. Frey and Osborne argue that in the next decade or so, 22–29 percent of U.S. jobs will be provided by offshore workers, who already perform tasks that do not require face-to-face encounters.

Writing for *USA Today*, Elizabeth Weise (2016) suggests the fear of robots and computers taking over most work in the next fifty years is real. Citing a survey by the Pew Research Center, "65 percent of American adults expect that by 2066, robots and computers will 'definitely' and 'probably' do much of the work currently done by humans" (Weise, 2016, p. 2B). According to the report, Americans who "fear the rise of digital workers are those who labor in government, education or at a non-profit" (Weise, 2016, p. 2B).

Researchers note that robotics may in the long run outperform humans at almost any task and job (Williams-Grut, 2016). World-famous futurist Stephen Hawking goes further to assert that artificial intelligence "would spell doom for the human race" (Williams-Grut, 2016). This reality has far-reaching implications for unions. Growth of robotics attracts investors in all regions including China, Australia, France, Germany, Italy, Japan, UK, and India. The proliferation of automation and robotics means, globally, income inequality will be on the rise (Williams-Grut, 2016). Economists predict that over 5 million jobs are at stake in fifteen major and developed or emerging economies (Brinded, 2016; World Economic Forum, 2016).

In a fascinating work, Derek Thompson (2015), a futurist and economic writer for the *Atlantic*, argues that few jobs are safe. Already millions of Americans aged twenty-five to fifty-four are not working in the traditional sense. Without jobs, people lose their sense of identity and status. An emerging class of workers who move from one job to the next is already commonplace in most advanced countries. This group has no bargaining rights, and lacks job security because much work is now automated. Ross (2016) adds that the industries of the future will continue to build on progress in areas such as genomics, robotics, and digital technology. To this list one may add a thorough understanding of the latest developments in virtual reality (VR), which Kevin Kelly (2016), considers a technological force that will shape the future. Given the connections in global economies, the lessons from the developed countries are relevant to Africa. In many ways, these are fields in which African countries need to invest more funds and develop expertise in order to engage the world. Without expanded investments in these fields, social stress and upheavals may arise.

More important is the concern with youth unemployment and the decline in the manufacturing industry in Kenya and other African countries. The situation is so dire that Kenya recently contemplated "exporting" labor to other countries. In 2016, the Jubilee government, through Labor Cabinet Secretary Phylllis Kandie, announced the country would export workers and create local jobs. The number of unemployed youths in Kenya is quite high. Those age eighteen to thirty-five are 35 percent of the population of 44 million. Of these, 10 million are unemployed (Standard, 2016). These trends mean unions have to be psychologically prepared to deal with the unintended consequences of the global economy, which will be fueled by automation and other products of artificial intelligence (AI).

The question will be whether African economies will cope with more unemployment and transformed manufacturing jobs that are largely driven by robots and other computer-mediated devices. Already, leading ethicists like Yale University's Wendel Wallach are calling for a global response to prevent technologies from becoming dangerous masters of human societies (Santini, 2016). Unions have to be in this discussion and to prepare for members' engagement with the new future. After all, today's knowledge-based economy is globally integrated and chances are that companies will continue to seek qualified individuals globally.

One of the reasons for this urgency is the reality of ICT-based job hunting. As Kenyans transfer their skills globally, workers need to be effective at personal networking and use ICTs for effective job searches. The Internet offers excellent recruiting functions and spaces. Unions ought to contribute to these resource. Unions have resources that workers need. Unions may provide information about career opportunities for individuals whose industries have ceased to exist. The Internet is also a key purveyor and facilitator of benchmarking, which requires workers to engage with others internationally. This means that workers have to acquire Internet fluency, especially the art of web surfing and productivity benchmarking. Contemporary union training curriculum must also address issues of the importance of workers observing proper social media etiquette.

Unions and Civil Society in Governance Networks

A stakeholder framework guides the ensuing discussion on why unions are a key component of the governance networks. The basic argument is that some groups have power, legitimacy, and urgency, which are the activities that stakeholders are involved in in support of membership goals. Identification of stakeholders starts with citizens and government officials. Since corporations and government workers, especially union members, are essential to the nation's productive capacity, they are involved in productivity negotiations upon which a nation's economy thrives. Not to mention, union members are citizens first, and, have every right to participate in social, economic, and political debate affecting them. This means unions have power, or the ability to influence political elites and impose members' will on others. While the traditional role of unions as a vehicle of collective bargaining on behalf of workers remains a key area of attention, focus on unions as defenders of the weak and champion for human rights has not changed. The legitimacy of unions comes from sources beyond their existing ability to influence decisions. Trade unions in sub-Saharan Africa, it must be observed, derived much legitimacy through historical circumstances.

Trade unions were active participants in the struggle for independence in Kenya, Ghana, Zambia, and other African countries. For example, the Ghana Trades Union Congress was a key supporter and collaborator of Kwame Nkurumah's struggle for freedom. Later on, TUC supported the formation of the All Africa Trade Union Federation (AATUF), which was the forerunner to the Organization of African Trade Union Unity (OATUU). With seventy-three affiliates in most African countries, OATUU represents the trade union movement and seeks to achieve trade union unity throughout the continent. OATUU has established goals to seek harmonization of labor legislation and to defend the material and moral interests of workers. The organization also has a mission to seek economic and social justice for African workers. COTU is an affiliate of this pan-African organization and therefore serves to remind workers of the need to be politically active.

As citizens, and members of civil society, union members individually and collectively are active in social movements. When unions participate in social movements, they help promote change. Their activism may be both formal and informal. In general, countries that have more open societies have had the most investments in ICTs. For example, South Africa, has higher levels of openness and investments from European and American IT corporations. In Kenya, ICT corporations like Safaricom drive the political process in a profound way. Safaricom, and other players in the ICT world, are players in finance (including political campaign finance solicitations through M-PESA) and in security matters as alluded to in previous chapters. Safaricom was a contractor in the installation of critical Closed-Circuit Television (CCTV) infrastructure that is part of the arsenal against religious and political fundamentalists now dominating political discourse.

In addition, the company directly contributed to the political recruitment process through support of the voting data. Safaricom was awarded a tender to supply Biometric Voter Registration (BVR) and Electronic Voter Identification Devices (EVID) after outbidding companies like EASCO Africa, ACIE Technologies, Charvins Limited, Estelle Distributors, and Nouvelle Technology (Republic of Kenya, AG, 2014, p. 177). Such direct participation in facilitation of political actions and processes is a defining feature of the political power of ICTs and must be understood in full by all stakeholders, including trade unions. The role of international IT corporations further illustrates the externalization of local politics through instant broadcasting results and enhancing global human rights, if the process is deemed fair and transparent.

It follows, therefore, the quality of democratization is also an important variable in the protection of IT investments. This can be seen in countries like Botswana and Mauritius, which have periodic elections. Although Kenya's election process is regular, as evident by periodic elections, there were challenges in the management of the IT infrastructure during the 2007 presidential election. However, the country's business community has benefited from a fairly open culture, exemplified by the existence of numerous publications, some of which are fairly critical of the government's policies (Marthoz, 2002, p. 42). As a result of liberal policy frameworks, Kenya's investment climate for ICTs has resulted in capital inflows leading to robust development of Internet and mobile phone platforms. These platforms provide avenues for networking among different elements of the civil society, including labor unions.

An aspect of networking for action is to strategize on their common interests. Through e-activism, unions as a group are increasingly being brought together to exchange information on workers' rights and terms and conditions of service. In some instances, union members use online resources for training, webinars, and learning from each other on types of content to provide to members. A visit to any union website reveals elements of mobilization for action and reiteration of missions and aspirations for workers. Besides, union e-newsletters are great informational resources for members.

Unions, as part of civil society, are also engaging their respective polities to utilize the Internet for expressing policy preferences in areas such as housing, food security, and social empowerment. Union websites have links to sites known to promote peace, empower women, and eliminate of racism.

Consider the example of KNUT, which has already signaled its support for digital literacy in Kenya. Regardless of the initial apprehension, the union has to utilize its resources to help promote the ideology of leveraging ICTs for navigating the new economy. Governments, on the other hand, have to provide enabling environments for unions to act responsibly especially by encouraging members to be advocates of using ICTs for empowerment. In other words, the labor movement should use ICTs to transform its activities for the benefit of workers.

At the level of campaigning for offices, union leaders have moved to social media to advertise their virtues. This implies e-campaigning is not just confined to political officials. Union leaders use ICT platforms to campaign for policy positions and strike decisions as part of their operations. Union websites, on some occasions, provide profiles of officials and their visions. Ordinary citizens also have opportunities to discuss labor union issues on social media. For example, in 2015, much commentary about union-engineered strikes occurred in social media like Facebook, WhatsApp, and Twitter. While politically motivated polling has not necessarily been employed for labor-related issues, social media also serves to have a sense of union position on various policy issues.

In the same breath, unions have not yet embraced e-voting techniques for their general meetings. Neither have unions in Kenya presented a cohesive statement on national elections moving toward automated or electronic referenda on debates over constitutional reforms. There was, however, a move by COTU and its affiliates to support reforms in the Independent Electoral and Boundaries Commission (IEBC), which supervises national elections in the country. Many union leaders and church clergy demanded the resignation of IEBC, arguing it was impartial and would not conduct free and fair elections in 2017. A more profound observation was that union leaders offered disjointed and tepid contributions to the formulation of the National ICT Policy document released in 2016. Unions were not effectively represented in consultative meetings leading to revisions of the draft National ICT Sector Policy.

In the spirit of shared governance, one would have expected firm statements on concerns over hacking of government websites that has been reported in Kenya. Issues such as cyber security and protection of workers' privacy and vital information and prevention of identity theft require vigilance from all stakeholders. Mobilization of union members and call to action through ICT forums has, however, been observed and widely reported.

Among the most successful union efforts at employing e-activism was evident during the September 2015 teachers strike in Kenya. Union members used a variety of social media including Facebook, WhatsApp, Youtube, and Twitter to organize collectively. Members also used creative codes in speeches meant to highlight their resolve and solidarity. For instance, during rallies, members were exhorted to use the "password" (slogan) 50–60 to remind the government that unions were demanding a pay raise of 50–60 percent as had been awarded by the industrial court.

Further examples were found in the increased use of text messaging among union leaders to announce actions like strikes and meetings. And the use of Yahoo! email accounts for operational purposes is quite common. In addition, unions use Internet activism to exchange idea on social media and in blogs. Kenya's labor movement has demystified the use of computer-mediated devices integrated with mobile phones. Furthermore, unions like COTU use their websites for e-civics purposes, to educate the masses about union roles in good governance and the history of unionism and its role in national politics. E-civics initiated through union websites adds to the volume of information on democratic governance. Union members have a host of tactics for engaging with the policy processes, where democratic space allows. In contemporary political dispensation, union members are accorded the freedoms of association and may also participate in elections just like other citizens. Beyond elections, union members are free to contact their senators, MPs, and other government officials. At the same time, unions may and have donated funds to *harambees* (fund-raising meetings), or advocated for change in social causes outside of collective bargaining.

Union E-Activism, Advocacy, and Social Change

Overall, the principle of engagement in policy areas has been well described. We discussed union activism in areas such as security and minimum wage legislation among other issues. But how do unions engage each other and mobilize for changes within the workers' movement in the face of emerging new technologies? How do unions leverage mobile telecommunications and other ICTs to effectively participate in both collective bargaining and social change?

When union members come together to advocate for a cause, or when members organize and provide support to other civil society groups, change happens. Unions have great potential to reshape civil society by focusing attention on the basic needs of the country's workers and also by exposing corruption in society. Unions are also strong advocates for collective action to promote social justice and increase freedoms. Kenya's history confirms just that.

At the international level, the 24/7 economies have made it much easier for unions to know of labor actions in other parts of the world. Unions in Kenya and other African countries have a unique capacity to adopt strategies learned from other parts of the world. Union internationalism goes beyond paying attention to collective action in individual countries to setting agendas for building solidarity against the growth of corporate power across the globe. This, then, means that unions in Kenya are stakeholders in the search for fair working conditions and the legitimacy of collective bargaining. By utilizing ICTs, unions in Kenya expect support from other workers' organizations and the protection of the legitimacy of their claims and interests.

Such support was reported in numerous occasions. Most recently, during the aforementioned teachers strike of September 2015, KNUT received support from the Danish Union of Teachers (DLFs), which wrote a letter to KNUT chairman Wilson Sossion and Secretary General Mudzo Nzili offering support for their cause. In DLF's letter, President Anders Bondo Christensen urged the government of Kenya to respect the ruling of the Supreme Court and not close public schools in Kenya. The messages were broadcast online and shared with millions of Kenyans.

KNUT's strike was prolonged and widespread. As a result, it affected the lives of students and ordinary citizens. Facebook and other social media showed examples of activities that students were engaged in in the absence of teachers. In addition, media carried several stories that depicted unionists as greedy and unselfish. Dissenting voices were heard in various online spaces including claims to the effect that unions had lost appeal among members, hence reluctance of some teachers to pay membership dues through payroll deductions. Union leaders countered by presenting narratives about government's failure to respect the rule of law by not honoring a court order to pay teacher's salary increases. Strike information messaging miniblogs through Twitter were also broadcast widely.

KNUT's Twitter feed had interesting comments. For example, Secretary General Wilson Sossion posted while in Ghana, attending an education forum in October 2015, that he appreciated Kenyans for recognizing the unions efforts. Union members also debated the issue of supporting candidates that supported their cause. KNUT posted on Twitter names of politicians that members should contact in efforts to boost the chances of realizing their goals. An interesting dimension of the Twitter activism was the re-tweeting of union endorsement of Hillary Clinton's presidential bid for the U.S. presidency in 2017. Using social media in campaigning and mobilization is not just confined to political recruitment processes, but for broadcasting the importance of unions in political development. That is the reality in Kenya where, for instance, KNUT's leadership seems to have been enthused by the National Education Association's (NEA) endorsement of Hillary Clinton's candidacy for the Democratic Party's nomination in 2016. KNUT tweeted that it was the responsibility of the union to guide citizens in electing candidates that would invest in children's future.

KNUT also used email to reach out to supporters worldwide. By using existing Yahoo! accounts, trade union leaders reached out to online databases of likeminded unionists to articulate their cause. So far, neither KNUT nor COTU have invested in sophisticated infernal computer networks, as do American universities. And neither KNUT nor KUPPET has identifiable listserves through which they can broadcast messages to members. The listserve model in the age of webinars can be used to support union conferences but has not been promoted in Kenya. Nevertheless, trade unions were able to take advantage of social media and other web-based labornets to promote public support for their trade union struggles.

KNUT members used open networks like Yahoo! and Hotmail (MSN-Microsoft) platforms to reach out to the outside world. Using these platforms, KNUT and other Kenyan unions put to use new technologies to alert the global community of the struggles of Kenyan teachers. As a result, there was overwhelming support from overseas unions.

As an example, a global union, Education International, which has 30 million members worldwide, wrote to President Kenyatta on September 28, 2015, requesting the government to implement court decisions confirming the pay raise demanded. Education International also asked the government of Kenya to engage in a meaningful dialogue with Kenya's teachers' unions, Kenya Union of Post Primary Education Teacher (KUPPET) and Kenya National Union of Teachers (KNUT). Of particular concern to Education International was its disapproval of the government's use of threats and abuse of freedoms of teachers to assemble and collectively bargain. Contents of the letter from Education International were rebroadcast in KNUT's Facebook forum. These examples of labor telematics only scratch the surface of what is certainly an extensive use of Internet and computer-mediated technologies in labor internationalism and building of networks for promoting workers' rights.

Unions in Kenya are affiliated to the International Labor Organization (ILO) and other international organizations. The ILO has been an important player in union development in Africa. In the past, the ILO helped establish forums for labor solidarity and founded the First of May movement (Sturmthal, 1972, p. 130). Today, ILO remains a key player in offering development programs for union leaders. Its overall focus is to raise living standards for working people and reduce exploitation of labor. In many ways, ILO sets the tone for unions to cooperate in the achievement of overall goals.

Although African unions have much to learn from their more experienced European counterparts, the methods of activism are not a direct copy of each other. Strategies adopted are a function of economic, political, and legal setting in each country. Moreover, globalization has impacted countries in varied ways. For example, export-processing zones in Kenya operate in situations of massive unemployment, and hence create much higher hurdles for union leaders.

In terms of political ability and strategy, unions in Kenya were based on the British model but experienced much transformation after independence. Before independence, unions saw themselves as part of the struggle against colonialism and as a key component of the struggle for independence. Anthony Clayton and Donald Savage (1974) illustrate that unions in East Africa were very much part of the international movement and sought affiliations and partnerships on matters affecting workers. Before independence, the World Federation of Trade Unions took a more leftist approach to workers' issues. The former Soviet Union and its allies dominated it. As a result, the Western countries formed, in 1949, the International Confederation of Free Trade Unions (ICFTU), which continued to have a strong Western European workers' agenda. ICFTU was dissolved in October 2006 after a merger with the World Confederation of Labor (WCL), resulting in the formation of the International Trade Union Confederation (ITUC). ITUC's African Regional Organization was formed in 2007. The regional group merged with DOAWTU and has close to 16 million members and 103 affiliated trade unions in Africa.

ICFTU had been proactive in setting an agenda for trade unions in the new millennium, especially setting out parameters for navigating the information economy, youth in the workplace, migrant workers, and union mergers. These agendas are a part of the conversation of much of labor activity in today's East Africa. In the contemporary Silicon Age, unions have to change strategy and methods. Not only have unions sought the support of the international solidarity movement, but have used international support in their endeavors.

KNUT and KUPPET are members of Education International (EI). There are also efforts to strengthen the capacity of the teachers' unions through exchange of knowledge and activities and engagement with the political leadership in matters concerning education. The East African Teachers Union leaders have a loose affiliation in which they have attempted to constitute forums for developing strategies to advance their common interests.

Other unions affiliated to Education International are the Kenya Union of Domestic, Hotels, Educational Institutions, Hospitals and Allied Workers (KUDHEIHA), and the Universities' Academic Staff Union (UASU). In addition, COTU is a member of the East African Trade Union Confederation (EATUC), a coalition of labor organizations from Kenya, Rwanda, Uganda, Tanzania, and Zanzibar. EATUC is concerned about protection of migrant workers and the free movement of persons in the region. One of its most important foci has been to articulate the interests of African workers, especially in the wake of trade deals with advanced countries. Notably, EATUC voiced its concern that the U.S. African

Growth and Opportunity Act (AGOA) lacked sufficient protections for the rights of East African workers. Also, one of its main tasks is to work toward harmonization of labor laws in the East African region.

COTU is also a member of the International Federation of Trade Union Organization (IFTUO). In that capacity, COTU joins other IFTUO members to promote employee welfare and safety in the workplace. COTU's activism is regulated through the Labour Relations Act of 2007, which also recognizes the union management structures in affiliate members. The Act, under section 26, as it stands permits unions to amalgamate for purposes of achieving their objectives (Republic of Kenya, 2007). This in itself reinforces the need for unions to leverage ICTs to build capacities for collaborative endeavors.

Along with the aforementioned affiliations, unions have much to gain from partnerships with each other. For instance, unions can network as a matter of building new values and economic necessity. Unions need each other to reestablish the position of the worker in relation to that of the corporate manager. All over the world, corporations have already reinvented themselves by alignments with sections of the political elite to weaken labor. Some authors argue that failure to "fit into the informational society" has contributed to the decline of unions (Naisbitt & Aburdene, 1985, p. 83). The question becomes just how do unions in East Africa leverage the information society to remain relevant in the twenty-first century?

One expects unions to build on networks already established to promote worker agendas. Mechanisms need to be in place to induce union participation in organizational learning. Learning can take place in cyberspace and in virtual communities or other forums. Eric Lee's (1997) work outlined the rise of labornets by tracing the use of the Internet since 1969. These labornets were forms of bulletin boards in cyberspace (p. 45). According to Lee (1997), trade unionists used computers during the early 1980s for communication, especially email and computer networking. Among the first online network was built in British Columbia in 1981. The British Columbia Federation of Teachers (BCTF) regarded the Internet as a communication channel for member mobilization and information exchange. BCTF gave out training and terminals to members as far back as 1983 (Lee, 1997, p. 51). Joining in the race to embrace ICT communications was the Canadian Union of Public Employees (CUPE), which represented civil servants. It was a pioneer in acquiring a computer mainframe for mailing mass mail to its members.

Later, Europeans trade unions established "labor telematics" in the mid-1980s. This took advantage of new platforms to articulate a vision that would counter the growing power of corporations. At this time, the labor movement needed strategies of e-activism against corporate policies that undermined workers' rights, including vacations, pensions, and other benefits. South Africa was first African nation to establish e-participation networks that concerned unions. Lee (1997, p. 46) reports that the first international gathering of online activists took place in Manchester, England, in April 1992, just a few years after online platforms crystallized into mature communication systems. At this time, a number of international trade secretariats including the International Federation of Chemical, Energy, and General Workers' Unions (ICEF) had built global networks, thereby ushering in new trends in networking.

Internationalization has meant that union databases and online e-learning platforms were now more than ever offering services to workers beyond their boundaries. Emerging electronic mail systems were now in place and were extensively utilized to enrich union movements across the nations. In the 1980s and 1990s, emails served as a medium through which distribution of information on union matters was facilitated. Moreover, unions could now exchange ideas on work-related hazards and policies, with the aim to improve working conditions of union members.

Networking is one element of building coalitions for improvements in workers' conditions worldwide. Yet that is not enough. Through use of social media, partnerships can be and have been negotiated with nonunion members and the public at large. During the September Teachers strike in Kenya, it was widely noticed that KNUT members received support from a section of the public through Facebook "likes" of the general principle that teachers' pay was low and needed to be raised, in accordance with previous agreed-upon principles. Union effectiveness can be boosted if the public is sympathetic to their cause. Conversely, without non-union-member support, political support, which is necessary for raising salaries of public employees, is considerably weakened or undermined.

As previously observed, ICTs enhance prospects for partnerships internationally. When unions champion their cause in terms of human rights, their grievances are likely to take on a different meaning. Acceptance of union points of view is enhanced in situations where union members have established stronger networks internationally. Partnership encompasses both individual and organizational levels, especially involving employee representatives and leaders. It has to be deliberate and intentional in order for unions to successfully engage the global community.

The relationship between information technologies and globalization of the workplace has become a focus for discussion among union leaders and academics. Most consider ICTs as a force that must be understood and engaged. From a social organization standpoint, ICTs create a borderless world in which foreign telecommunication corporations will dictate production activities in ways beyond the control of traditional union frameworks. And still, union members must understand their limitations, especially if brought to bear through the lack of ICT resources or dimensions of the digital divide.

While globalization is making it possible for African villages to be wired, unwired worlds are vulnerable in the sense that workers in those areas are off mainstream collective bargaining activities. ICTs are well known to promote digital democracy, and workers who are excluded inevitably bargain and mobilize from a weakened position. To engage the ICTs, union leaders and members must exploit the opportunities available through the new media. The unions must design processes that interrogate technologies.

In preparation for engaging ICTs, union leaders must be capable of expanding their human capital base. One cannot leverage information and communication technologies from an ignorant point of view. Understanding the state of the art in ICTs requires revisiting the questions of organizational structure and pathways taken to engage the new platforms. Unions have a window of opportunity to link their activities to the new platforms. This is the new paradigm for unionization. It entails the removal of barriers to learning about ICTs as a user and a tool for social learning in new spaces. Unions need to recognize that protest and strike actions, in this new digital era, are global real-time events. Global audiences are assured through simple tools like mobile phones and the Internet.

Moreover, the same platforms are avenues for creating communities. Union members are now members of virtual communities that can exchange ideas about organization and strategy. The new infrastructure creates alternative models of collaboration and internationalization of activities. Collaborative models are now possible, across borders. The prevailing state of the ICT world makes it possible for information to be shared in two-way directions, from managers to the bottom, and from the grassroots to the top. The new platforms also provide avenues for horizontal engagements with different employer organizations.

Way Forward: Changes in Organizational Structures and Internal Dynamics

In the past century, organizations were the dominant structures in society. Today, virtual organizations are key to societal functioning because ICTs have been absorbed into our psyche. A good part of what we do in society is digitized and archived in the new media. Nearly all communications are in digital format and careers are built around ICT platforms. The story of ICTs is the story of human society in the twenty-first century. Without the power of ICTs, businesses cannot have investors. And once ICTs are available, the Internet is the most efficient form for articulating its vision and purpose. With ICTs, trade unions can recruit members and help socialize them into constituents for the cause of labor. Growing the membership base takes place if unions effectively utilize their ICT platforms.

According to observers, technology now shapes how organizations function. And nearly all significant organizations adopt some kind of ICT or the other. The transformation is rapid and it is anticipated that at some point, the digital divide will be narrow and proliferation of key ICTs in most countries assured. Information technology has much to do with globalization, and it is increasingly clear that almost all businesses will be marketed through some kind of digital platform. No question, technology is playing a huge role in shaping organizations, and academic studies are well underway to determine and identify the most consequential ways in which ICTs shape trade union and other organizational structures.

Since union management structure starts from the local level in workplaces, the majority of elected leaders, including the shop steward, use social media for networking and communications. Social networking has been a vital ingredient in the election of shop stewards. Likewise, communication between different trades is facilitated through the new ICTs. As an umbrella body, COTU affiliates are now part of a virtual community in pursuit of common goals.

Rapid growth of the ICT sector means the focus on collective bargaining may also be impacted. New techniques and new skills have to be factored into collective bargaining decisions. Someone has to do ICT jobs, for example chief information officers (CIOs) in various government departments and companies.

The identity of traditional management has changed. Budgeting and Human Resource Management Systems (HRIS) have forced all organizations, including unions, to change work policies, processes, and structures. HRIS applications are broad and include keeping track of employee metrics for reporting and compliance purposes. Armed with appropriate software, organizations can accumulate information about their capacities, accomplishments, and strategic objectives all in a dashboard. From a data perspective, organizations are concerned with data to ensure efficient and effective ways to retain system-wide accuracy.

Without data-driven strategies, human resource managers are not going to do a good job tracking down ethnicity or tribalism at public offices. HRIS allow organizations to follow cases of discrimination based on religion or sexism and tribalism. HRIS are valuable for human resource development as well. Through HRIS, managers can register employees in training and track salary deductions and offer opportunities for evaluation of training programs. HRIS are also helpful for tracking employee disciplinary records, especially where unions are affected. For their part, unions should also be able to access some of the data used by employers across organizations. Unions must have capacities to engage organizations such as the National Social Security Fund (NSSF), which embrace HRIS platforms to manage workers' retirement funds. In many instances retirement funds are invested in private and state-owned corporations, which are linked to global corporations, especially by way of consumption of IT software and hardware products. In this networked world, union leaders cannot afford to ignore changes in the global arena.

Without doubt, corporations such as Safaricom are players in complex systems of collaborative governance. The clear implication is that cross-sector collaboration means unions have to be an informed partner in finding solutions to problems that affect both government and private sectors. For example, downsizing, brought about through corporate reorganization following globalization, means that trade unions have to find new ways of understanding the rights of union members. There is significant evidence to illustrate that workplace processes are impacted by forces outside the purview of workers. An immediate example that is visible in government offices is the urge to automate through devices run by computer software. For instance, the modern workplace does not require as many operators as used to be the case, I mention the case of lift (elevator) operators or copy machine operators. Most modern machines have digital switches that can be operated by anyone with access codes and passwords. Trade unions have to take into account the changed organizational work processes, forms and structures. Unions also must be informed about the changed workplace and embrace new, but relevant technologies in their operations. Unions should use ICT to share experiences. When members belong to multiple digital communities, members can tap into available resources from the many virtual platforms and networks. Unions in Kenya and other parts of Africa are beginning to recognize the huge potential benefits of collaboration, especially when larger unions with greater resources provide a helping hand.

CONCLUSIONS

In conclusion, union strategies in both public and private sectors have to be cognizant of the existing realities in the global economy. Currently, alliances between unions and other organizations are the norm and have been institutionalized. Through forces of globalization, an ICT-driven economy exists and has a direct impact on collective bargaining processes. In the new economy, networks and partnerships have been established and solidified in virtual organizations. Whether unions are small or large, they have to make adjustments in the age of ICTs. Because unions represent workers in various occupations, their aim is to protect the jobs and rights of members. And unions, as stakeholders in governance structures, are expected to offer leadership in navigation of the new economic production arenas and activities. The effectiveness of unions in exerting energies for collaborations is a function of union leadership. More profoundly, through collaborative structures and networks, unions have to explore ways through which members can constructively explore all aspects of their problems, including differences among unions and their members, and chart out workable solutions. Through ICTs, collaborative governance processes that include exchanges of ideas and member education on social media and union websites are now a common feature in unionism. And because changes in how work is done have already taken place, ICTs are at the forefront of these new ways of work. Constant informational exchanges on strategies for mobilization and interest articulation will be necessary for union activity at both local and international levels.

References

Aaron, B. (1965). Government restraints on featherbedding. In P. A. Weinstein (ed.), *Featherbedding and technological change* (pp. 11–16). Boston, MA: DC Heath and Company.

Acemoglu, D., & Verdier, T. (1998). Property rights, corruption, and the allocation of talent: A general equilibrium approach. *Economics Journal* 450, 1381–403.

Achuka, V. (2015, February 15). Fierce battle for billions slams on the brakes from cashless fare system. *Daily Nation*. Retrieved from http://www.nation.co.ke.

———, & Okoth, E. (2016, October 30). Concerns raised about overall health of Kenya's economy. *Daily Nation*. Retrieved from http://www.nation.co.ke/news/reports-raise-concern-about-overall-health-of-economy/1056–3434768–17f4nlz/index.html.

Adams, D. A., Nelson, R. R., & Todd, P. A. (1992). Perceived usefulness, ease of use, and usage of information technology: A replication. *MIS Quarterly* 16 (2), 227–47.

African Union. (2004). *Strategic plan of the commission of the African Union: 2004–2007*. Addis Ababa: African Union.

Aidt, T. (2009). Corruption, institution and economic development. *Oxford Review of Economic Policy* 25, 271–91.

Ali, A. (2007, July 3). Our terms for electing Kibaki. *Standard*. Retrieved from http://www.standard.media.co.ke.

Alic, J. A. (1997). Knowledge, skill, and education in the new global economy. *Futures* 29(1), 5–16.

Ally, J. (2013, March 18). Atwoli to head new global labor body. *Standard*. Retrieved from http://www.standardmedia.co.ke.

Amishadai, L. A. (1965). *The civil service in new African states*. New York: Frederick Praeger.

Amutabi, M. N., & Oketch, M. (2003). Experimenting in distance education: The African Virtual University (AVU) and the paradox of World Bank in Kenya. *International Journal of Educational Development* 23, 57–73.

Andersson, M., & Karlsson, C. (2007). Knowledge in regional economic growth. *Industry and innovation* 14, 129–49.

Anguka, J. (1998). *Absolute power*. London: Zed Books.

Anner, M. (2009). Two logics of labor organizing in the global apparel industry. *International Studies Quarterly* 53 (3), 545–70.

Anyanzwa, J. (2014, May 28). Laptops cash used to pay Anglo Leasing debt. *Standard Digital News*. Retrieved from http://www.standardmedia.co.ke.

Asian Development Bank. (1998). *Asian development outlook*. Mandaluyong City, Philippines: Information Office.

Assane, D., & Grammy, A. (2003). Institutional framework and economic development: International evidence. *Applied Economics* 35, 1811–17.

Atwoli, F. (2011, June). Conference speech: Remarks at the 100th session of the ILO conference, Geneva, Switzerland Retrieved from http://www.cotu-kenya.org/index.php?src=30.

———. (2014, January 30). Jeff Koinange Live. YouTube. KTN News. Retrieved from https://www.youtube.com/results?search_query=Atwoli+the+Bench+Koinange.

Ayitei, G. 1992. *Africa Betrayed*. New York: Palgrave Macmillan.

Azam, J. (1997). *Bypassing the state: economic growth in Kenya, 1964–1990*. Organization for Paris: Economic Cooperation and Development.

Babu, R. B. (ed.). (1996). *Changing global political context and Afro-Asia. strategies for development*. New Delhi: South Asian Publishers.

Baily, P. J. H. (2008). *Procurement principles and management*. Harlow, England: Prentice Hall Financial Times.

Ball, K. S. (2001). The use of human resource information systems: a survey. *Personnel Review* 30(6), 677–93.

Barclay, C., & Duggan, E. W. (2008). Rethinking the digital divide: Towards a path of digital effectiveness. Proceedings of the 41st Hawaii International Conference on System Sciences. IEEE Computer Society. Retrieved from http://www.computer.org/csdl/.../hicss/.../30750129.pdf.

BBC. (1998). South Korea: economic reforms run into difficulty. (May 27). Retrieved from http://news.bbc.co.uk/2/hi/special_report/1998/asian_economic_crises/45476.stm.

———. (2014a, November 20). Kenya orders probe into 12,000 "ghost workers" on payroll. Retrieved from http://www.bbc.com/news/world-africa-30137326.

———. (2014b, September 30). Kenya's economy grows by 25% after recalculation. Retrieved from www.bbc.com/news/business-29426575.

Bellamy, C., & Taylor, J. (1994). Introduction: Exploiting IT in public administration-towards the Information Polity? *Public Administration Review* 72(1–2).

Berg, I., & Kuhn, J. (1962). The assumptions of featherbedding. *Labor Law Review Journal* 13(4), 277–83.

Berg-Schlosser, D. (1992). Ethnicity, social classics and the political process in Kenya. In W. O. Oyugi (ed.). *Politics and Administration in East Africa* (244–96). Nairobi: Konrad Adenauer Foundation and English Press.

Berman, E. M., Bowman, J. S., West, J. P., & Van Wart, M. R. (2016). *Human resource management in public service: Paradoxes, processes, and problems*.

Berry, L., Mirabito, A., & Baun, W. (2010). What's the hard return on employee wellness programs? *Harvard Business Review* 88(12), 104–12.

Beukes-Amiss, M. (2014). Into the heart of the global economy. The eLerning report Africa 2014. Berlin, Germany: ICWE. Retrieved from http://www.eLearningafrica.com.

Bhattacherjee, A., & Premkumar, G. (2004). Understanding changes in belief and attitude toward information technology usage: A theoretical model and longitudinal test. *MIS Quarterly* 28(2), 229–54.

Boughanmi, A. (2009). Human development and economic growth. *The Business Review of Cambridge* 13, 252–59.

Bovaird, T., & Loffler, E. (2009). *Public management and governance*. London: Routledge.

Bowman, W. (2010). Governance, technology and the search for modernity in Kenya. *William and Mary Policy Review* 1, 87–116.

Brademas, J., & Heimann, F. (1998). Tackling international corruption: No longer taboo. *Foreign Affairs* 77(5), 17–20.

Brinded, L. (2016, January 18). Robots, automation, will replace 5 million human jobs by 2020. *Business Insider*. January 18. Retrieved from http://www.businesinsider.com.

Broos, A. (2005). Gender and information and communication technologies (IT) anxiety: male self-assurance and female hesitation. *CyberPsychology & Behavior* 8(1), 21–31.

Brown, J. (2015, February 25). Internet of Things expected to quadruple in size by 2020. *Governing Magazine*. Retrieved from http://www.governing.com/templates/gov/gov_id.

Brown, W., & Walsh, J. (1991). Pay determination in Britain in the 1980s: The anatomy of decentralization. *Oxford Review of Economic Policy* 7, 44–59.

Callaghy, T. M. (1988). The state and the development of capitalism in Africa: Theoretical, historical and comparative reflections. In Chazan, N. & D. Rothchild (eds.), *The precarious balance: State and society in Africa*. Boulder, CO: Westview Press.

Campbell, J. R. (1994). Creating technology capacity: The changing role of the Korean state since the Third Republic [PhD Dissertation]. Miami University, Oxford, OH.
Carson, T. (2015). *Work simply: Embracing the power of your personal productivity Style* [E-Book, MP3 CD]. Charlotte, NC: Brilliance Audio.
Castells, M. (1996). *The rise of the network society (The information age: Economy, society and culture, Volume 1)*. Malden, MA: Blackwell Publishers.
———. (2000). *The rise of the network society*. Oxford, England: Blackwell Publishers.
CBS Dallas. (2015, February 11). Apple sets record with $710 billion value. Retrieved from http://dfw.cbslocal.com/2015/02/11/apple-sets-record-with-710-billion-value/.
Chaison, G. N. (1996). *Union mergers in hard times: The view from five countries*. Ithaca, NY: Cornell University Press.
Chazan, N. (1988). Patterns of state-society incorporation and disengagement in Africa. In Chazan, N., & D. Rothchild (eds.), *The precarious balance state and society in Africa*. Boulder, CO: Westview Press.
Chege, M. (1987). The state and labour in Kenya. In P. A. Nyongo (ed). *Popular struggles for democracy in Africa* (pp. 248–64). London: Zed Books.
Chepkoech, A. (2015, December 24). Atwoli hints at working with Raila in 2017 elections. *Daily Nation*. Retrieved from http://www.nation.co.ke/Atwoli-hints-at-union-with Raila/.
Clarke, R. Y. (2015, October). Smart cities and the Internet of everything: The foundation for delivering next generation citizen services. IDC Government Insights. #G1243955. White Paper. CISCC. Framingham, MA: International Data Corporation, IDC.
Clayton, A., & Savage, D. C. (1974). *Government and labor in Kenya, 1895–1963*. London, England: Frank Cass.
CNN (1998). Cable News Network, Focus Money Link, TV program aired November 17, 7:30 EST.
Compa, L. A., & Diamond, S. F. (1995). *Human rights, labor rights, and international trade: Law and policy perspectives*. Philadelphia, PA: University of Pennsylvania Press.
Cooper, R. (2002). To organize wherever the necessity exists: The activities of the organizing committee of the labor council of NSW, 1900–1910. *Labor History*, 83, 43–64.
COTU. (2003, May 26–28). Report of trade union experiences with PRSP in Kenya-presented at the ICFTU-AFRO Sub-regional seminar on PRSPs in East Africa. Nairobi, Kenya.
Coughlin, P., & Ikiara, G. K. (eds.). (1988). *Industrialization in Kenya: In search of a strategy*. London: James Currey.
Cullen, R. (2006). E-government and the digital divide. In Hernon, P., Cullen, R., & Relyea, H. (eds.), *Comparative perspectives on e-government: Serving today and building for tomorrow* (pp. 289–313). Lanham, MD: Scarecrow Press.
Daily Nation. (2008, June 25). Editorial: An illiterate society is an abomination. Retrieved from http://www.nation.co.ke.
———. (2012, April 9). War against cattle theft goes hi-tech. Retrieved from http://www.nation.co.ke.
———. (2013, June 13). Sh 53 .2 billion for the free laptop program. Retrieved from http://www.nation.co.ke.
———. (2014, December 14). 22 Million Kenyans languish in poverty. Retrieved from http://www.nationmedia.co.ke.
———. (2015, February 12). House team casts doubts on police ability to use CCTV cameras in war on crime. Retrieved from http://www.nation.co.ke.
———. (2015, March 9). Kenya's women close digital gap. Retrieved from http://www.nation.co.ke.
Dareel, E. (2015, April 7). Kuppet asks teachers to leave volatile regions. News 24 Kenya. Retrieved from http://m.news24.com/kenya/MyNews24/Kuppet-asks-teachers-to-leave-volatile-regions-20150407.

Darkoh, M. K. (2015). Industrialization and rural development in the Anglophone African countries. *Journal of Developing Societies* 3 (3), 358–84.

Davis, F. D. (1989). Perceived usefulness, perceived ease of use, and user acceptance of information systems. *MIS Quarterly* 13 (3), 319–40.

———, Bagozzi, R. P., & Warshaw, P. R. (1989). User acceptance of computer technology: A comparison of two theoretical models. *Management Science* 35(8), 982–1003.

De Argaez, E. (2016). Internet World Stats: Usage and population statistics, 2015. Miniwatts de Columbia Ltda. Bogota, Colombia. Retrieved from http://www.internetworldstats.com/.

De Donk, W. B. H., & Tops, P. W. (2006). Informatization and democracy: Orwell or Athens? A review of the literature. In E. E. Otenyo & N. S. Lind (eds.). *Comparative Public Administration: The essential readings* (pp. 635–66). Oxford, UK: Elsevier.

De Leon, P. (1993). *Thinking about political corruption*. New York: M. E. Sharpe.

Denning, P. J. (1996, May 27–31). The university's next challenges. *Communications of the ACM* 39(5).

Derbyshire, H. (2003, January 25). Gender issues in the use of computers in education in Africa. *Imfundo*. Retrieved from http://imfundo.digitalbrain.com.

de Vaal, A., & Ebben, A. (2011). W. Institutions and the relation between corruption and economic growth. *Review of Developmental Economics* 15, 108–23.

Devani, A. (2003, November 5). Anticipated challenges and possible intervention. Paper presented at the Technical, Industrial, Vocational and Entrepreneurship Symposium, Nyeri, Kenya.

———. (2003, November 6). Anticipated challenges and possible intervention. Paper presented at Conference in Nyeri. National Symposium for Technical, Industrial, Vocational and Entrepreneurship. Retrieved from http://www.standardmedia.co.ke.

Diamond, L. (1987). Class formation in the swollen African state. *The Journal of Modern African Studies* 25 (4), 567–96.

Digischool Secretariat, ICT Authority. 2016. Digischool access to learning project, Nairobi: ICT Authority. Retrieved from http://www.digischool.icta.go.ke.

Dobo, N. (2014, December 29). School buses bring Wi-Fi to Impoverished families. The Hechinger Report. Retrieved from http://www.centerdigitaled.com/news/School-Buses-Bring-Wi-Fi-to-Families.html.

Drucker, P. F. (1994). *Post-capitalist society*. New York: Harper Collins.

Ducker, P. (1991). The new productivity challenge. *Harvard Business Review* 69, 69–79.

Durndell, A., & Thomson, K. (1997). Gender and computing: a decade of change? *Computers & Education* 28 (1), 1–9.

Durst, S. L., & De Santis, V. S. (1997). The determinants of job satisfaction among federal, state, and local government employees. *State and Local Government Review* 29(1), 7–16.

Dyck, J. L., & Smither, J. A. (1995). Older adults' acquisition of word processing: The contribution of cognitive abilities and computer anxiety. *Human Behavior* 12(1), 107–99.

Edwards, M. R. (1990). A joint effort leads to accurate appraisals. *Personnel Journal* 69, 122–28.

Emeka-Mayaka, G., & Samwel, K. (2009, February 6). Why employers interested in where you got your degree. *Daily Nation*. Retrieved from http://www.nation.co.ke.

Ernest, S. (2014, June 11). Over 50pc of EA graduates half-baked. *The Citizen*. Retrieved from www.thecitizen.co.tz.

Ernst & Young. (2009). Africa connected: Telecommunication growth story. Retrieved from https://webforms.ey.com/Content/vwWFPreview/GL/en/Africa_Connected_-_A_telecommunications_growth_story?OpenDocument.

Etta, F. E., & Elder, L. (2005). *At the crossroads: ICT policy making in East Africa*. Nairobi, Kenya: East African Educational Publishers.

———. (2005). At the crossroads: ICT policy making in East Africa. Nairobi, Kenya: East African Educational Publishers.

Evans, P. (1995). *Embedded autonomy: States and industrial transformation*. Princeton, NJ: Princeton University Press.

———. (2014). National labor movements and transnational connections: Global labor's evolving architecture under neoliberalism. IRLE Working Paper no. 116–14. (September). Retrieved from http://www.irle.berkeley.edu/workingpapers/116–14.pdf.

Fairbrother, P., O'Brien, Junor, A., O'Donnell, M., & Williams, G. (2012). *Unions and globalization: Governments, management, and the state at work*. London: Routledge.

Faye, A. N. (1989). Evaluating employees by computer. *Personnel Administration* 34, 67–72.

Feather, V. (1971). *Essence of trade unionism*. London: The Bodley Head.

Federal Communications Commission (FCC), (2016, January 29). Broadband progress report, Retrieved from http://www.fcc.gov.

Federation of Kenya Employers, (FKE). (2016, June 29). Employers' body elects new leaders as jobs and politics remain key concerns. Retrieved from http://fke-kenya.org/index.php/about-us/245-employers-body-elects-new-leaders-as-jobs-and-politics-remain-key-concerns.

Fishbein, M., & Ajzen, I. (1975). *Belief, attitude, intention and behavior: An introduction to theory and research*. Reading, MA: Addison Wesley.

Flood, L. G. (1995). Unions and policy problems. In L. G. Flood (ed.)., *Unions and public policy; the new economy, law, and democratic politics* (pp. 3–10). Westport, CT: Greenwood Press.

———, Scheuerman, W., & Plotkin, S. (1995). Public sector unions and the ideological struggle for the state. In L. G. Flood (ed.)., *Unions and public policy; the new economy, law, and democratic politics* (pp. 149–64). Westport, CT: Greenwood Press.

Fredland, R. A. (2000). Technology transfer to the public sector in developing states: Three phases. *The Journal of Technology Transfer* 25(3), 265–75.

French, H. W. (2014, May 16). Into Africa: China's wild rush. *New York Times*. Retrieved from http://www.nytimes.com/2014/05/17/opinion/into-africa-chinas-wild-rush.html?_r=0.

Frey, B. C., & Osborne, M. A. (2013, September 17). The future of employment: How susceptible are jobs to computerization? Oxford University. Retrieved from http://www.oxfordmartin.ox.ac.uk/downloads/academic/The_Future_of_Employment.pdf.

Frundt, H. J. (2002). Central American unions in the era of globalization. *Latin American Research Review* 37(3), 7–53.

Fuujita, K. H. (1997). Auto industrialization in Southern Asia: national strategies and local development. *ASEAN Economic Bulletin*, 13, 312–22.

Galbraith, K. (1967). *The new industrial state*. Boston, MA: Houghton Mifflin.

Garson, D. G. (2006). *Public information technology and e-governance: Managing the virtual state*. Sudbury, MA: Jones and Bartlett Publishers.

Gathura, G. (2015, January 28). Burnout by Kenyan medics at alarming level. *Standard*. Retrieved from http://www.standardmedia.co.ke.

Gefen, D., Karahanna, E., & Straub, D. W. (2003). Trust and TAM in online shopping: an integrated model. *MIS Quarterly* 27 (1), 51–90.

Gellerman, S. W. (1968). *Management by motivation*. New York: American Management Association.

Gereffi, G., & Wyman, D. (1987). Determinants of development strategies in Latin America and east Asia. *Pacific Focus* 2(1), 5–33.

Gereffi, G. (1990). Big business and the state: East Asia and Latin America compared. *Asian Perspective* 14(1), 5–29.

Gerschenkron, A. (1962). *Economic backwardness in historical perspective: A book of essays*. Cambridge, MA: Harvard University Press.

Gisesa, N. (2015, March 6). Over 65 per cent of manufacturing firms in Kenya don't survive. *Standard Digital News*. Retrieved from http://www.standardmedia.co.ke.

Goldstein, J. (2015, February 12). How the electronic spreadsheet revolutionized business. NPR: *All Things Considered, Planet Money*. Retrieved from http://www.npr.gov.

Goulden, M., Mason, M. A., & Frasch, K. (2011). Keeping women in the science pipeline. *The Annals of the American Academy of Political and Social Science* 638, 141–62.

Government Technology. (2015, February 10). Japan will be the first country to do what with robots? Retrieved from http://www.govtech.com/question-of-the day/.

Greer, I., & Hauptmeier, M. (2008). Political entrepreneur and co-managers: Labor transnationalism at four multinational auto companies. *British Journal of Industrial Relations* 46, (1), 76–97.

Grosh, B. (1991). *Public enterprise in Kenya: What works, what doesn't and why*. Boulder, CO: Lynne Rienner.

GSMA. (2015). Bridging the gender gap: Mobile access and usage in low and middle income Countries, Report. Retrieved from http://www.gsma.com/connectedwomen/wp-content/uploads/2015/02/GSM0001_02252015_GSMAReport_FINAL-WEB-spreads.pdf.

Guguyu, O. (2015, June 19). Workers threaten to strike over NHIF rates. *Daily Nation*. Retrieved from http://www.nation.co.ke.

Guto, S. (1980). The rule of law and the Republic in Kenya. Seminar paper presented at the Law Society of Kenya, Mombasa. December 10–11.

Gyorgy, A. A. (1998). Women and tigers: Effects of rapid industrialization on women in Asia. *Synthesis/Regeneration*, 16–19.

Hailey, L. (1942). Native administration and political development in Africa. *British Government Tropical Africa Report*, 1940–42, 252–56. London: Government Printers.

Hakken, D. (1993). Computing and social change: New technology and workplace transformation, 1980–1990. *Annual Review of Anthropology* 22, 1107–32.

Hays, S. W., & Lavigna, R. (2009). Human resource metrics in government: Measuring the impacts of HRM. In S. W. Hays, R. C. Kearney, & J. D. Coggburn (eds.), *Public human resource management: Problems and prospects* (pp. 160–78). New York: Longman.

Heller, P. S. (1997). *Aging in the "Asian Tigers": Challenges for fiscal policy*. Washington, DC: IMF.

Hempstone. S. (1997). *Rogue ambassador: An African memoir*. Sewanee, TN: University of the South.

Herzberg, F., Mauser B., & Snyderman, B. B. (1959). *The motivation to work*. New York: Wiley.

Himbara, D. (1994). *Kenyan capitalists, the state, and development*. Boulder, CO: Lynne Rienner.

Horton, R. D. (1976). Productivity and productivity bargaining in government: A critical analysis. *Public Administration Review*, 407–14.

Huang, A. H. (2002). E-mail communication and supervisor-subordinate exchange quality: an empirical study. *Human Systems Management* 21, 193–204.

Huntington, S. (1968). *Political order in changing societies*. New Haven, CT: Yale University Press.

Huxhold, W. E. (1991). *An introduction to urban geographic information systems*. New York: Oxford University Press.

ILO. (2001, June). World employment report. Geneva, Switzerland: ILO. Retrieved from http://www.ilo.org/public.

iMlango (2016). The unique iMlango programme. London: Avanti Communications. Retrieved from http://www.imlango.com/.

International Confederation of Free Trade Unions (ICFTU). (1998). Nairobi trade union statement adopted by the conference on defending workers' human rights in the global economy. Nairobi, Kenya: ICFTU, African Regional Organization.

International Monetary Fund (IMF). (1995). Unproductive public expenditures: A pragmatic approach to policy analysis. *Pamphlet Series 48.* Washington, DC: IMF Fiscal Affairs Department.

International Telecommunication Union (ITU). (2014). Measuring the information society report. *United Nations. ITU Report*, Retrieved from http://www.itu.int/en/ITU-D/Statistics/Pages/publications/mis2014.aspx.
Itika, J. S. (2011). *Fundamentals of human resource management: Emerging experiences from Africa*. African Studies Centre, Groningen: University of Groningen.
Iungai, E. (2015, March 13). Patients evacuated from Vihiga Hospital as health workers strike enters day 3. *Standard*. Retrieved from http://www.standardmedia.co.ke.
Jackson, L. A., Ervin, K. S., Gardner, P. D., & Schmitt, N. (2001). Gender and the Internet: Women communicating and men searching. *Sex roles* 44 (5–6), 363–79.
Jamah, A. (2015, March 12). Nowhere to hide as Kenya automates citizens' data. *Standard*. Retrieved from http://www.standardmedia.co.ke.
Jreisat, J. (2012). *Globalism and comparative public administration*. Boca Raton, FL: CRC Press.
Jubat, A. (2014, October 10). Employees told to stay at work stations all the time. Standard. Retrieved from http://www.standardmedia.co.ke/thecounties/article/2000137658/employees-told-to-stay-at-work-stations-all-the-time?pageNo=1.
———. (2015, June 4). North Eastern region faces education crisis as 95 schools shut over insecurity. *Standard*. Retrieved from http://www.standardmedia.co.ke.
Jules-Rosette, B. (1990). *Terminal signs: computers and social change in Africa*. Berlin, Germany: Mouton de Gruyter.
Juma, C. (2010, January). Information and communication technologies in Africa: Challenges and prospects for development. Paper presented at the 14th Ordinary Summit of the African Union (AU) heads of state, Addis Ababa. Retrieved from http://vancouverethiopian.wordpress.com/2010/06/10/kenyan-born-harvard-professor-calestous-juma-invest-in-high-speed-internet-says-scholar-to-african-leaders/.
Justus, W., & Sigei, J. (2013, July 2). Publishers cry foul over laptop project. *Daily Nation*. Retrieved from http://www.nationmedia.co.ke.
Kadel, R. (2005). February. How teacher attitudes affect technology. *Learning and Leading with Technology* 39(5), 34–47.
Kaffenberger, M. (2014, April 10). M-Shwari in Kenya: How is it really being used? CGAP. Retrieved from http://www.cgap.org/.
Kagwe, S. (1986). The ecology of public administration in Africa: A review. In *The Ecology of Public Administration and Management in Africa*. African Association for Public Administration and Management (AAPAM), (pp. 18–31). New Delhi, India: Vikas Publishing House.
Kahihu, N. (2015, March 1). Align technical training to Industry needs. *Daily Nation*. Retrieved from http://www.nationmedia.co.ke.
Kajilwa, G. (2016, March 2). Heavy drinking, low pay leading factors in teacher absenteeism in Kenya. *Standard*. Retrieved from http://www.standardmedia.co.ke/article/
Kamau, J. (2015, April 3). KNUT asks state to permanently close Kenyan University over terror attack. *Standard*. Retrieved from http://www.standardmedia.co.ke.
Kamau, M. (2015, February 13). Karira Mission Hospital gets scanning machine. *Standard*. Retrieved from http://www.standardmedia.co.ke.
Kaoma, M., & Ikombo, G. (2009). ICTs in Zambia. In Ikombo, G., & Kaoma, M. (eds.), *The challenge of change in higher education in the 21st century* (p. 184). Amherst, NY: Cambria.
Kaplinsky, R. (ed.). (1978). *Readings on MNC in Kenya*. Nairobi: Oxford University Press.
Kariuki, J. (2014, December 30). 1.8 million Kenyans are obese, says new report. *Daily Nation*. Retrieved from http://www.nationmedia.co.ke.
Kariuki, N. (2015, April 19). Kenya among top data collectors, reveals research. *Daily Nation*. Retrieved from http://www.nation.co.ke.
Karshoda, M., & Waema, T. (2007). *ICT strategy brief based on findings of E-readiness survey of higher education institutions in Kenya*. Nairobi: Kenya Education Network (KENET).

Kenyatta, U. (2015, February 10). Speech given at Precious Blood Secondary School, Riruta, to mark Safer Internet Day. Speech read by Cabinet Secretary, Judy Wakhungu. Reported in Macharia, M. The Internet should be made safe for the children, urges President Uhuru Kenyatta. *Standard Digital News*. Retrieved from http://www.standardmedia.co.ke.

Kay, R. (2006). Addressing gender differences in computer ability, attitudes and use: the laptop effect. *Journal of Educational Computing Research* 32(2), 187–211.

Kay, T. (2005). Labor transnationalism and global governance: The impact of NAFTA on transnational labor relationships in North America. *American Journal of Sociology* 111(3), 715–56.

Keefe, J. H. (1991). Do unions influence the diffusion of technology? *Industrial and Labor Relations Review* 44(2), 261–74.

Kelly, K. (2016). *The inevitable: Understanding the technological forces that will shape our future*. New York: Viking.

Kelly, P. (1998, February 18). Swiss scientist warns of robot Armageddon. CNN. Retrieved from http://www.cnn.com/TECH/science/9802/18/swiss.robot/.

Kemp, T. (1989). *Industrialization in the non-western world*. London: Longman.

Kenya, Republic of. (1965). *Sessional paper no. 10*. Nairobi: Government Printer.

———. (1966). *National development plan. 1966–1970*, Nairobi: Government Printer

———. (1970). *National development plan, 1970–1974*. Nairobi: Government Printer

———. (1979). *National development plan, 1979–1983*. Nairobi: Government Printer.

———. (1984). *Development plan, 1980–1988 5th development plan*. Nairobi, Kenya: Government Printer.

———. (1989). *Development plan, 1989–1993 6th development plan*. Nairobi, Kenya: Government Printer.

———. (2007). *Kenya vision 2030. A competitive and prosperous Kenya*. Nairobi, Kenya: Government Printer.

———. (2016). National information and communication technology (ICT) policy. June. Ministry of Information and Communications Technology. Nairobi: Government Printer.

Kenyatta, U., (2013, September 17). President of Kenya. Speech on September 17, 2013 during the Official Opening of the High-level economic conference on Kenya, Norfolk Hotel, Nairobi.

Kestenbaum, D. (2015, June 3). Experts debate: Will computers edge people out of entire careers? National Public Radio (NPR) *Planet Money*. Retrieved from http://www.npr.org.

———. (2015, June 3). Experts debate: Will computers edge people out of entire careers? National Public Radio (NPR) *Planet Money*. Retrieved from http://www.npr.org.

Kettl, D. F. (2005). *The global public management revolution*. Washington, DC: The Brookings Institution.

Kibaki, M. (2010, April 26). Performance contract [Speech]. Kenyatta International Conference Center. Retrieved from http://kenyauptodate.blogspot.com/2010/04/performance-contract.html.

Kiggundu, M.N. (1989). *Managing organizations in developing countries: An operational and strategic approach*. West Hartford, CT: Kumarian Press.

Kigotho, W. (2009, January 3). Conspiracy of the rich in the education system. *Standard Digital News*. Retrieved from http://www.standardmedia.co.ke.

The Economist. (2013, May 27). Why does Kenya lead the world in mobile money? Retrieved from http://www.economist.com/blog.

Killick, T., & Sharpley, J. (1985). Extent, causes and consequences of disequilibria in developing countries. In T. Killick (ed.), *The quest for economic stabilization: The IMF and the third world* (pp. 15–54). Brookfield, VT: Gower, Overseas Development Institute, London.

Kimutai, V. (2013, July 10). Education: It's tablets for pupils now as laptops headed for "archives." *Standard Digital News*.

Kinyanjui, K., & Okuttah, M. (2011, June 13). Access Kenya launches web filtering tool. *Daily Nation*. Retrieved from http //www.nationmedia.co.ke.
Kiplangat, J. (2015, February 5). Bill: Gates: Mobile money innovation to "trickle up" to developed countries. *Daily Nation*.
Kipsang, W. (2015, February 15). Union seeks Sh. 270m. for Mandera victims. *Daily Nation*. Retrieved from http://www.nation.co.ke.
Kirsh, B.S. (1964). *Automation and collective bargaining*. New York: Central Book Company.
Kisero, J. (2014, May 20). When France Telecom quits Kenya, are we ready for the inevitable loss? *Daily Nation*. Retrieved from http://www.nation.co.ke.
Kithi, N. (2014, October 10). Kenya loses Sh 69 b annually to corruption. *Standard*. Retrieved from http://www.standardmedia.co.ke.
Klingermann, H. D. & Fuch, D. (1988). *Citizens and the state*. New York: Oxford University Press.
Klotz, R. J. (2004). *The politics of Internet communication*. New York: Rowman & Littlefield.
Kobrin, S. J. (2000). Development after industrialization: Poor countries in an electronically integrated global economy. In N. Hood & S. Young (eds.), *The globalization of multinational enterprise activity and economic development* (pp. 133–49). New York: St. Martin's Press.
Koross, K. (2013, November 25). KNUT delivers its promise to teachers despite all odds. *Standard*. Retrieved from http://www.standardmedia.co.ke.
Kozma, R. B. (2008). Comparative analysis of policies for ICT in education. In Voogt, J. & Knezek, G. (eds.). *International handbook on information technology in education* (pp. 1083–91). New York: Springer.
Kraemer, K. L., & Perry, J. L. (1999). Innovation and computing in the public sector: A review of research. *Knowledge, Technology and Policy* 12(1), 3–18.
Kraemer, K. L., & Dedrick, J. (1994). Payoffs from investment in information technology: Lessons from the Asia-Pacific region. *World Development* 22(12), 1921–31.
——— (1997). Computing and public organizations. *Journal of Public Administration Research and Theory* 7(1), 89–112
Kranenburg, R. V. (2008). *The Internet of Things*. Amsterdam, Netherlands: Institute of Network Cultures.
Kubania, J. (2015, February 3). Labour CS Kazungu Kambi dissolves industrial training board. *Daily Nation*. Retrieved from http://www.nation.co.ke.
———. (2015, February 17). Sh 17 bn for laptops to be diverted, says Rotich. *Daily Nation*. Retrieved from http://www.nation.co.ke.
Kurzweil, R. (2005). *The singularity is near*. New York: Viking.
Landes, D. S. (1969). *The unbound prometheus: Technological change and industrial development in Western Europe from 1750 to the present*. Cambridge, MA: Cambridge University Press.
Langdon, S. W. (1981). *Multinational corporations in the political economy of Kenya*. London: Macmillan.
Langevin, M. S. (2010). Between fragmentation and globalization: U.S. public sector Unions and International Labor Cooperation. *Labor Studies Journal* 35 (3), 364–85.
Lederer, A. L., Maupin, D. J., Sena, M. P., & Zhuang, Y. (2000). The technology acceptance model and the World Wide Web. *Decision Support Systems* 29 (3), 269–82.
Lee, A. C. K. (2003). Undergraduate students' gender differences in IT skills and attitudes. *Journal of Computer Assisted Learning* 19(4), 488–500.
Lee, C. (2007). Labor unions and good governance: A cross-national, comparative analysis. *American Sociological Review* 27(4), 585–609.
Lee, E. (1997). *The labour movement and the Internet: The new internationalism*. London, England: Pluto Press.
Lee, G. (1999). The performance impacts of information technology in public organizations: The case of state governments [PhD dissertation]. Indiana University.

Lett, N. (1964). Economic development through bureaucratic corruption. *American Behavioral Sciences* 8, 8–14.
Leys, C. (1975). *Underdevelopment in Kenya*. London: Heinemann.
Li, N., Kirkup, G., & Hodgsn, B. (2001). Cross-cultural comparison of women students' attitudes toward the Internet and usage: China and the United Kingdom. *CyberPsychology & Behavior* 4(3), 415–26.
Liaw, S. S. (2002). An Internet Survey for perceptions of computers and the World Wide Web: Relationship, production, and difference. *Computers in Human Behavior*, 18(1), 17–35.
Ligami, C. (2014, November 1). Kenya plans $145 m e-registration of adults, children by October 2015. *East African*. Retrieved from http://www.theeastafrican.co.ke/news/-/2558/2507646/-/53i6uoz/-/index.html.
Linard, A. (2002). The brain drain: Losing one's head. In the challenge of globalization in Africa: The trade union response. *Labour Education* 123, 47–49. Retrieved from http://www.ilo.org/dyn/infoecon/docs/199/F506945503/123e.pdf.
Lindell, I. (2010). Informality and collective organizing: Identities, alliances, and transnational activism in Africa. *Third World Quarterly* 31 (2), 207–22.
Linington, D. (2014, November 6). Tanzania: Trade Union unveils mobile money transfer platform. *IT News*. Retrieved from http://www.itnewsafrica.com/2014/11/tanzania-trade-union-unveils-mobile-money-transfer-platform.
Liqiang, H. (2015, July 17–23). Seeds of Industry: Africa has a chance to follow in China's footsteps by planting special economic zones. *China Daily, Africa Weekly*.
Lucas, H. C., Jr. (1999). *Information technology and the productivity paradox*. New York: Oxford University Press.
Lundall, P., & Howell, C. (2000). *Computers in schools: A national survey of information technology in South African Schools*. Cape Town: Education Policy Unit of the University of Western Cape.
Magarinos, C. (1998). UNIDO Director Genera's remarks, Quoted in paper. *Daily Nation*. October, 6, 1998. Retrieved from http://www.nation.co.ke.
Manono, G. (2012, September 9). New Kenya: Business process outsourcing, destination Nairobi. *Kenya Today*. Retrieved from https://www.kenya-today.com/technology/ew-kenya-business-process-outsourcing-destination-nairobi.
Marthoz, J. (2002). African press and globalization: An unfinished transformation. In International Labor Organization (ILO), The Challenge of globalization in Africa: The trade union response, *Labor Education*, no. 123 (pp. 42–46). Geneva, Switzerland: ILO. Retrieved from http://www.ilo.org/dyn/infoecon/docs/199/F506945503/123e.pdf.
Martin, N. D., & Brady, D. (2007). Workers of less developed world unite? A multilevel analysis of unionization in less developed countries. *American Sociological Review*, 27(2), 562–84.
Masinde, J. (2015, February 18). Mobile Money transactions hit Sh 2.4 trillion. *Daily Nation*. Retrieved from http://www.nation.co.ke.
———. (2015, January 29). Kenya IT firms to benefit from Sh 100 m fund. *Daily Nation*. Retrieved from http://www.nationmedia.co.ke.
Masta, J., & Mwamadzingo, M. (2012). Trade unions services and benefits in Kenya. In Kaluposa, T., Otoo, K. N., and Shindondola-Mote, H. (eds.). *Trade unions and benefits in Africa*. (pp. 169–203). Accra: Africa Labour Research Network.
Mathieson, K. (1991). Predicting user intentions: Comparing the technology acceptance model with the theory of theory of planned behavior. *Information Systems Research* 3 (3), 173–91.
Mathiu, M. (2015, March 15). There is no excuse for the negligence of cancer treatment in this country. *Daily Nation*. Retrieved from http://www.nation.co.ke.
Matiangi, F. (2016, March 3). Education CS Fred Matiangi announces KCSE 2015 Results. Speech by Cabinet Secretary. Retrieved from https://www.youtube.com/watch?v=04gAiGRfIwA&feature=youtu.be.

Mauro, P. (1995). Corruption and growth. *Quarterly Journal of Economics* 110(3), 681–712.
Maxfield, S. (1994). Financial incentives and Central Bank authority in industrializing nations. *World Politics* 46, 58–88.
Mbatiah, S. (2015, March 22). Illiteracy, poverty, to blame for insecurity in Baringo, Says Senator John Lonyangapuo. *Daily Nation*. Retrieved from http://www.nation.coo.ke.
———. (2015, May 12). Uhuru Kenyatta moves laptop project to Fred Matiangi. *Daily Nation*. Retrieved from http://www.nation.co.ke.
Mboya, T. (1963). *Freedom and after*. New York: Little, Brown.
McFellin, A. (2013). Labor unions in the new economy. *Common Dreams*. Retrieved from www.commondreams.org/views/2013/03/24/labor-unions-new-economy.
McKinsey Consultants. (2013). Lions go digital: The Internet's transformative potential for Africa. *McKinsey Global Institute Report* (November). Retrieved from http://www.mckinsey.com/insights/high_tech_telecoms_internet/lions_go_digital_the_internets_transformative_potential_in_africa.
Mclleland, D. C., Atkinson, J., Clark, R. A., & Lowell, E. L. (1953). *The achievement Motive*. New York: Appleton-Century-Crofts.
Medina, A. T. (1996). *Asian Economic Tigers: A Philippine comparison*. Washington, DC : University Press of America.
Migdal, J. S. (1988). *Strong societies and weak states: State-society relations and capabilities in the third world*. Princeton, NJ: Princeton University Press.
Mikkelsen, B. (1987). Formation of an industrial labour force in Kenya: Experiences of labor training in the metal manufacturing industries. University of Nairobi, Institute of Developmental Studies (IDS) Occasional Paper no. 49.
Milakovich, M. E. (2012). *Digital governance: New technologies for improving public service and participation*. London: Routledge.
Ministry of Defense, (2014, October 31). High level seminar on national security strategy. Nairobi: Ministry of Defense, Government of Kenya. Retrieved from http://www.mod.go.ke/?p=3800.
Mitchell, S., Villa, N., Stewart-Weeks, M., & Lange, A. (2015). The Internet of Everything for cities: Connecting people, process, data, and things to Improve the 'Livability' of cities and communities. CISCO White Paper, 1–221. San Jose, CA: CISCO.
Mo, P. (2000). Corruption and economic growth. *Journal of Comparative Economics* 40, 66–79.
Moe, T. M., & Chubb, J. E. (2009). *Liberating learning: Technology, politics, and the future of American education*. San Francisco, CA: Jossey-Bass.
Moore, B. (1966). *The social origins of dictatorship and democracy: Lord and peasant in the making of modern world*. Boston, MA: Beacon Press.
Morris, M. G., & Dillon, A (1997). How user perceptions influence software use, decision support systems. *IEEE Software* (July–August), 58–65.
Morrison, N. (2014, July 31). Forget Bitcoin, a university education is the new global currency. *Forbes*. Retrieved from http://www.forbes.com/sites/nickmorrison/2014/07/31/forget-bitcoin-a-university-education-is-the-new-global-currency/#5f70ad7424f7.
Mudasiru O. Y., & Modupe R. B. (2011). Student-teachers' competence and attitude towards information and communication technology: A case study in a Nigerian University. *Cedtech.net. Contemporary Education Technology* 2 (1), 18–36.
Mugonyi, D. (2008, February 23). Githongo tells of fights with ministers. *Daily Nation*. Retrieved from http://www.nation.co.ke.
Mugwe, D. (2012, July 11). Posta's fortunes dip further as Kenya Internet users grow. *Daily Nation*. Retrieved from http://www.nationmedia.co.ke.
Muller, R. (1973). The MNC and the underdevelopment of the third world. In Wilber, C. K. (ed.), *The political economy of development and underdevelopment*. New York: Random House.

Mumo, M. (2012, June 4). Google slips into Kenya e-payment market. *Daily Nation*. Retrieved from http://www.nationmedia.co.ke.
———. (2014, March 5) Scandals mar dream of Konza technopolis. *Nation Media*. Retrieved from http://www.nationmedia.co.ke.
Munda, C. (2014, October 1). Now Kenya joins the ranks of the middle income countries. *The Star*. Retrieved from http://allafrica.com/stories/201410011159.html.
Munene, G. A., & Nyaribo, Y. M. (2013). Effect of social media pertication in workplace on employee productivity. *International Journal of Advances in Management and Economics*, (2), 141–50.
Munene, I. (1997). The struggle for faculty unionism in a stalled democracy: Lessons from Kenya's public universities. *Journal of Third World Studies* 14(1), 91–114.
———. (2014). The problem with public university salaries in Kenya. *International Higher Education*, *77*, 21–22.
———. (2007). Experiments in distance education: The African Virtual University (AVU) and the paradox of the World Bank in Kenya—A rejoinder. *International Journal of Educational Development* 27, 77–85.
Mungai, C. (2015, January 5). Laptops in Africa's classrooms: Saviour or waste of good money? *Mail and Guardian*. Retrieved from http://www.mgafrica.com.
Munyakho, D., and Kareithi, P. (1982). The pineapple industry debate, *Daily Nation*, June 25, pp. 11–13.
Musambi, E. (2014, June 12). Budget: Gov introduces e-procurement to cut wastage. *Daily Nation*.
Mutambo, A. (2016, May 2). Cotu differs with employers' body on pay rise formula. *Daily Nation*. Retrieved from http://www.nation.co.ke.
Mutegi, Juliet. (2015) Kenya's women close digital gap. *Daily Nation*. March 9. Retrieved from http://www.nationmedia.co.ke.
Mwakio, P. (2015, April 5). NBK taps into cashless matatu payment. *Standard Digital News*. Retrieved from http://www.standardmedia.co.ke.
Mwamadzingo, M. (2003). Bridging Africa's digital divide: the role of trade unions in English-speaking Africa. Geneva: International Labour Office, Bureau for Workers' Activities. Geneva: ILO.
Mwangi, J. (2015, February 26). CCTV men were asleep during Muchai murder. *Standard*. Retrieved from http://standardmedia.co.ke.
Mwangi, W. (2015, April 13). New app to root out cargo delays. *Daily Nation*. Retrieved from http://www.nation.co.ke.
Mware, L. (2014). Kenya's 'false start' with big bang school laptops. (Opinion). eLearning Africa Report 2014. Berlin, Germany: ICWE. Retrieved from http://www.eLearningafrica.com.
Mwembe, K. (1989). Kenya labor: The post-colonial era. *Labor* (May) 10 (5). Retrieved from http://www.multinationalmonitor.org/hyper/issues/1989/05/mwembe-labor.html.
Mwesiga, R. (2015, January 23). Uganda sued in landmark medical "brain drain" case. *Daily Nation*. Retrieved from http://www.nationmedia.co.ke.
Naisbitt, J., & Aburdene, P. (1985). *Reinventing the corporation*. New York: Warner Books.
Ndemo, B. (2013, December 2). The story behind Kenya's open data. *Daily Nation*. Retrieved from http://www.nation.co.ke.
———. (2014). Is modernity destroying African education? eLearning Africa Report 2014. Berlin, Germany: ICWE. Retrieved from http://www.eLearningafrica.com.
Ndii, D. (2016, August 13). Lessons from Asian Tigers that you won't hear from political leaders. *Daily Nation*. Retrieved from http://www.nation.co.ke.
Nduati, C., & Bowman, W. (2005). Forging a new path: The role of the Kenya ICT Federation. In L. Elder & F. Etta (eds.), *At the crossroads: ICT policymaking in East Africa* (pp. 56–67). Ottawa, Canada: International Development Research Center.
Neef, D. (2001). *E-Procurement: From strategy to implementation*. New York: Free Press.

Ngare, P. (2008, June 25). School heads demand hefty salary increase. *Daily Nation*. Retrieved from http://www.nation.co.ke.
Ngethe, N. (1995). Strongmen, State Formation, Collapse and Reconstruction in Africa. In Zartman, I. W. (ed.), *Collapsed state and restoration of legitimate authority* (p. 251). Boulder, CO: Lynne Rienner.
Ngethe, V. (2016, March 3). Only two out of five students reach form four, statistics show. *Daily Nation*. Retrieved from http://www.nation.co.ke/newsplex/school-dropout-kcse/2718262–3101106-lw3mir/index.html.
Ngila, D. (2015, February 25). Embrace ICT or die, Fred Matiang'i tells postal firms. *Daily Nation*. Retrieved from http://www.nation.co.ke.
Nguli, P. N. (2013, August 28). Fred Kubai was one of the pioneer trade unionists. *Standard*. Retrieved from http://www.standardmedia.co.ke.
Nissen, B. (1995). Combating plant closings in the era of transnational corporations. In L. Flood (ed.), *Unions and public policy: The new economy, law and democratic politics* (pp. 131–47). Westport, CT: Greenwood Press.
Njagih, M., & Kimutei, G. (2015, July 14). Rift MPs, in new bid to sack Kimenyi. *Standard Digital News*. Retrieved from http://www.standardmedia.co.ke.
Njiru, J. (2014, October 2). Cadbury to shut Nairobi factory at end of month. *Daily Nation*. Retrieved from http://www.businessdailyafrica.com/Corporate-News/Cadbury-to-shut-Nairobi-factory-this-month/-/539550/2472588/-/mdnghlz/-/index.html.
Nordlinger, E. (1970). *Politics and society: Studies in contemporary political sociology*. New Jersey: Prentice Hall.
———. (1981). *On the autonomy of the democratic state*. Cambridge, MA: Harvard University Press.
Nyabiage, J. (2015, February 1). Pain as multinationals axe hundreds. *Standard Digital News*. Retrieved from http://www.standardmedia.co.ke.
Nyanchama, M. (2015, February 22). Kenya as Silicon Savannah—The need to do more! Paper presented during the National ICT Innovation Forum. Ministry of Information Communication and Technology and ICT Authority. Kenyatta International Conference Center, KICC Conference theme: Silicon Savannah! Mind the gap! Close the Gap.
Nyassy, D. T. (2014, February 25) Union leaders trade accusations as dockers dump COTU to new outfit. *Daily Nation*. Retrieved from http://www.nation.co.ke.
Nyassy, D. T., & Cicobi, M. (2015, June 19). School heads oppose union leaders on evaluation of teachers. *Daily Nation*. Retrieved from http://www.nation.co.ke.
Nyongo, P. A. (1996, June 10–16) Commentary, *The East Africa*. Retrieved from http://www.theeastafrican.co.ke.
Nzomo, M. (1992). External influence on the political economy of Kenya: the Case of MNCs. In Oyugi, W. (ed.), *Politics and administration in East Africa* (pp. 429–67). Bonn: Konrad Adenauer Foundation.
Obama, B. (2014, January 28). State of the Union Address, U.S. Congress. Retrieved from http://www.whitehouse.gov/the-press-office/2014/01/28/president-barack-obamas-state-union-address.
———. (2015, January 20). State of the union address. Congress of the United States [Video Transcript]. Retrieved from http://www.mediaite.com/online/president-obamas-2015-state-of-the-union-address-full-transcript/.
Oblinger, D. G., & Rush, S. C. (1997). *The learning revolution: The challenge of information technology in the academy*. Bolton, MA: Anker.
Obradovic, S. (2009). Education and economic growth. *Economic Series* 1, 377–85.
Ochieng, L. (2015, April 30). ICT Sector continues on upward trajectory to emerge second, *Daily Nation*. Retrieved from http://www.nation.co.ke.
———. (2015, July 2). Rules could split Safaricom's revenue arms. *Daily Nation*. Retrieved from http://www.nation.co.ke.
———. (2015, June 22). Team given 6 months to deliver online content for laptop project-Video. *Daily Nation*. Retrieved from http://www.nation.co.ke.

———, & Kipruto, N. (2015, May 11). KUPPET wants security in learning institutions. *Standard*. Retrieved from http://ww.standardmedia.co.ke.
Ochuodho, S. J. (2010, December 11) Speech in Juba, Sudan. Augustine Oduor, Honouring the man who linked Kenya to world. *Standard*. Retrieved from http://standardmedia.co.ke.
———. (2012). *Dawn of a Rainbow: The untold intrigues of Kenya's first coalition government*. Nairobi: Adage Publishing and Information Services.
Odunga, D. (2015, March 3). Francis Atwoli asks President Kenyatta to end TV switch impasse. *Daily Nation*. Retrieved from http://www.nationmedia.co.ke.
Oduor, A. (2011, May 31). ICT answer to teacher shortage, says Ministry. *Standard Digital News*. Retrieved from http://www.standardmedia.co.ke.
———. (2013, June 13). Teachers vow to thwart State laptops scheme. *Standard Digital News*.
———. (2015, April 30). Uhuru goes for tablets to cure laptop headache. *Standard Digital News*. Retrieved from http://www.standardmedia.co.ke.
———. (2015, January 8). Labor Cabinet secretary Kazungu Kambi tells teachers to report to work, says strike illegal. *Standard*. Retrieved from http://www.standardmedia.co.ke.
———. (2015, May 13). Education teachers' unions oppose new NHIP deductions. *Standard*. Retrieved from http://www.standardmedia.co.ke.
———. (2015a, June 16). No Promotions for lazy teachers, Teachers Service Commission warns. *Standard*. Retrieved from http://www.standardmedia.co.ke.
———. (2015b, February 6). Why half of Kenyan teachers want to leave their profession. *Standard*. Retrieved from http://www.standardmedia.co.ke.
Oduor, A., & Weru, J. (2013, June 14). Job Teachers cry foul after Treasury "snubs" demands. *Standard Digital News*. Retrieved from www.standardmedia.co.ke.
Ogemba, P. (2015, March 4). Ex-ministers, top officials charged over Anglo Leasing. *Daily Nation*. Retrieved from http://www.nationmedia.co.ke.
Ogeto, A. (2016, January 18). Social Media has linked us more but reduced direct interaction. *Daily Nation*. Retrieved from http://www.nation.co.ke.
Ojanji, W. (2006, December 10). Kenya hardest hit by brain drain. *Standard*. Retrieved from http://www.Standardmedia.co.ke.
Okendo, B. (2014, March 12). Tough questions Uhuru must ask over laptops. *Standard Digital News*. Retrieved from http://www.nation.co.ke.
Okoth, J. (2014, October 22). Safaricom emerges Kenya's biggest taxpayer for the 7th consecutive year. *Standard Digital News*. Retrieved from http://www.standardmedia.co.ke.
Olowu, D. (1987). Bureaucratic Decay and the prospects of regeneration in Nigeria. *Corruption and Reform* 2(3), 215–19.
Ombati, C. (2014, January 10). Police fight for better equipment. *Standard*. Retrieved from http://www.standardmedia.co.ke.
Ombuor, J. (2008, December 6). Nurses' struggle to find better life abroad. *Standard*. Retrieved from http://www.standardmedia.co.ke/business/article/1144001021/nurses-struggle-to-find-better-life-abroad.
Omollo, K. (2014, June 18). KNUT trashes literacy report. *Standard Digital News*. Retrieved from http://www.Standard.co.ke.
Omondi, D. (2016, March 26). Graft scaring away investors, World Bank warns. *Standard*. Retrieved from http://www.standardmedia.co.ke.
Omwansa, K. T., & Sullivan, P. N. (2012). *Money, real quick—The story of M-PESA*. London: Guardian Books.
Onis, Z. (1991). Review article: The logic of developmental state. *Comparative Politics* 24, 109–26.
Orvis, S. (1997). *The Agrarian question in Kenya*. Gainesville, FL: University Press of Florida.

Otenyo, E. (2016). Labor unions and public law. In A. Farazmand (ed.), *Global Encyclopedia of public administration, public policy, and governance*. Springer International Publishing. doi:10.1007/978-3-319-31816-5_1088-1.

———. (1998). Au coeur de l'accumulation kenyanne du bon usage des banques en politique (1985–1995). In F. Grignon, & G. Prunier (eds.), *Kenya contemporarain* (pp. 272–82). Paris: Editions Karthala.

———. (2000). Kenyan students' attitudes toward democracy, authority, equality, and multiculturalism: Insights into a failed political socialization project. *Politics, Groups, and the Individual* 9 (1&2), 35–42.

Otenyo, E., & Lind, N. (2011). *E-Government: The use of information and communication technologies in Administration*. Youngstown, NY: Teneo Press.

Otieno, D., & Ngethe, V. (2016, August 20). The pitfalls in Kenya's high Internet penetration. Retrieved from http://www.nation.co.ke/newsplex/kenya-fixed-broadband-internet/2718262-3352180-q5r79vz/.

Owuor, O. (1994, June 16). Otula Owuor Columnist, Daily Nation. Retrieved from http://www.nation.co.ke.

Peacock, A. T. (1983). Public X-Inefficiency: Informational and institutional constraints. In H. Hanusch (ed.), *Anatomy of Government Deficiencies*. Berlin: Springer.

Pearson, D. S. (1969). *Industrial development in East Africa*. Nairobi: Oxford University Press.

Peitchinis, S. G. (1983). The attitude of trade unions toward technological change. *Industrial Relations* 38(1), 104–19.

Pempel, T.J. (1998). *Regime shift: Comparative dynamics of the Japanese political economy*. Ithaca, NY: Cornell University Press.

Perry, J. L., & Rainey, H. G. (1988). The public-private distinction in organization theory: A critique and research strategy. *Academy of Management Review* 13, 182–201.

Perry, M. J. (2016). Putting America's ridiculously large $18T economy into perspective by comparing US state GDPs to entire countries. (June 6) Washington, DC: American Enterprise Institute. Retrieved from http://www.aei.org/publication/.

Peters, G. B. (2001). *The future of governing*. Lawrence: University of Kansas Press.

Phillips, M. A. (1997). Into Africa. *Wall Street Journal*, September 18, p. R 6.

Plato, O. O. (2015, April 1–8). 21st Century Africa must increase its intellectual capital or perish. *The African Executive*. Retrieved from http://www.africanexecutive.com/modules/magazine/articles.php?article=8337&magazine=544.

Poggi, G. (1978). *The development of the modern state: A sociological introduction*. Stanford, CA: Stanford University Press.

Porter, L., and Lawler, E. (1968). What job attitudes tell about motivation. *Harvard Business Review* 46(1), 118–28.

Potter, B. (1985). *Beating job burnout: How to transform work pressure into productivity*. Berkeley, CA: Ronin Publishing.

Powell, W. W., & Snellman, K. (2004). The Knowledge Economy. *Annual Review of Sociology* 30, 199–220.

PSCU. (2015, May 1). President Uhuru Kenyatta raises minimum wage by 12 percent. *Daily Nation*, through the Presidential Strategic Communication Unit (PSCU). http://mobile.nation.co.ke/news/Uhuru-Kenyatta-Labour-Day-Minimum-Wage/-/1950946/2703112/-/format/xhtml/item/1/-/9n45rt/-/index.html.

———. (2015, May 22). Focus on market oriented courses, President Uhuru tells University Chancellors. *Standard*. Retrieved from http://www.standardmedia.co.ke.

Queally, J. (2015, January 15). Arguing for faster Internet, Obama goes to bat for municipal broadband. *Common Dreams*. Retrieved from http://www.commondreams.org/news/2015/01/15/arguing-faster-internet-obama-goes-bat-municipal-broadband.

Reddick, C. G. (2012). *Public administration and information technology*. Burlington, MA: Jones & Bartlett.

Reid, J. D., Jr. (1990). Future unions. *Industrial Relations* 31, 122–36.

Republic of Kenya, (2014). Office of the Auditor General Special Unit on Procurement of electronic voting devices for the 2013 General Election by the Independent Electoral and Boundaries Commission, (June 6). Nairobi: Government of Kenya.

———. (2015). *The 2015 Economic Survey*, National Bureau of Statistics. Nairobi: Government Printer.

———. (2007). Labor Relations Act No 14 of 2007. Laws of Kenya. Nairobi: National Council for Law. Retrieved from http://www.kenyalaw.org/kl/fileadmin/pdfdownloads/Acts/LabourRelationAct_No14of2007.pdf.

———. (2016). National information and communication technology (ICT) policy. Nairobi: Ministry of Information Communication and Technology. Retrieved from http://www.information.go.ke/wp-content/uploads/2016/06/Draft-National-ICT-Policy-20June2016.pdf.

Reuters. (2010, March 19). Reuters Interview with Michael Joseph. *Standard Newspapers*, Safaricom's Michael Joseph eyes retirement in 2010. Retrieved from http://www.standardmedia.co.ke.

Rice, A. (1995). International Labor Federation. *Occupational Environmental Health* 1(2), 215–22.

Roach, S. S. (1988). Technology and the service sector: The hidden competitive challenge. *Technological forecasting and social change*, 34, 387–403.

Rodan, G. (ed.). (1996). *The political opposition in industrialising Asia*. London: Routledge.

Rodrik, D. (2011). *The globalization paradox: Democracy and the future of the world economy*. New York: W.W. Norton.

Rogers, E. (1994). Bhutto chases the Asian Tigers. *Middle East Economic Digest*, 38, 2–3.

Roscorla, T. (2015, March 10). 10 Privacy principles for student data. Center for Digital Education. Retrieved from http://www.centerdigitaled.com.

Roseberg, C. G., & Jackson, R. H. (1994). The political economy of African personal rule. In Apter, D. E., & Roseberg, C. (eds.), *Political development and the new realism in Sub-Saharan Africa* (pp. 291–322). Charlottesville, VA: University Press of Virginia.

Ross, A. (2016). *Industries of the future*. New York: Simon and Schuster.

Rostow, W. W. (1971). *The Stages of Economic Growth*. Cambridge, England: Cambridge University Press.

Rothchild, D., and Chazan, N. (eds.). (1988). *The precarious balance: State and society in Africa*. Boulder: West Press.

Rouben, I., & Donalds, S. (2005). The impact of investment in IT on economic performance: Implications for developing countries. *World Development* 33(5), 681–700.

Rubin, R. (1998). Statements reported in *Daily Nation* July 18.

Ruechemeyer, D., Everlyn H., & Stephens, J. (1992). *Capitalist development and democracy*. Chicago, IL: University of Chicago Press.

Santini, J. (2016, February 14). Intelligent robots threaten millions of jobs. AFP. Retrieved from http://www.france24.com/en/20160214-intelligent-robots-threaten-millions-jobs.

Schlosser, D. B. (1992). Ethnicity, social classes and the politics process in Kenya. In W. Oyugi (ed.), *Politics and administration*. Nairobi: East African Educational Publishers.

Schneider, R. (1998). Business-government relations: Review Article. *Comparative Politics* 31(1), 103–8.

Scott, J. (1972). *Comparative political corruption*. Englewood Cliffs, NJ: Prentice Hall.

———. (1998). *Seeing like a state*. New Haven, CT: Yale University Press.

Sennett, R. (2006). *The culture of the new capitalism*. New Haven, CT: Yale University Press.

Shafritz, J. M., Russell, E. W., & Borick, C. P. (2013). *Introducing Public Administration*. New York: Pearson.

Shahonya, E. (2012, June 25). How ICT sector can benefit from Sh 7.2 bn budget boos. *Daily Nation*.

Shaikh, A. (2010). Should we worry about internal brain drain? *UN Dispatch*, United Nations News and Commentary, Global News Forum. Retrieved from https://www.undispatch.com/should-we-worry-about-internal-brain-drain/.

Shimoli, E. (2016, May 26). Left behind: How South Korea overtook Kenya in development. *Daily Nation*. Retrieved from http://www.nation.co.ke.

Shiundu, A. (2012, June 6). Githae: Kenya set to register businesses online. *Daily Nation*. Retrieved from http://www.nationmedia.co.ke.

Shostak, A. B. (1991a). *Robust unionism: Innovations in the labor movement*. Ithaca, NY: ILR Press.

———. (1991b). *Cyberunion: Empowering labor through computer technology*. Armonk, NY: M.E. Sharpe.

Siddiqi, M. (1997). The birth of a new star? After burning their fingers in South East Asia, a number of international investors are now taking cautious peeks at Africa's emerging markets. *African Business*, 28–31.

Silva, E. (1997). *The State and capital in Chile: Business elites, technocrats, and market economies*. Boulder, CO: Westview.

Simler, N. J. (1965) The economics of featherbedding. In Weinstein, P. A. (ed.), *Featherbedding and Technological Change* (pp. 55–65). Boston, MA: DC Heath and Company.

Smith, H. (1998). The determinants of manufacturing protection in Taiwan. *The Developing Economies* 36(3), 305–31.

Smith, K. (1999). *Improving the effectiveness of service delivery by fighting corruption*. Pretoria, South Africa: Unisa Press.

Smith, Michael. (1979). Documenting employee performance. *Supervisory Management* 24(9), 31–35.

Snellen, I., & Thaens, M. (2008, January 15). From E-Government to M-Government: Towards a new paradigm in public administration. Seminar paper, Italian Department for Public Administration and Formez. Bologna, SPISA Via Belmeloro, 10–40126, Bologna.

So, A. Y. & Chiu, S. W. K., (1995). *East Asia and the world economy*. Thousand Oaks, CA: Sage.

Solow, R. M. (1987, June 12). We'd better watch out. *New York Times Book Review*.

Sossion, W. (2016, February 3). Privatization is a big threat to quality of learning in Kenya. *Daily Nation*. Retrieved from http://www.nation.co.ke.

Spires, H. A. (2012, October 24). Pondering the digital divide across the globe. World View Global Education Symposium. Retrieved from http://www.slideshare.net/haspires/world-view-2012-digital-divide-final.

Standard. (2015, April 1). Atwoli urges anti-graft commissioners to stay put. Retrieved from http://www.standardmedia.co.ke.

Standard, Editorial. (2015, February 19). Shelving laptop project a disappointment, but sensible. *Standard Digital News*. Retrieved from http://www.standardmedia.co.ke/article /2000152126.

———. (2015, February 16). There's more than meets the eye in switch-off of TV stations. Retrieved from http://www.standardmedia.co.ke.

———. (2016, February 19). Exporting labor makes little economic sense. Retrieved from http://www.standardmedia.co.ke.

Standard Digital News. (2014, June 11). Nyanza sugar factories face closure for lack of market.

Standard Digital Reporter. (2013, April 16). Uhuru insists on laptop plans for class one pupils. *Standard Digital News*. Retrieved from http://www.standardmedia.co.ke.

Standard Reporter. (2015, March 5). M-Shwari crosses 10 million customer mark. *Standard Digital News*. Retrieved from http://www.standardmedia.co.ke.

Steger, M. B. (2003). *Globalization: A very short introduction*. New York: Oxford University.

Stein, H. (ed.). (1995). *Asian industrialization and Africa: Studies in policy alternatives to structural adjustment*. New York: St. Martin's.

Stern, B. J. (1937). Resistance to the adoption of technical innovations in technological trends and national policy. *National Resources Committee* 39, 55.

Sturmthal, A. (1972). *Comparative labor movements: Ideological roots and institutional development*. Belmont, CA: Wadsworth Publishing Co.

Sum, A. (2014, July 21). COTU Secretary General Francis Atwoli alleges Sh. 1.7 billion lost at NSSF. Standard. Retrieved from http://www.standarmedia.co.ke.

Sunday, F. (2011, September 9). Government bid for IT in education fails to click with teachers. *Daily Nation*. Retrieved from www.nationmedia.co.ke.

———. (2012, March 21). Tablet computers still out of reach for most Kenyans despite hype. *Daily Nation*. Retrieved from http://www.nation.co.ke.

———. (2014, June 8). Government reaching out to IT multinationals for skills. *Standard Digital News*. Retrieved from http://standardmedia.co.ke.

———. (2014, September 29). Matiangi raises alarm on high-end ICT skills gap. *Standard*. Retrieved from http://www.standardmedia.co.ke/business/article/2000136459/matiang-i-raises-alarm-on-high-end-ict-skills-gap.

———. (2015, April 16). Safaricom bets on local servers to revamp M-PESA. *Standard Digital News*. Retrieved from http://www.standardmedia.co.ke.

Swainson, N. (1980). *The development of corporate capitalism in Kenya*. London: Heinemann.

Swanson, R. A., & Holton, E. F., III. (2009). *Foundations of human resource development*. San Francisco, CA: Berrett-Koehler.

Tannenbaum, S. I. (1990). HRIS: User group implications. *Journal of Systems Management* 41(1), 27–32, 36.

Tanzer, A. (1998, March 23). Asia will rise again. *Forbes*, p. 114.

Tauman, Y., & Weiss, Y. (1987). Labor unions and the adoption of new technology. *Journal of Labor Economics* 5(4), 477–501.

Teo, T. S. H., Lim, V. K. G., & Lai, R. Y. C. (1999). Intrinsic and extrinsic motivation in Internet Usage. *Omega* 27 (1), 25–37.

Teo, T. S. (2001). Demographic and motivation variables associated with Internet usage activities. *Internet Research* 11 (2), 125–37

———. (2008). Pre-service teachers' attitude towards computer use: A Singapore survey. *Australasian Journal Educational Technology*, 24(4), 413–24.

Teproff, C. (2015, March 18). Miami-Dade animal services launches pet finder App with facial recognition. *Miami Herald*. Retrieved from http://www.govtech.com.

Thite, M., & Kavanagh, M. J. (2009). Evolution of human resource management and human resource information systems: The role of information technology. In M. Kavanagh & M. Thite, *Human resource information systems basics, applications, and future directions* (pp. 3–24). Thousand Oaks, CA: Sage.

Thompson, D. (2015, July/August). A world without work. *The Atlantic*. Retrieved from http://www.theatlantic.com/magazine/archive/2015/07/world-without-work/395294/.

Throupe, D. W., & Hornsby, C. (1998.) *Multi-Party Politics in Kenya. The Kenyatta and Moi States and the Triumph of the System in the 1992 Election*. Athens, OH: Ohio University Press.

Tilya, F. (2008). IT and education policy in the Sub-Saharan African region. In Voogt, J., & Knezek, G. (eds.). *International Handbook on Information Technology in Education* (pp. 1145–54). New York: Springer.

Todaro, M. (1992). *Economics for a developing world: An introduction to principles, problems, and policies for development,* 3rd edition. New York: Prentice Hall.

Toffler, A. (1981). *The third wave*. New York: Bantam Book.

Transparency International (TI). (2014). Corruption Perception Index, 2014. Retrieved from http://www.transparency.org/cpi2013/results.

Trubek, D. M., Mosher, J., & Rothstein, J. S. (2000). Transnationalism in the regulation of labor relations: International regimes and transnational advocacy networks. *Law and Social Inquiry* 25, (4), 1187–211.

Trucano, M. (2009, August 14). Making ICT and educational policy. Edu Tech: A World Bank Blog. Retrieved from http://blogs.worldbank.org.
United Nations, Economic and social commission for Asia and the Pacific (1997). *The industrial and technological development news for Asia and the Pacific*. New York: UNO.
United Nations. (2005). *World Summit on the information society: Tunis commitment*. New York: United Nations.
Vandemoortele, J. (1984). *The wage policy in Kenya: past, present, and future*. Institute for Development Studies. Nairobi, Kenya: University of Nairobi.
Vaughn, P., Fengler, W., & Joseph, M. (2012). How Kenya became a world leader for mobile money. Scaling-up through disruptive business models—The inside story of mobile money in Kenya. Washington, DC: Brookings.
Venkata Ratnam, C. S. (2007). Trade unions and wider society. *Indian Journal of Industrial Relations* 42(4), 620–51.
Verizon. (2015). *State of the market. The Internet of Things 2015*. New York: Verizon, USA.
Versi, A. (1995). Kenya: first of the African "Tigers"?. *African Business*, 13–15.
Verweyen, G. (2012, March 5). Kenya: Unequal access to the School System. *Deutsche Welle*. Retrieved from http://www.dw.de/Kenya.
Villalon, L., & Huxtable, P. (eds.). *The African state at a critical juncture: Between disintegration and reconfiguration*. Boulder, CO: Lynne Rienner.
Villalon, L. (1998). The African state at the end of the twentieth century: Parameters of the critical juncture. In Villalon, L., and Huxtable, P. (eds.), *The African state at a critical juncture: Between disintegration and reconfiguration*. Boulder, CO: Lynne Rienner.
Wabuyele, L. C. (2003). *Understanding teachers' and administrators perceptions and experiences towards computer use in Kenyan classrooms: A case study of two schools*. Athens, OH: Ohio University.
Wachira, C. (2014, June 4). Airtel challenges Safaricom supremacy in money transfer industry. *Daily Nation*. Retrieved from http://www.nationmedia.co.ke.
Wade, R. (1988). The role of government in overcoming market failure: Taiwan, Republic of Korea, and Japan. In Hughes, H. (ed.), *Achieving industrialization in East Asia*. Cambridge, MA: Cambridge University Press.
———. (1998, August). The Asian debt and development crisis of 1997: Causes and consequences. *World Development*. Retrieved from http://www.wright.edu/~tdung/wade-wd-9808.htm.
Waitathu, N. (2014, November 26). Safaricom finally links Sh 15 billion security deal with Kenya Government. *Standard*. Retrieved from http://www.standardmedia.co.ke.
Wakabayashi, D. (2015, February 10). Apple: $710 Billion and Counting. *Wall Street Journal*. Retrieved from http://www.wsj.com.
Wallerstein, I. (1974). *The modern world system: Capitalist agriculture and the origins of European world economy in the sixteenth century*. New York: Academic Press.
———, and Gutkind, P. C. W. (1976). *The Political Economy of Contemporary Africa*. Beverly Hills, CA: Sage.
Walubengo, J. (2014, February 25). Where is that report—Social media and workplace productivity. *Daily Nation*. Retrieved from http://mobile.nation.co.ke/blogs/-/1949942/2220684/-/format/xhtml/-/ba1f7ez/-/index.html.
———. (2015). Why isn't Internet in Kenya affordable? *Daily Nation*. (June 2). Retrieved from http://www.nation.co.ke.
Wamae, R. G. (1995). *The nature of labor in the newly Industrialized developing countries: Focus on Kenya*. Nairobi, Kenya: Westlands.
Wanjira, K. (2009). Educational development in Kenya and the role of information and communication technology. *International Journal of Education and Development Using ICT* 15, 2. Retrieved from http://ijedict.dec.uwi.edu/viewarticle.php?id=740&layout=html.

———. (2015a, April 28). Kaimenyi: Over 2 million children not learning. *Daily Nation*. Retrieved from http://www.nation.co.ke.

———. (2015b, May 7). Majority want school computer labs. *Daily Nation*. Retrieved from http://www.nation.co.ke.

———. (2016). 5,000 tablets from China for class one pupils. *Daily Nation*. Retrieved from http://www.nation.co.ke.

Wanyoro, C. (2015, February 20). Dons union calls for police protection after protest at Eldoret University. *Daily Nation*. Retrieved from http://www.nation.co.ke.

Wanzala, O. (2014, June 29). Cashless fare: Matatus seek time. *Daily Nation*. Retrieved from http://www.nation.co.ke.

———. (2015, November 28). TSC orders teachers to verify union membership. *Daily Nation*. Retrieved from http://www.nation.co.ke.

———. (2015a, May 20). Pay to peg teachers' pay on performance. *Daily Nation*. Retrieved from http://www.nationmedia.co.ke.

———. (2015b, February 7). Treasury extends online tenders to parastatals. *Standard*. Retrieved from http://www.standardmedia.co.ke.

———. (2015c, June 4). Kaimenyi tells off Knut in wrangle. *Daily Nation*. Retrieved from http://www.nation.co.ke.

Ward, S., & Wainer, L. (2002, April 4–7). Dinosaurs in cyberspace? British trade unions and the Internet. Paper prepared for presentation at Political Studies Association Annual Conference, University of Aberdeen.

Warner, G. (2015, June 3). A taxi App aims to build trust where crime is high. National Public Radio (NPR). Retrieved from http://www.npr.org/sections/alltechconsidered/2015/06/03/411538709/a-taxi-app-aims-to-build-trust-where-crime-is-high.

Webb, S. & Webb, B. (1920). *The history of trade unionism*. London: Longman Green.

Weinstein, P. A. (1965). Featherbedding: A Theoretical Analysis. In Weinstein, P. A. (ed.), *Featherbedding and technological change* (pp. 44–54). Boston, MA: DC Heath and Company.

Weise, E. (2016, March 11). Looming job fear: Robots keeping us up at night. *USA Today*, Money, p. 2B.

Weiss, L. (1998). The Myth of the powerless state. Ithaca, NY: Cornell University Press.

Wesangula, D. (2012, January 7). Crossing the great digital divide. *Daily Nation*. Retrieved from http://www.nationmedia.co.ke.

Whitley, B. E. (1997). Gender differences in computer-related attitudes and behavior: A meta-analysis. *Computers in Human Behavior*, 13, 1–22.

Williams-Grut, O. (2016, February, 15). Robots will steal your job: How can AI increase unemployment and inequality, *Business Insider*. Retrieved from http://www.businesinsider.com.

Wokabi, C. (2014, November 25). Nairobi tops index of most strategic city for multinationals eyeing Africa. *Daily Nation*. Retrieved from http://www.nation.co.ke.

Wong, S. L., & Hanafi, A. (2007). Gender differences in attitudes towards information technology among Malaysian student teachers: A case study at Universiti Putra, Malaysia. *Educational Technology & Society* 10 (2), 158–69.

Woodfield, R. (2000). *Women, work and computing*. Cambridge: Cambridge University Press.

World Bank. (1989). *Sub-Sahara Africa. From crisis to sustainable growth: A long-term perspective study*. Washington, DC: World Bank.

———. (1997). *World Development Report: The state in a changing world*. New York: Oxford University Press.

———. (2003). *ICT and MDG: A World Bank perspective*. Washington, DC: World Bank.

———. (2012). *2011–2012 Doing Business Report. International Finance Corporation Report*. Washington, DC: World Bank.

———. (2014, September 30). Kenya a bigger better economy. Retrieved from http://www.worldbank.org/en/news/feature/2014/09/30/kenya-a-bigger-better-economy.

———. (2015). *Kenya's education achievement and challenges*. September Report. Washington, DC: World Bank.

———. (2015, March 5). Kenya among the fastest growing economies in Africa. Press Release. World Bank. Retrieved from http://www.worldbank.org/en/news/press-release/2015/03/05/kenya-among-the-fastest-growing-economies-in-africa.

World Economic Forum, (WEF), (2016). The future of jobs, report. Retrieved from http://www.weforum.org/reports/the-future-of-jobs.

World Wide Web Foundation. (2015). Women's right online: Translating access into empowerment. (October 20). Report. Retrieved from http://webfoundation.org/about/research/womens-rights-online-2015/.

Wresch, W. (1996). *Disconnected: Haves and have-nots in the information age*. New Brunswick, NJ: Rutgers University Press.

Wrong, M. (2009). *It's our turn to eat: The story of a Kenyan whistle-blower*. London, England: Harper.

Youn-Suk, K. (1997). Korea and developing countries: Lessons from Korea's industrialization. *Journal of East Asian Affairs* 11, 417–29.

Zartman, I. W. (1995). *Collapsed states: The disintegration and restoration of legitimate authority*. Boulder, CO: Lynne Rienner.

Index

About the Author

Eric Edwin Otenyo is a professor in the department of politics and international affairs at Northern Arizona University. His core interests are in the field of public administration, management, and governance in Africa. Professor Otenyo earned his PhD in political science from Miami University, Oxford, Ohio. He previously attended graduate school at the Maxwell School of Citizenship and Public Affairs, Syracuse University where he received his MPA. His teaching experience is broad; he has taught at the University of Nairobi and Illinois State University.

Professor Otenyo has a broad list of publications, including articles in several journals, including, *International Journal of Services, Economics and Management; Public Resistance: International Journal of Public Administration; Studies in Conflict and Terrorism; African Security Review; Journal of Asian and African Studies; Journal of Public Terrorism; Journal of Public Administration and Management; Public Organization Review; Global Encyclopedia of Public Administration, Public Policy, and Governance* (Springer); and *Cornell University's IAD Occasional Papers Series*. His published books include: *E-Government: The Use of Information and Communication Technologies in Administration* (Youngstown, NY: Teneo Press, 2011); *Comparative Public Administration: The Essential Readings* co-editor with Nancy Lind (Oxford, UK: Elsevier, 2006); and *Ethics and Public Service in Africa;* Friends of the Book Foundation (Rockefeller Foundation Supported, 1998).

www.ingramcontent.com/pod-product-compliance
Ingram Content Group UK Ltd.
Pitfield, Milton Keynes, MK11 3LW, UK
UKHW012037150926
475560UK00001B/51

9 781498 548793